Lynchings, Murders, and Other Nefarious Deeds

A Criminal History of Greene County, Mo.

Larry Wood

Hickory Press

Joplin, Missouri

ISBN: 9781733471411

Library of Congress Control Number: 2020921664

Published by
    Hickory Press
    Joplin, MO

Table of Contents

Preface

The subtitle of this book is *A Criminal History of Greene County*, but the main title, *Lynchings, Murders, and Other Nefarious Deeds*, is more indicative of the book's contents, because I do not represent it to be a comprehensive history of crime in the county. Instead, the book is simply a compilation of some of the more notorious crimes in the annals of Greene County.

One might ask why one criminal episode was included and another excluded. I did have certain criteria in mind as I chose the incidents to be chronicled in the book. Generally speaking, the more infamous the crime, the more likely it was included in the book. A murder with an element of intrigue or premeditation was more likely to be selected than one committed spontaneously during a barroom brawl. A homicide involving multiple victims was more likely to be included than one with a single victim. If no one was killed as a result of an incident, it was unlikely to be included—with at least one notable exception. Bonnie and Clyde's kidnapping of Tom Persell was included because of the infamy of the criminals, even though Persell was finally released unharmed.

Some readers may notice that the book contains comparatively few incidents from the last fifty years. That omission is by design. I prefer to write about events from long ago rather than recent ones. The recent ones, the ones I remember reading or hearing about as current events, seem less like history to me. In addition, a few well-known fairly recent criminal cases, such as the Feeney murder case and the disappearance of "the Springfield Three," were omitted for the simple reason that they remain officially unsolved. However, I did include two or three relatively recent crimes to lend the book a sense of proportion.

Acknowledgements

Historical research is easier than it used to be. Years ago, I often made trips to the State Historical Society of Missouri in Columbia, the Missouri State Archives in Jefferson City, and similar facilities when I was working on a writing project. I still make such trips, but they have become much rarer because many historical documents that used to be accessible only in person are now available online. The easy accessibility of these documents has also reduced my correspondence with librarians, archivists, and research assistants. Consequently, I have less personal contact during my research and, thus, fewer people to thank afterward. Still, there are a few individuals whom I would like to acknowledge for their ready assistance while I was researching and writing this book.

Steve Haberman of the Greene County Archives and Records Center was very helpful during my trip to that facility, and archives director Connie Yen sent me a photo for use in the book. Officer Rob Schroeder of the Springfield Police Department and Springfield Police Museum went above and beyond in providing numerous images. The Reference Staff of the Missouri State Archives furnished mugshots and register information on several penitentiary inmates. Ingrid Lennon Pressey of the Yale University Beinecke Library helped with my Wild Bill Hickok research. Thanks to all of them and to my wife, Gigi, for serving as a proofreader.

1
Two Pre-Civil War Murder Cases

Violent crime was relatively rare in Greene County's very early days, in large part because of the sparseness of the population, but the rarity of violent crime made it noteworthy when it did occur. Two murder cases, in particular, both predating the Civil War, have received considerable attention in local histories, such as Holcombe's 1883 *History of Greene County*, largely because they represented firsts. Compared to some of the other crimes chronicled in this book, these two early-day crimes do not strike one as especially dramatic or intriguing, but I feel obligated to mention them for the same reason Holcombe and others have—because they were considered noteworthy at the time they happened.

A relative dearth of primary sources makes it difficult to shed any new light on these pre-war crimes. Many early-day newspapers and other contemporary records were burned or otherwise destroyed. If one is going to write about these two incidents, secondary sources such as the aforementioned Holcombe's history must necessarily provide much of the information. So, while I feel obliged to mention these early-day crimes, my accounts are brief summaries that rely largely on what other historians have already written, and they offer little, if any, new information or insight into the cases. For this reason, I have lumped these two pre-Civil War murder cases together in a single chapter rather than trying to treat them extensively in separate chapters.

Charles S. Yancey's Killing of John Roberts

The very first murder in Springfield was an infamous case involving several of the leading citizens of Greene County. The sequence of events leading up to the crime began when John Roberts appeared before Charles S. Yancey, presiding judge of the Greene County Court, on a minor charge in the fall of 1836. John P. Campbell, the founder of Springfield and a man with whom Roberts had recently feuded, happened to be present at the time.[1]

Roberts, who owned a mill and a distillery at Jones Spring east of Springfield near present-day Highway 65, had served as the first coroner of the county. However, he had been involved in at least two serious affrays and was considered a rough character, especially if he'd been drinking, which was not an infrequent occurrence. In 1833, he was charged with assault with intent to kill, apparently for stabbing Thomas Horn (later sheriff of Greene County). Although the criminal case was dropped the following year, Horn, with Yancey acting as his attorney, sued Roberts for trespass and assault. Roberts counter-sued, and the case was settled in his favor. Then, in 1835, Roberts went to trial on a new charge of assault with intent to kill after slitting the ear of Kindred Rose, but the jury failed to reach a verdict.[2]

Campbell had testified against Roberts in both assault cases against him, and the two men renewed their feud when they met in Yancey's court in 1836. They began exchanging heated words, and Yancey ordered them to settle down. Campbell obeyed, but Roberts turned his ire toward the bench, reportedly telling the judge that he would say what he damn well pleased, in Yancey's court or any other. Yancey fined Roberts twenty dollars for the outburst.[3]

Roberts paid the fine, but afterwards he began making threats against the judge and taunting him whenever he happened to see Yancey in public. Yancey bore Roberts's insults for several months, walking away from confrontations on more than one occasion. In the spring of 1837, Roberts also filed a suit against Yancey. Although it is not known whether the suit had anything to do with the fine Yancey had levied against Roberts, it was settled in Yancey's favor, which might have exacerbated Roberts's ill feeling toward the judge.[4]

One day in the late summer of 1837, Roberts again appeared on the streets of Springfield, and upon learning that his old nemesis was in town, Yancey determined not to back down this time. He told fellow lawyer Littleberry Hendricks that he would not let Roberts intimidate him again. Hendricks advised Yancey to go home in order to avoid a confrontation, and the two men started together toward the judge's house. Near the northwest corner of the square, however, they ran into Roberts, who again began taunting the judge. The two adversaries briefly exchanged words, and then Yancey told Roberts not to follow him any farther and started to walk away. As he turned, he noticed Roberts, who was known to carry a big knife, reach his hand beneath his coat. Judge Yancey, thinking Roberts was going for the weapon, pulled out a pistol and shot him. He then pulled out a second pistol and was in the act of firing again when Hendricks knocked the weapon upward, sending the ball into the air. According to an account of this incident that appeared in the *Springfield Missouri Weekly Patriot* years later, Roberts shouted, "Don't shoot, I am a dead man now," as he collapsed and died.[5]

LITTLEBERRY HENDRICKS
JUDGE 1862–1863

Littleberry Hendricks tried to prevent the confrontation between Yancey and Roberts. *Courtesy of the Greene County Archives and Records Center.*

In 1838, Yancey was charged with manslaughter in Roberts's death. At Yancey's trial during the April 1839 term of court, his friend Littleberry Hendricks served as the prosecuting attorney. Although Roberts had apparently been reaching not for a knife at the time he was killed but rather for a glasses case that he had been in the habit of snapping at the judge, Yancey was found not guilty. Later, he was appointed a judge of the Greene County Circuit Court.[6]

The Hanging of Willis Washam

In the early 1850s, Willis Washam was charged with killing his stepson in Taney County, but the case was tried in Greene County on a change of venue. Willis was found guilty in July 1854, and he was hanged the following month from a gallows at the northeast edge of Springfield on the north side of Jordan Creek. It was the first legal hanging in Greene County, and for this reason, it is noteworthy in the criminal annals of the county, even though the crime itself occurred elsewhere.[7]

Washam scratched out a living on a farm on the White River near Forsyth. Some years earlier, he had married a woman, considerably younger than he was, who already had a son at the time. According to one version of the story, the boy was born after the marriage, but Washam always denied he was the lad's father. The stepson was now twelve to fourteen years old, and the couple also had a son of their own who was about eight. Although some sources refer to Washam as an "old man," he was only about forty-five.[8]

The Washam family was "not a model one," according to Holcombe's history. Washam and his wife often quarreled, and both of them mistreated the older boy. However, the youngster occasionally "showed fight" and had been known to hit his mother with a hoe or a metal bar.[9]

One morning, Washam and his stepson went down to Bee Creek to fish. According to the story the "old man" told, they soon separated, each claiming a different fishing hole. When it came time to head to the house, Washam couldn't locate the boy, and he went home alone. A search for the lad was promptly launched, and a day or two later the boy's body was found at the bottom of Bee Creek, weighted down with a heavy rock. The body bore signs of violence, including a place on the lad's head where he had apparently been struck with a blunt instrument.

Washam himself pulled the body ashore, and as he did so, Mrs. Washam rushed up to him and immediately accused him of killing her son. Two men fording the creek saw Washam pull the body out of the water and witnessed the ensuing argument between the old man and his wife. They sided with the wife, as it seemed apparent that the boy had been foully dealt with. The youngster had left home with his stepfather, no one else had been seen in the area, and Washam was known to mistreat the boy. So, it was assumed he'd probably stuck and killed the youngster during a fit of anger.[10]

When a warrant for his arrest on a charge of murder was issued, Washam decided not to hang around. Fleeing not only the law but also rumblings that Judge Lynch might take matters into his own hands, Washam took his eight-year-old son and absconded to Arkansas, riding his celebrated horse, Tom Benton. Washam took a job working on a cotton plantation near the Arkansas River, but after a few months, the boy started missing his mother and begged to see her. Risking arrest, Washam brought the boy back to Taney County.[11]

When he arrived, he was surprised to be warmly received by his wife. She told him that he was no longer suspected of killing the stepson and that charges against him had been dropped. As soon as Washam fell asleep, however, Mrs. Washam hurried to Forsyth to report her fugitive husband to authorities. Washam awoke to discover his wife had left, and suspecting that she had gone to turn him in, he again mounted Tom Benton and took flight.[12]

He had not gone far, however, before he was overtaken by the Taney County sheriff and arrested. The sheriff said later that, on the way back to Forsyth, Washam offered to give him Tom Benton if he would let him escape. Washam claimed the sheriff himself brought up the subject, offering to "look the other way" if Washam would give him his horse.[13]

Washam was indicted for first-degree murder in Taney County, but the trial was moved to Greene County on a change of venue. The case came up at the July 1854 term of the Greene County Circuit Court with Judge Yancey, the same man who'd faced a murder charge himself fifteen years earlier, presiding. Mrs. Washam was the star witness against her husband, but most of the evidence against him was circumstantial. After a two-day trial, the jury came back on July 21 with a verdict of guilty, and the next day Yancey sentenced the prisoner to be hanged on August 25. Littleberry Hendricks, Washam's lawyer, moved for a new trial, for an arrest of judgment, and for the sentence to be suspended until the case could be heard by the state supreme court, but Yancey refused to take any action.[14]

A huge crowd from all over southwest Missouri streamed into Springfield to witness the hanging on August 25. The site was slightly east of present-day Jefferson on the north side of Jordan Creek. Washam was driven to the scene in a horse-drawn cart, which was positioned under an overhanging beam of the gallows. (The gallows had no platform as later ones did.) Standing in the cart, the condemned man made a brief speech denying his guilt and saying that he could clear himself if had the money to hire a big-time lawyer. He blamed his "old woman" for swearing his life away and said he was ready to die, even though he was not guilty. A rope was looped around Washam's neck and the other end tied to the cross beam of the gallows. After Washam had finished his speech, the cart was pulled out from under him, and he swung into eternity. After Washam was dead, his body was cut down and given to Dr. A. W. Chenoweth to use for scientific study.[15]

Some years after Washam's execution, a story circulated that Mrs. Washam had confessed on her deathbed that her husband was not guilty of the crime for which he had died. Instead, she had killed her own son and contrived to fix the guilt on Washam. An embellishment on this story held that she and the Washams' hired man had killed the boy because he had caught the two of them "in compromising circumstances" and that, after Washam's death, his wife married the hired hand. Although many people were eager to believe the yarn of Mrs. Washam's confession, more sober observers thought the story was made up and was first told by an unscrupulous lawyer who, in seeking to get his client acquitted of murder, dubiously cited the Washam case as an example of wrongful conviction. Indeed, the Washam example was repeatedly cited in Greene County as an argument against capital punishment until the early 1930s, when the county finally staged its second legal execution.[16]

SPRINGFIELD MAN RECALLS HANGING OF WILLIS WASHAM

L. A. Gardner Tells Story Which Has Never Before Been Published.

This headline from a 1923 issue of the *Springfield Daily Leader* shows that the Willis Washam execution was remembered in the city long after it occurred.

2
The Lynching of Mart Danforth

Cases such as that of Martin "Mart" Danforth, a black man who was lynched in Springfield in August of 1859, were not rare in the mid-1800s to early 1900s. Mart was accused of raping a white woman, supposedly confessed to the crime, and was strung up by a mob before any legal punishment could be meted out. Nothing incited white men to violence against blacks more readily than the idea that "their women" might be violated by a black man.

John Morrow was away from home on business when a black man stopped at his house five or six miles south of Springfield on Saturday evening, August 13, 1859, and demanded entrance. When Morrow's young wife, who was home alone except for one or two small children, refused to open the door, the man tried to gain entrance through a window, but Mrs. Morrow managed to repulse him. The man then retrieved an ax, broke the door down, and burst inside. The terrified woman threw hot water on the intruder, but it was not scalding enough to disable him. He grabbed her hands and held them with one of his while he choked her into insensibility with the other. He then "accomplished his hellish purpose, and left her senseless on the floor."[1]

After the young woman regained her wits, she walked with her little children through the rain to the nearest neighbor, about a quarter mile from her house. When she reported what had happened, people throughout the neighborhood grew indignant and turned out to search for "the scoundrel."[2]

Over the next couple of days, several black men on whom the least bit of suspicion fell were brought before Mrs. Morrow one after another, but they were all turned loose when she failed to identify any of them. Then someone mentioned the name of Mart Danforth, a slave who belonged to the estate of Finley Danforth, deceased. The Danforth place was located several miles east of Springfield, but recently Mart had been engaged in hauling goods in the Springfield area. His route regularly took him past the Morrow home, and, therefore, those searching for the guilty culprit reasoned that Mart had probably known the young woman was home alone the previous Saturday night. On Wednesday, August 17, a posse of men went to where he was working and grilled him with questions. He allegedly admitted his guilt without any "force or threats" and readily told what had happened. His story of the rape agreed in almost every particular with the facts of the case as related by Mrs. Morrow. In addition, his chest and stomach were blistered, as though from hot water, such as Mrs. Morrow had thrown on her assailant. As a final check of his guilt, the posse took him before Mrs. Morrow, and she promptly identified him as "the boy" who had attacked her.[3]

Mart was kept under guard near the place where he was arrested until Thursday morning, August 18, at which time he was taken to Springfield. The circuit court was in session at the time, and Mart's case was immediately brought before that body. The sheriff was ordered to take the alleged rapist into custody until the court could act, and the prisoner was held in a room at the Temperance Hall on the east side of the square.[4]

A special grand jury was called, and a true bill was returned against Mart charging him with rape. Before the case could be tried, however, a mob of three or four hundred men gathered around the Temperance Hall and broke in. They went to an upstairs room where Mart was being held and ushered him out with a rope around his neck. They hurried him through the streets, crossed to the north side of Jordan Creek, and strung him up to a tree near where present-day Benton Avenue crosses the creek. (It was near the same spot where Washam had been legally hanged five years earlier.) Mart died within a few minutes, and his body was cut down and given "a hasty burial."[5]

MISSOURI.

EXCITEMENT IN SPRINGFIELD.

We are informed by a gentleman just from Springfield, that the citizens of that place hung a negro on the 18th inst., for the commission of an outrage upon the person of a Mrs. Morrow.— [*Neosho Herald.*]

Brief story about the Danforth lynching in a Neosho newspaper, reprinted in the *Fort Scott (KS) Bulletin.*

Observers in the immediate wake of this incident were, not surprisingly, more outraged by the rape of Mrs. Morrow than by the lynching of Mart Danforth, and they used the former to justify the latter. The *Boonville Observer*, for instance, blamed the extralegal hanging at least partly on the laxity of Missouri law, which at the time stipulated castration as the usual punishment for rape. Until rape was made a capital offense, it would be "a seeming necessity" for the public "to take the law into their own hands as a terror to evil-doers."[6]

Twenty four years later, the author of the 1883 *History of Greene County* was even blunter in defending the action of the mob that lynched Mart Danforth:

> In view of the circumstances, without justifying mob violence in general, it is proper to state that there was excuse for this one act of lawlessness on the part of those who hung Mart Danforth. Negro men were prone to commit offenses of the most terrible character upon unprotected and defenseless white women, and it is said that many a crime of this description was perpetuated in the quarter of Missouri that went unpunished, because of the unwillingness of the poor victim to make public her horrible misfortune. Women were afraid to be left alone or to travel unprotected, and this was the state of affairs not to be borne with complacency. The law then provided no punishment, save a mutilation that rendered the commission of a second offense of the kind impossible, and this was not considered a penalty at all adequate to the gravity of the offense.[7]

Even in 1915, fifty-four years after the fact, local historians Jonathan Fairbanks and Edwin Tuck thought the Danforth lynching was understandable, attributing it to "that ever-present menace where there is a large negro population, the assault committed upon a white woman by a black man."[8]

After the lynching of Mart Danforth, twice more in the subsequent history of Springfield white men would be excited to violence against black men to the point of executing them extralegally, and each time the immediate catalyst for the mob violence was an alleged assault on a white woman. A black man molesting a white woman was the ultimate challenge to white, male authority.

3
A Shocking Civil War Tragedy
The Murder of Miss Mary Willis

When tragedy befell the Mary Willis family in Springfield during the Civil War, a local newspaper reported that the widow Willis was a Union refugee from the White River country of northern Arkansas and that she'd come to Springfield to escape the depredations her family had suffered at the hands of their Southern-sympathizing neighbors. That Mary came to Springfield seeking asylum is no doubt true, but if she and her family ever lived in northern Arkansas, it must have been for a very brief period because, prior to the war, the Willises had lived in southern Missouri for over twenty years.[1]

Mary and her husband, Solomon, came to Missouri from Tennessee shortly after their 1835 marriage and settled in Taney County. In 1850, they were living near Ozark in that part of Greene County that later became Christian. By 1860, Mary was a widow living in Christian County near Highlandville with twelve children ranging in age from twenty-four years to six months.[2]

At the outbreak of the Civil War, Mary's four oldest sons all joined the Greene and Christian County Home Guards under Captain Jesse Galloway. They enlisted in Taney County on May

28, 1861. Not long after this date, notorious Confederate guerrilla Alf Bolin shot and killed the eldest son, William, as he was carrying corn to feed a family horse. According to an 1862 report from a Springfield correspondent to the *New York Times*, another son, Harvey, was also killed during the latter part of 1861 after he left home to find work. (Census records do not show a son of Mrs. Willis named Harvey, but this was perhaps a reference to Henry, who would have been about twenty-one or twenty-two years old at this time.) Another son, Samuel, was also killed during this same time frame by gunfire from passing Rebel marauders as the eighteen-year-old lad sat in a doorway of the Willis home.[3]

Perhaps the Springfield correspondent conflated or confused one or more of these incidents, but it's almost certain that Mary Willis had lost at least two sons to the Civil War by the time she moved to Springfield in the late winter of 1861-1862. Yet her suffering was far from over. In March of 1862, Mary's twenty-year-old son, David, who was one of the brothers who'd joined the home guard early in the war, enlisted in the 24th Regiment Infantry Volunteers in Springfield, and he, too, would become a casualty of the war. But not before another tragedy struck the Willis family even sooner and closer to home.[4]

When Mary and her family first arrived in Springfield, they were placed in a house on the east side of town that had previously been occupied by a "squad of accommodating girls." Not aware that the place had changed hands or that the occupants were of a different character than their predecessors, many soldiers continued to call at the home expecting to be entertained. The Willis family complained to military authorities, who responded by placing a two-man guard at the house to ward off unwelcome visitors.[5]

Captain John R. Clark was officer of the day at the Springfield post on Wednesday, May 21, 1862, but he didn't let that stop him from imbibing while on duty. That evening about dark, he and his orderly, both intoxicated, called at the Willis home and demanded supper. When Mary refused to admit them, Clark and the orderly, A. J. Rice, drew their pistols and, swearing angrily, tried to force their way into the house anyway. One of the guards promptly shot Clark through the body, and he stumbled back a couple of steps and fell dead. Rice then fired at the guard who'd shot Clark but missed and, instead, hit Mary's twenty-four-year-old daughter in the head, killing her instantly. The other guard then shot Rice in the breast, severely wounding him as the ball passed up through his shoulder and badly shattered the bone. Miss Willis, whose name was also Mary, bore an excellent reputation and was engaged to a Union soldier at the time of her death. According to one report, her betrothed was one of the men guarding the Willis home on the day of the deadly encounter.[6]

Although the deceased Clark was from northern Missouri, he was captain of a company in the Fifth Kansas Cavalry. A veteran of the Mexican War and a two-term sheriff of Mercer County, he raised a company of men in and around Grundy and Mercer counties and was commissioned a captain in the Kansas regiment when it was formed. Despite Clark's dubious conduct leading to his death, he was buried in Springfield the day after the incident with both military and Masonic honors.[7]

The captain was certainly not without his critics, though. J. T. Townsend, a soldier in a different company of the Fifth Kansas, called Clark a "beastly border ruffian" who was "destitute of all manly instincts." Rice, Townsend added, "rivaled his captain in wanting every qualification of a gentleman." Townsend claimed Clark only joined the Union Army because he wanted to be a cavalry officer and that the colonel of the Fifth Kansas heard of his ambition and offered him a commission because he needed the men. Clark was actually "a pro-slavery brute," according to Townsend, who "ought to have joined the rebels instead of our side."[8]

Terrible Tragedy.

From the St. Louis News, May 31.

On Wednesday of last week, a deplorable tragedy occurred at Springfield, in this State. Capt. John B. Clark, of Co. F, Fifth Kansas cavalry, being officer of the day, called ,in company with one A. J. Rice, both in a state of intoxication, at the house of Mrs. Willis, a widow lady, to get their supper. Mrs. Wil-

A St. Louis newspaper recounts the murder of Mary Willis, reprinted in the *Muscatine (IA) Weekly Journal.*

In the immediate aftermath of the shooting incident, observers thought Rice, who was gravely wounded, would likely not recover. He lived long enough, however, to be charged in Greene County Circuit Court with murder in the death of Miss Mary Willis. In August of 1862, the case was transferred on a change of venue to Phelps County. Rice was convicted at Rolla in late October, but he was granted a new trial, scheduled for the April 1863 term. However, the case was continued at that time, and there seems to be no record of the case after the continuance. Perhaps Rice died before the case could be decided, because the 1883 *History of Greene County* says that the wound he suffered at the Willis house "eventually proved fatal."[9]

Mary Willis's suffering was still not over, even after the untimely shooting death of her oldest daughter. Her son David, who'd joined the 24th Regiment Infantry Volunteers shortly after the family's arrival in Springfield, died on December 2, 1862, while serving with the regiment on the Black River in

southeastern Missouri. How long Mrs. Willis continued to live
in Springfield is unknown, but by 1870, she was living in
Morgan Township of Dade County. Of the twelve children
who'd lived with her ten years earlier in Christian County, the
five youngest were still in the household, two or three had left
home and were living on their own, but at least four and probably
five were dead either directly or indirectly as a result of the Civil
War. As the Springfield correspondent of the *New York Times*
observed shortly after the tragic death of Mary's daughter, "The
tender mercies of secession are cruel.... Such are the trials of
loyal citizens in the border slave states."[10]

4
Wild Bill Hickok and Dave Tutt Shoot It Out on the Springfield Square
The First Gunfight of the Wild West Era

It was late afternoon of July 21, 1865, in the frontier town of Springfield, Missouri. James Butler "Wild Bill" Hickok, a Colt navy revolver at his side, stood beside the Robertson and Mason Dry Goods store, located on the west corner of South Street and the public square. Hickok kept looking north across the square, keeping a vigil to see whether Dave Tutt came across the open area wearing Hickok's gold Waltham watch. Hickok had told the man not to wear the watch in public, and he meant to make sure he didn't. Someone had said Tutt was at the livery in the northeast corner of the square, and Hickok kept peering in that direction. More likely the man was at Worrell's saloon next door to the livery, if Hickok knew Dave Tutt, and he'd done enough drinking with him to know. Either way, if Tutt started across the square wearing the watch, there was going to be hell to pay. Sometimes a man's honor eclipsed even friendship.[1]

Born in Homer (now Troy Grove), Illinois about 1837, Hickok came west in the mid-1850s when he was eighteen or

Wild Bill Hickok. *Author's collection.*

nineteen years old. He spent a few years in Kansas Territory, where he aligned himself during the late fifties with free-soil Kansans in their border troubles with proslavery ruffians from Missouri. Somewhere along the line he picked up the nickname Bill and later Wild Bill. The outset of the Civil War found Hickok working for a freight company in southeast Nebraska as a stock hand at Rock Creek, a waystation along the Oregon Trail. In July of 1861, Hickok got involved in a shootout that left Dave McCanles, former owner of the waystation, and two of his sidekicks dead. Hickok and two other employees of the freight company were arrested for murder but were found not guilty by reason of self-defense. Hickok then drifted into Missouri, where he signed on at Sedalia as a teamster with the Union Army. By the mid-part of the war, he had landed in Springfield as a special policeman for the Union provost marshal. Later he worked as a Union spy and scout roaming through southwest Missouri and into northern Arkansas. Some say that's how he first met Dave Tutt, a former Confederate soldier from Yellville, Arkansas.[2]

What's known for sure is that Tutt, a member of the family that had been involved in the infamous Tutt-Everett feud during the 1840s, came to Springfield during the mid to latter part of the Civil War with his mother, his half-brother, and other family members. The twenty-six-year-old Tutt and Wild Bill became gambling and drinking buddies, and both earned reputations as rowdy young men. Court records show that Tutt, Hickok, and a few other young men were associated with each other and sometimes went each other's bail when one of them got in trouble.[3]

Although some accounts say jealousy over a woman played a part in the falling out between Tutt and Hickok that led to their showdown on the public square, the best evidence suggests that the rift between them stemmed directly from a dispute over a debt that Hickok owed Tutt. On the afternoon of July 21, 1865, Dave, Wild Bill, James W. Orr, and probably one or two other men were playing cards in Hickok's upstairs room at the Lyon House a block and a half off the square on South Street. (At least one version of the story says Tutt was merely an onlooker during this particular game, although this seems unlikely.) When the game ended, Tutt reminded Hickok of a previous debt, and they argued over the amount. Tutt claimed Bill owed him $35, while Bill said he owed only $25. Hickok remarked that he had a memorandum book showing the amount, and as he searched his pockets for the book, he lay his gold pocket watch on the table. Tutt picked it up and said he'd keep it as collateral until the debt was paid. Angered that Dave had picked up his watch, Hickok said the memorandum book was probably downstairs, and the men adjourned to the saloon on the first floor. When Hickok still couldn't find his notation, Tutt said the debt was actually $45 but he'd accept $35. This no doubt made Hickok even madder, and he insisted he owed only $25. (Most accounts of the card game say it took place on the night of July 20, but this is incorrect. Witness statements in the coroner's report on Dave Tutt and Union post commander Albert Burnitz's diary make it clear the shootout occurred the same day as the card game. Besides, it stands to reason the game took place during the daytime, as most card games did until electric lights became readily available.)[4]

Depiction of Hickok card game. *From Harper's New Monthly Magazine.*

Continuing to debate the matter, the men went outside and sat on a bench in front of the hotel. A man named Eli Armstrong happened by at about five o'clock and asked what the trouble was. Learning of the dispute over money between Hickok and Tutt, the thirty-two-year-old Armstrong tried to act as a peacemaker. He called each man aside to talk to him in private. Tutt said he'd settle for thirty-five dollars rather than fight over the difference, and Hickok agreed to pay twenty-five now and the remaining ten when he found his memorandum book if the book showed he owed it. After his private parley with Armstrong, Tutt remarked that, even though he was settling for $35, he still thought Hickok actually owed him $45. Hickok then told Tutt he'd "rather have a fuss with any man on earth" than him because Tutt had "always accommodated (him) more than any man in town." He'd borrowed money from Tutt numerous times, and they'd never had a dispute before. Tutt agreed and said that he didn't want any difficulty either. "Boys, that settles it then," Armstrong announced. He suggested they all go inside and have a drink to seal the deal. Once they got inside, though, no money exchanged hands, and Tutt gulped down his drink without saying anything or returning the watch. As he got up to leave, Hickok warned him not to wear the watch in public. Tutt retorted, as he walked out, that he'd wear it across the public square if he wanted to.[5]

Armstrong followed Tutt out the door and down to the square, where he saw Tutt heading toward the livery. After Orr left to go home for supper, Hickok also left the Lyon House and ambled toward the square. When he heard that Tutt had gone toward the livery, Bill took up a vigil at the Robertson and Mason corner, waiting to see whether Dave dared to come across the square wearing his watch after he'd been warned not to.[6]

Springfield public square looking southeast, as it appeared circa 1865. *Courtesy Springfield-Greene County Library.*

This photo, taken about ten years after the gunfight, looks south from the square. The Richardson building where Hickok kept his vigil at the corner is on the right. *Courtesy Rob Schroeder and the Springfield Police Museum.*

Shortly after Hickok took up his position on the corner, Oliver Scott, who was headed to the post office just off the square on South, stopped to ask Bill what was going on. Hickok explained his dispute with Tutt and warned that Dave "should not cross the square with his watch." Hickok then told Scott, who had sat down on a bench or chair, that he needed to "get away from there." Heeding the warning, Scott got up and went on his way.[7]

Alfred T. Budlong happened along about the time Scott moved off, and Hickok repeated the same story he'd told Scott about his dispute with Tutt. He said Tutt was over by the courthouse in the northwest corner of the square and that he was waiting for him. Tutt, Hickok warned, "should not carry his watch up that street."[8]

Meanwhile, Tutt was overheard to say, as he lingered in the northwest corner of the square, that it would "take a better man than Haycock (sic) to make him give up the watch."[9]

Hickok was still keeping his vigil when James Orr came back downtown about 6:00 p.m. after going home for supper. Orr stopped to talk and again tried to smooth things over between Hickok and Tutt. Hickok thought Orr was taking Tutt's side in the dispute, and he was in no mood for negotiation. Hickok told Orr to tell Tutt to bring the watch back within an hour and he would pay $25 now and pay the other $10 later if he owed it. Otherwise "something else would be done." When Orr balked at the assignment, Hickok warned him to move on out of the way then. Orr retorted that the corner belonged to him as much as it did to Hickok. But Orr didn't want any trouble, so he walked away.[10]

Frederick W. Scholten came up while Hickok was still talking to Orr and overheard the last part of their conversation. After Orr had left, Tutt's half-brother stepped up and told Hickok he was sorry there was a difficulty between him and

Dave and that, if Hickok would go with him to see Dave, he thought they could settle the matter. But the time for negotiations was past. Hickok spotted Tutt in the northwest corner of the square, and he started off to the west along the boardwalk in front of the stores on the south side of the square, with Scholten tagging along. They had gone but a few paces when Hickok stepped out to meet Tutt and called for him to halt. "David, you cannot come any further and pack my watch."[11]

Tutt halted as he drew even with the courthouse, and Hickok stopped to face him about seventy-five paces away. With his hand on or near the butt of his revolver, Tutt made some reply, but none of the witnesses understood exactly what he said. Both men drew and fired about the same time. Tutt missed, but Hickok didn't. Tutt had turned as he fired, and Hickok's bullet struck him in the right side. He cried out, "Boys, I am killed," as he ran toward the courthouse. He fell just outside the doorway and died within a minute or two.[12]

Depiction of Hickok-Tutt gunfight. *From Harper's New Monthly Magazine.*

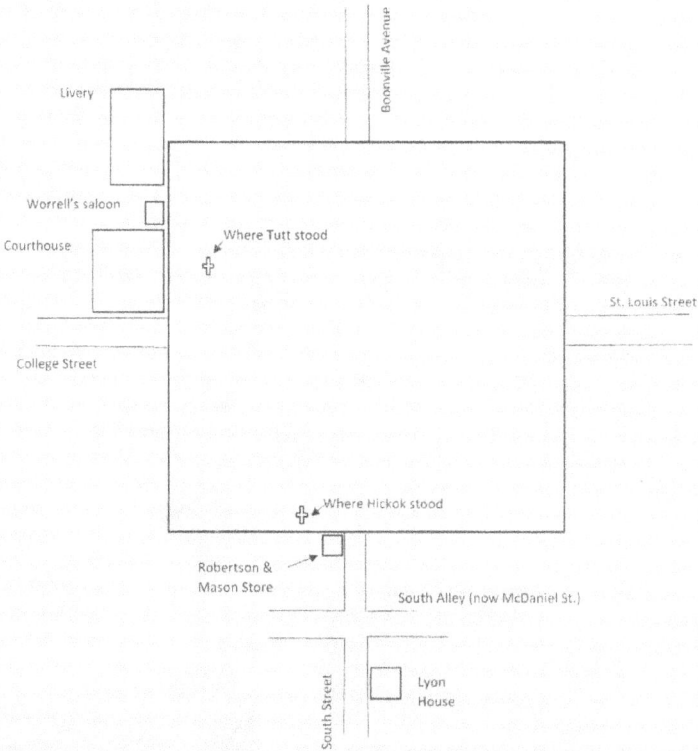

Diagram of the Springfield Public Square showing where Hickock and Tutt stood during their gunfight there on July 21, 1865. *By the author.*

Scholten remarked to Hickok immediately after the shooting that his action was "rather hard." Hickok retorted that "it was two (sic) late now and he was not sorry."[13]

Tutt's body was taken to his mother's house on South Street, and Coroner J. F. Brown summoned a jury that same night. After hearing witness testimony, the jury returned a verdict the next day, July 22, that Davis Tutt "came to his death by a pistol shot" fired "by a certain James B. Hickok." Tutt was buried in the city cemetery on State Street but was later moved to Maple Park Cemetery.[14]

Meanwhile, Hickok turned himself in to military authorities immediately after the shooting and was handed over to the Greene County sheriff. Hickok was charged with manslaughter and released on $2,000 bond. According to one report, he was seen just minutes after the shooting "riding leisurely up South Street."[15]

Tutt gravesite in Maple Park Cemetery. Newer headstone on left and older one on right. *Photo by the author.*

The gunfight between Hickok and Tutt merited only a small column in the next issue of the *Springfield Missouri Weekly Patriot*:

> David Tutt, of Yellville, Ark., was shot on the public square, at 6 o'clock, P. M., on Friday last, by James B. Hickok, better known in Southwest Missouri as "Wild Bill." The difficulty occurred from a game of cards. Hickok is a native of Homer, Lasalle County, Ills., and is about twenty-six years of age. He has been engaged since his sixteenth year, with the exception of about

two years, with Russell, Majors & Waddill, in Government service, as scout, guide, or with exploring parties, and has rendered signal service to the Union cause, as numerous acknowledgments from the different commanding officers with whom he has served will testify.[16]

Hickok's trial took place in early August, just two weeks after the shootout. Some accounts of the gunfight between Hickok and Tutt intimate that their having been on opposite sides during the Civil War might have contributed to their dispute. While there is reason to believe some ill will might have existed between the two men prior to the Lyon House card game, there is even less evidence that the grudge had anything to do with the Civil War than there is for the notion of a romantic rivalry between the two men. However, the post-shootout legal proceedings against Hickok were indeed stained by political sentiment.[17]

Approximately a month and a half before the gunfight, Missouri citizens had narrowly passed what was known as the Drake Constitution. Promoted by Radical Republicans, the new constitution stipulated that no one who had ever been in Confederate service or sympathized with the Confederacy could vote, serve on a jury, or hold certain occupational positions such as teacher, preacher, or lawyer. In order to be accorded the full rights of citizenship, those whose loyalty was uncertain were required to take what became known as the "Ironclad Oath," stating that they had never engaged in disloyal behavior and that they fully supported the Union. Of course, most Confederate sympathizers could not, in good conscience, swear such an oath, and, thus, they were disenfranchised. So, all the officials and all the jurors in Hickok's trial were staunch Union men. In fact, the judge, S. H. "Pony" Boyd; the prosecutor, Robert W. Fyan; and Hickok's lawyer, John S. Phelps; were all former Union officers.

To use a gambling metaphor, the cards were stacked in Hickok's favor.[18]

Prosecutor Fyan seems to have made an earnest effort to convict Hickok, even though they'd been on the same side during the war. Fyan asked the court to instruct the jury that they could not acquit on the grounds of self-defense or justifiable homicide if the defendant willingly engaged in the fight and made no effort to avoid it. Fyan also asked the court to instruct the jury to disregard any evidence as to the loyalty or disloyalty of the deceased, any evidence pertaining to his moral character, and any threats he might have made against Hickok prior to their argument at the Lyon House. In his final charge to the jury, however, Judge Boyd adopted a decidedly different set of instructions. He told the jury that they could consider the reputation of the deceased as a fighting man and any prior threats he might have made against the defendant. Boyd said that, if the defendant thought the deceased meant to do him great bodily harm and was advancing toward him, he was not obligated to retreat or "to stand with his arms folded until it was too late." If the jury believed that the defendant acted to prevent a "threatened impending injury," they should acquit.[19]

Considering the judge's instructions, the jury understandably came back, at the conclusion of the trial on August 5, with a not guilty verdict after only ten minutes of deliberation. However, the verdict met with "general dissatisfaction" on the streets of Springfield, according to the next issue of the *Springfield Missouri Weekly Patriot*. The citizens were "shocked and terrified at the idea that a man could arm himself and take a position at a corner of the public square, in the centre of the city, and await the approach of his victim for an hour or two, and then willingly engage in a conflict with him which resulted in his instant death." The 1883 *History of Greene County* recalled that a prominent attorney even got up on the balcony of the courthouse and "denounced the verdict as against the evidence and all decency, and there were threats of lynching Bill, but nothing was done."[20]

Not only was the deck stacked in Hickok's favor during his trial, the *Weekly Patriot*'s coverage of the case also reflected a Union bias. After reporting the general dissatisfaction with the verdict among Springfield citizens, many of whom were no doubt disenfranchised Southern sympathizers, the newspaper chastised them for their outrage. The newspaper said that few, if any, of the people who professed to be "shocked and terrified" by the idea that a man could get away with lying in wait for another man before gunning him down in a shootout made any attempt to intervene. If they failed to speak out to try to prevent the tragedy, they "are partly to blame themselves" and "should not complain of others."[21]

The pro-Union *Patriot* also defended the court officials and the jury against the public censure they had encountered since the trial ended. Although public outrage over the verdict was mainly directly at the jury, the *Patriot* took special pains to defend Judge Boyd. He had "conducted himself impartially throughout the trial," said the editors, and his rulings "gave general satisfaction." As "evidence of the impartiality of his Honor," the editors added, "we copy the instructions given to the jury." The only problem is the list the newspaper provided was not Judge Boyd's list at all. Either unwittingly or in a deliberately disingenuous attempt to shield the judge from criticism, the editors listed the instructions Prosecutor Fyan had requested that the judge deliver to the jury and identified them as the judge's own instructions. After giving the mislabeled list, the *Patriot* concluded, "The Court instructed the jury" that Hickok "was not entitled to an acquittal on the grounds of self-defense unless he was anxious to avoid the fight, and used all reasonable means to do so; but the jury seems to have thought differently."[22]

Of course, that's not at all what Judge Boyd had said in his final instructions, but how many people on the streets of Springfield were aware of the deception?

On September 13, a little over a month after his acquittal, Hickok was defeated in an election for city marshal of Springfield. The winner got 107 votes, Wild Bill received 63, and three other candidates split 61 votes among them. Although not an overwhelming defeat for Hickok, the outcome of the election shows that his duel with Tutt had not made him particularly popular in Springfield. This seems especially true, if we keep in mind that Southerners were excluded from voting.[23]

About the time of the election, George Ward Nichols arrived in Springfield to write what turned out to be a highly exaggerated account of Hickok's adventures for *Harper's New Monthly Magazine*. In the Nichols narrative, Wild Bill supposedly killed ten men singlehandedly in the Rock Creek affair at the beginning of the Civil War when, in fact, only three men died at Rock Creek and it's not certain that Hickok killed any of them. Nichols's main source for details about the Tutt gunfight was "Captain Honesty," who in real life was Captain Richard B. Owen, a Union quartermaster who had employed Hickok during the war and who had been one of his bondsmen when he was charged with manslaughter. Although Nichols claimed Captain Honesty was "unprejudiced," his story of the gunfight was biased in favor of Hickok, whom he depicted as a hero, while Tutt served in the role of villain. Wild Bill himself no doubt contributed to the larger-than-life portrait Nichols painted of him. According to Nichols, for instance, Hickok told him how he came to be a crack pistol shot by shooting at dimes when he lived in the mountains prior to the war.[24]

In late January 1866, Springfield policeman John Orr shot and killed a man named James Coleman during a brawl. Orr was arrested, and Hickok, who was an eyewitness to the affair, gave testimony in the case. After Orr was released on bond, however, he skipped town and was never heard from again.[25]

Shortly after the Coleman killing, Hickok left Springfield at the invitation of Captain Owen, who had been named acting quartermaster at Fort Riley, Kansas. Hickok got a job there as a government detective. When Nichols's embellished story of Hickok's adventures was published in early 1867, Wild Bill became an overnight legend, the most famous figure in America's Wild West. And he spent the rest of his life trying to live up to his reputation. Most people in Springfield, though, were unimpressed. When Hickok came back to Springfield in the fall of 1872 and spent several months boarding at the St. James Hotel, his presence was scarcely noted in the local press. When he was finally killed in Deadwood, South Dakota, in 1876, Springfield newspapers again paid little attention, with the *Weekly Patriot* simply rerunning a notice of the shooting that had appeared previously in a Chicago newspaper.[26]

In the 1920s, a number of reminiscent accounts by old-timers were published in Springfield newspapers of Hickok's local exploits, primarily the Tutt gunfight. In direct contrast to the Nichols article, most of these reminiscent accounts cast Hickok in an unfavorable light. No doubt some of them were written by Southern men who'd been disenfranchised at the time the incident occurred and who were now venting their still lingering resentment. Others were written by men who weren't even old enough to have witnessed the gunfight that had occurred over fifty-five years earlier.[27]

In 1975 metal plaques were placed in the street on the Springfield public square showing where Hickok and Tutt stood when they drew down on each other. The marker showing where

Tutt stood is accurate, but Hickok stood well west and slightly south of where his marker is located.[28]

5
If Not Cruel, Certainly Unusual Punishment
The Reign of the Regulators

About daylight on the morning of May 23, 1866, three "Regulators" sneaked onto the farm of Green B. Phillips two miles northeast of Cave Spring in Greene County and took up hiding places near his barn. At sunup, the thirty-six-year-old Phillips emerged from his house to do his morning chores, going into a crib behind the barn to get corn to feed his animals. As he began husking the corn, he glanced up and saw the shadowy shapes of the three men lurking in the semi-darkness outside the crib, each with a revolver poking through the cracks of the building. While two of the men kept Phillips covered, one of them came to the door and ordered him out.[1]

The three men marched Phillips toward a gate that led into some timber. Two of them walked on either side of their captive holding his arms while the third goaded him from behind. The group had gone about twenty feet when the powerful Phillips jerked loose and started running. He dashed about thirty feet before stumbling over a hog lying in his path that he failed to see in the dull morning light. As he climbed quickly to his feet, the Regulators opened fire. Phillips was struck twice in the body and died almost instantly.[2]

During the Civil War, Missouri had been the scene of a vicious guerrilla warfare that often pitted neighbor against neighbor. Roving bands of bushwhackers and irregular soldiers took advantage of the civil unrest to loot, plunder, and sometimes murder. Although treaties had been signed in the spring of 1865 officially ending the war, lawlessness persisted in many parts of the state, including Greene County. Theft and other crime continued to plague the northwest part of the county, in particular, even a year after the war had ended. In the spring of 1866, a group of prominent citizens from in and around Walnut Grove, exasperated that civil authorities had thus far been unable to suppress the lawlessness, got together to organize a "law and order" group to look after their own interests and to help law enforcement officials put an end to the crime. During the first meeting at Cave Spring on March 21, Stephen H. Julian was appointed president. Other members included John Small and Thomas W. Coltrane. The resolutions adopted stressed the group's intent to work with civil authorities to end the depredations in the area.[3]

But several of the members were unconvinced that law and order could be restored through ordinary means. Few of the area's lawbreakers had thus far been caught, and even when they were, they were rarely punished. Instead, they were let go on the sworn testimony of their friends or on some technicality. Small, Coltrane, and others soon broke with the original group and formed a more militant organization called the Honest Men's League, which adopted resolutions emphasizing the group's intent to take the law into its own hands if necessary in order to stop the outbreak of lawlessness in Greene County and surrounding areas. Notably, Julian, leader of the original organization, did not join the Honest Men's League, or the Regulators as the group was usually called.[4]

Green B. Phillips was the Regulators' first victim, but it's not clear why he was chosen. Unlike a number of vigilante groups in Missouri and elsewhere during the aftermath of the Civil War, the Honest Men's League was motivated little, if any, by political sentiments carried over from the war. Most of its members were former Union soldiers or sympathizers, but so was Phillips. He had been a captain in the Enrolled Missouri Militia, and his company had helped in the defense of Springfield during the Battle of Springfield in January 1863. He had also served as a township constable in the early 1850s and had run for state representative in 1864. According to Holcombe's 1883 *History of Greene County*, many people claimed, after Phillips was killed, that he had never committed any crimes or induced others to do so and that the only possible justification for his murder was that he had befriended certain men accused of criminal activity. This assertion, though, was off the mark, because, despite Phillips's prominence, he did have a checkered past. During the war, General Egbert G. Brown, commanding the Southwest District at Springfield, threatened to disband Phillips's company because he'd received reports that some of the men of the company had been guilty of looting, robbery, and even murder. However, the same was true of John Small's company; so Phillips was probably targeted for reasons unrelated to his military service. During the war and the months immediately after it, Phillips was sued in civil court on more than one occasion for non-payment of debts, and he was charged with horse stealing on one occasion. In addition, he was one of several bondsmen who bailed out a man accused of manslaughter in 1865. So, while the immediate motive of the Honest Men's League for singling out Phillips is not known, there is evidence to suggest that he might well have had enemies with a personal grudge against him. In any case, on or about May 20, 1866, the Regulators selected Phillips as their first target, three men were appointed to carry out the attack, and now he lay dead.[5]

On Saturday, May 26, 1866, three days after Phillips was killed, two of his acquaintances, John Rush and Charles Gorsuch, went into Walnut Grove, where they denounced the killing and made threats against two of the Regulators whom they accused of being the assassins. Gorsuch had been a member of Phillips's militia company during the war, and Rush, also a former Union soldier, was Gorsuch's father-in-law.[6]

It so happened that a meeting of the Regulators was taking place that very day at the Rice schoolhouse just northeast of Walnut Grove in Polk County. Someone sent word to the meeting of Rush and Gorsuch's presence in town and of the threat they'd made. The group immediately "went into executive session" to hold a drumhead trial. The impromptu "jury" pronounced a sentence of death on the two men and set out to execute it. They captured Rush and Gorsuch at a store in Walnut Grove, took them a mile southwest of town, and strung them up to a redbud tree.[7]

In justifying their action, the Regulators claimed Rush and Gorsuch were "ringleaders of the thieves." It's true the two men had been charged with hog stealing in Greene County court earlier in 1866, and the case was still pending at the time they were hanged. However, their outspoken denunciation of Phillips's murder likely had as much to do with their fate as did their alleged criminal activity.[8]

On Monday, May 28, two days after Rush and Gorsuch were lynched, the Regulators, over two hundred strong, rode into Springfield about one o'clock in the afternoon to give an account of the actions they'd taken. Still on horseback, they arranged themselves in a box formation in front of the courthouse on the public square, and one of their leaders, J. M. Brown, stood on a wagon, drawn up as a makeshift dais, and addressed the crowd who'd gathered to hear what he had to say. A Presbyterian minister, Brown explained what the Honest Men's League had done so far in the name of law and order and declared that the group aimed to rid the region of thieves and robbers through legal means if possible but that, if necessary, they would "execute justice upon the guilty in their own way."[9]

The public square in early-day Springfield was often a busy place, as it was when the Regulators occupied it on May 28, 1866, and on the day this photo was taken a few years later. *Courtesy History Museum on the Square.*

Levi P. Downing, another leader of the Regulators, took the stage next and spoke along the same line as Brown. The Regulators then invited several prominent Springfield citizens to offer their thoughts on the actions taken thus far by the league to alleviate the lawlessness existing in and around Greene County.[10]

Former Union officer James Baker generally lauded the Regulators but didn't openly endorse their vigilante action. Baker vouched for the character of many of the men in the group, and he was sure they had suffered greatly at the hands of thieves and robbers, just as Springfield citizens had. Ideally, punishment should be inflicted on wrongdoers through legal channels, but he thought the motives of the men in forming their organization were pure. State senator J. W. D. L. F. "Alphabet" Mack followed Baker to the podium and seconded his remarks.[11]

Both former Missouri secretary of state John M. Richardson and former US congressman John S. Phelps strongly condemned the group's taking of the law into its own hands. Phelps, who, like Richardson, was a former Union colonel, urged the Regulators not to carry out any further acts of vigilantism but instead to let the courts "remedy the evil and punish those guilty of crime." If the current officers of the law were insufficient to do the job, "that could be remedied through the ballot-box."[12]

In a counterpoint to Phelps's closing remarks, the editors of the *Springfield Missouri Weekly Patriot* said they didn't think the officers or the courts were at fault for the lawless condition existing in the region but rather it was a lingering effect of the Civil War. The disintegration and demoralization of society caused by the war made it difficult to bring to justice those who would band together and take advantage of the chaos for criminal purposes. Remedying the evil and punishing those guilty of crime took "an extraordinary effort on the part of the honest portion of the community." However, the newspapermen stopped short of sanctioning the Regulators' mob action, saying they deeply regretted that the honest citizens of the league did not make a stronger effort to punish the lawbreakers by legal means instead of lynching them. The *Patriot*'s conservative rival, the *Springfield Southwest Union Press*, also defended the Regulators to some extent. "Their deportment, while in the city, was all that could be desired," said the *Press*. "Each one attending to his own business and letting bad whiskey alone."[13]

John S. Phelps, later governor of Missouri, addressed the Regulators when they descended upon Springfield on May 28, 1866. *Author's collection.*

Perhaps in deference to the admonitions of Phelps and the other Springfield dignitaries, the Regulators did make a token effort to work within the law during the days immediately following their visit to the city. On June 6, 1866, the Honest Men's League assisted Greene County deputy Isaac Jones in rounding up eight accused thieves in the northwest part of the county and bringing them to Springfield to face charges. The names of the alleged thieves were Joseph Mullenax, Jackson Smith, Samuel Richards, Jasper Fly, James Davis, John Perryman, Donnell Cochran, and Marion Fortune. Most of these men were probably associates of Green B. Phillips. It's known, for instance, that Mullenax was a brother-in-law to Phillips, and Perryman had served in Phillips's company during the war.[14]

But the Regulators again resorted to mob rule on June 9, just three days after helping arrest Mullenax and company. On June 3, James W. "Boss" Edwards, and another "hardened customer" named Parton had stolen two horses in Christian County and fled in the direction of Arkansas. They had to turn back at the White River because they were unable to cross. They released the animals and made their way back to Christian County. Pursuing the thieves, the sheriff found the horses and then followed the trail of Edwards and his sidekick back to Christian County, where they were placed under arrest and lodged in jail at Ozark. On the 9th, about one hundred Regulators came down from Greene County and took Edwards from the jail by force. They took him out on the Forsyth road a short distance from Ozark and hanged him from a large oak tree at the side of the road. The body was left hanging until noon the next day, when family members came and cut it down.[15]

As was the case with Phillips, the question of why the Honest Men's League selected Edwards is not clear. Like the previous victims, he was a former Union soldier, but he lived in Christian County and seemingly had little, if any, connection to the men from northwest Greene County who were lynched or arrested. Edwards was surely a casualty of bad timing, because he committed his crime during a period when the effort of the Regulators to rid the region of thieves and robbers was at its peak. But that doesn't explain why his partner in crime was spared. However, Edwards, who was known as "a most desperate character and a terror to the country," apparently had a worse reputation than Parton. In addition, Edwards had reportedly threatened some of the men guarding him at Ozark that he would kill them if he ever got free again. The Regulators didn't give him a chance to carry out his threats but instead decided to make an example out of him.[16]

The Honest Men's League was next heard from after the group learned that some of the men they'd helped round up and lodge in jail had been bailed out, and they issued a declaration warning against such action. The notice was written at Walnut Grove on June 16 and was reprinted in the *Weekly Patriot* on June 21:

> *To the Citizens of Southwest Missouri:*
> We, the Regulators, organized to assist in the enforcement of the civil law, and to put down an extensive thieving organization, known to exist in our midst, having succeeded in arresting and committing to jail and number of persons charged with grand larceny, robbery and general lawlessness, whom we believe to be bad men; and finding several of them have been bailed out, thereby extending to them an opportunity of again putting into execution their diabolical purposes of robbing, plundering and murdering their neighbors; Therefore, we hereby give notice, that all persons bailing such parties out of jail, will be regarded as in sympathy if not in full cooperation with such, and will be held strictly responsible for the conduct and personal appearance at court for trial, of all persons thus bailed out of jail. Emphatically by the
>
> REGULATORS[17]

The lynching of Edwards had essentially ended the violent reign of the Regulators, but a war of words continued between its members and those individuals brave enough to speak out against the vigilante organization. On July 28, 1866, the Honest Men's League met at Cave Spring to elect officers and draft resolutions expressing the sentiments of the group. Among the officers chosen were Levi Downing and Thomas Coltrane. The resolutions that were adopted pointed once again to the unusual state of lawlessness existing in Greene and surrounding counties to justify the organization's existence, and they reiterated the group's determination to rid the region of thieves and robbers "through the forms of law, if we can, but without the forms of law, if we must." The document declared that "the hanging of certain notorious thieves" had been very beneficial to the community and that the group had only adopted such extreme measures out of "stern necessity." The group also denounced "would-be political leaders" who kept up a pretended regard for law and order and an allegiance to the Radical Union party while secretly sympathizing with and encouraging thieves.[18]

This jab at would-be political leaders was likely aimed mainly at Stephen Julian, who had, in fact, run unsuccessfully for the state legislature earlier in 1866. Julian, a friend and neighbor of Green B. Phillips, wasted little time in responding to the barb. After the resolutions of the Honest Men's League were published in the August 9 issue of the *Weekly Patriot*, Julian called a meeting of his original law and order group, and it met at Cave Spring on August 17, although with many fewer members than it had back in March. Julian opened the meeting, but Daniel Mallicoat, who had been at the first meeting, was selected as the new president. The group adopted a series of resolutions strongly condemning the Regulators as nothing more than "an organized mob." Julian and company also denounced the resolutions that the Regulators had adopted at their July meeting. Other resolutions reiterated some of the basic Constitutional rights of US citizens, such as the right to free speech and the right to trial by jury, rights that the Regulators were thwarting.[19]

Taking his protest another step, Julian wrote a letter on August 20 from Walnut Grove defending himself and condemning the Regulators, and it was published in the *Patriot* three days later. Pointing out that the Regulators were composed of men of all persuasions, from rebels and copperheads (i.e. men who professed loyalty to the Union but secretly sympathized with the Confederacy) to radicals and preachers of the gospel,

Julian had words of rebuke for all the different groups. The rebels were at least consistent in that they were still defying civil authority just as they did when they seceded in 1861. Julian cut the copperheads no such slack. They had balked during the war at punishing rebels who committed atrocities but were now all-too-willing to punish Union men accused of theft. The Union men in the Honest Men's League, Julian asserted, were being used like a "cat's paw" to do the dirty work of the rebels and copperheads. Many of them had fought for three years to put down the rebellion and restore civil authority, but now they had joined the rebels, copperheads, and conservatives to shoot down Union men, "or thieves as they call them." Lastly, the preachers of the gospel, supposed to be followers of Jesus, whose message was one of mercy, were showing no mercy whatsoever but instead were acting as the primary spokesmen and apologists for a group that had hanged at least two men contrary to the Constitution and the statutes. Julian ended his letter by reminding his readers that hanging was an extraordinary punishment for stealing. If it wasn't cruel punishment, it was certainly unusual punishment. He signed the letter, "S. H. Julian, would-be politician."[20]

On September 21, Levi Downing responded to Julian in a letter of his own that appeared in Springfield newspapers shortly afterward. He accused Julian of being a sore loser, still upset at having lost his bid for state office, who was trying to inject politics into the controversy surrounding the Regulators by suggesting that the group's intent was to punish Union men. To the contrary, Downing said, the Honest Men's League was apolitical, organized only in the interest of restoring order and dispensing justice to lawbreakers.[21]

Downing's letter basically ended the public war of words between the Regulators and their critics, but the group met twice more, once in early April 1867 at Cave Spring. John Small chaired the meeting, and the group adopted resolutions justifying the actions it had taken over the past year to rid the area of criminals and vowing to work closely with civil authorities now that they were more capable of enforcing the law. At the group's final meeting in early May 1868 at Ash Grove, the Regulators adopted resolutions reaffirming that it was a nonpartisan organization, in answer to persistent accusations to the contrary.[22]

Each of the widows of the first three men killed by the Regulators; Clotilla Phillips, Caroline Gorsuch, and Mary Rush; brought suit against the group's members seeking financial damages for the deaths of their husbands. Among those named in Mary Rush's suit were John Small, Thomas Coltrane, A. C. Sloan, and Levi Downing. All three suits named principally the same individuals. Whether any of the women ever won a monetary settlement is unclear, but none of the Regulators were ever charged in criminal court for the lynchings they carried out.[23]

6
A Jargon of Voices Crying for His Blood
The Lynching of Bud Isbel

About two o'clock on the afternoon of June 19, 1871, a young black man named Joseph "Bud" Isbel stopped at the home of Peter Christian, in northwest Springfield near the intersection of present-day Kansas Expressway and Brower Street. Keeper of a boarding house in downtown Springfield, the thirty-eight-year-old Christian was not home, but his twenty-year-old wife, Martha Lou, was, along with the couple's infant child. Bud asked Martha for a drink of water, and she gave him a dipper and pointed him toward the well. When he came back to the house to return the dipper, he looked Martha "full in the face" and asked her if she'd like to make five dollars. Insulted by the insinuation, Martha ordered the man off the premises.[1]

Instead of leaving, the twenty-one-year-old Isbel grabbed the young woman by her arms and threw her to the floor. Overpowering her, he "forced her to submit to his will." Described in a Springfield newspaper as "a small, frail woman," Martha was unable to fight off the desperate "fiend," and her screams for help went unheeded, as she lived in an open field about a half-mile from her nearest neighbor.[2]

Isbel fled after he had "accomplished his purpose," and Martha hurried to a neighbor's house, from where word was sent to Christian of the outrage on his wife. The police were also notified, and from the description Martha gave them, they were confident that her attacker was Bud Isbel, who allegedly had also assaulted an eleven-year-old black girl a couple of miles east of Springfield five days earlier. Search parties were quickly organized, and Christian, an immigrant from Norway, offered a hundred dollar reward for the capture of the suspect. Isbel was described as being about five feet and five inches tall and "poorly clothed."[3]

Although Isbel was reportedly spotted in Springfield on Boonville Street the morning after the rape, the suspect, if indeed it was Isbel, slipped away without being apprehended, and no other good leads turned up in the immediate wake of the crime. For several days, citizens around Springfield kept an eye out for Isbel, and some formed into posses to go out looking for him. "Every road and bush in the vicinity of the city was watched and guarded," said the *Springfield Leader*. "From every section of the county reports were received that he had been seen, first here, there and 'away over yonder' until we began to believe him endowed with ubiquity." Then on June 23, four days after the attack, word was received in Springfield that Isbel and his mother had been spotted near Newtonia, and two men set out for Newton County to bring him back. When they arrived in Newtonia late that evening, they found Isbel already in the custody of the town marshal, and after spending the night, the men boarded a train with the fugitive and brought him back to Springfield on Saturday morning, June 24.[4]

Martha Christian was brought to the depot, where she identified Isbel as her attacker. He was then brought to the public square and guarded in a wagon by eight to ten armed men, as a few others looked on. Most of those present seemed "determined to dispose of him summarily," said the *Leader*, but lacking a general agreement, the mob was not yet big enough to overcome the objections of the few. The debate over Isbel's fate went back and forth for thirty minutes.[5]

Law officers and city officials made no effort to break up the mob, even though the sheriff, the city marshal, and the mayor were all on the square during the "early stages of the proceedings," according to the *Springfield Missouri Weekly Patriot*, and "their authority would probably have been respected" at that time.[6]

As the dispute over Isbel's fate continued, word of his capture ran "like wild fire" through the streets of Springfield, and hundreds of people thronged onto the public square until it became "a sea of foaming, indignant humanity." Cries of "Hang him!" rent the air, and an occasional exhortation to burn or torture the captive echoed across the plaza. As Isbel stood in the wagon with the threatening mob pressing in around him, he appeared "as cool and indifferent as an iceberg," said a *Springfield Leader* reporter. Gazing upon "the physiognomy of the doomed wretch," the newspaperman described Isbel as "about five feet and eight inches in height, square shoulders, heavy frame, large oval head, broad nostrils and sensual lips."[7]

The reporter overheard someone standing nearby ask Isbel whether he was guilty of the crime he was charged with and urged him to tell the truth in view of what appeared to be his impending doom. "I am not," Isbel replied.[8]

The newsman remained unconvinced, though, because those who'd captured Isbel and brought him to Springfield claimed he confessed to them and that he also admitted perpetrating several similar attacks and many petty crimes in the Springfield area.[9]

The mood of the mob gathering on the square grew uglier with each passing minute, and finally Isbel stood on "the very brink of eternity." Only one man in the crowd dared to offer "an extenuating voice...in behalf of the friendless negro...amid the jargon of voices that were crying for his blood." Isbel's "champion" tried to plead for the doomed man's life, but "he was flung out like the whirlwind wafts the feather."[10]

"After making a public exhibition of Bud Isbel for half an hour," the mob marched him down Boonville Street to "an alley north of Schmook's mill" (probably present-day Phelps Street) with many curious onlookers traipsing behind. Turning east, the mob took Isbel into the Jordan Creek valley just east of Benton Avenue, about equidistant from two nearby African-American churches. Mart Danforth had been lynched twelve years earlier in the same immediate vicinity.[11]

"The crowd gathered around the spot," said the *Leader*, "thirsting like Moloch, hungry for human blood." Despite the ominous threat of the murderous crowd, Isbel "retained his self possession with wonderful composure, never moving a muscle or fibre of his countenance."[12]

R. B. Chappel, a former Union major, tried to plead with the crowd to conduct a further investigation to make sure Isbel was the guilty party, and he also suggested that the hanging, if it had to occur, should take place farther out of town away from houses. But he was shouted down and several revolvers drawn on him.[13]

Presently, someone produced a bed cord, and one end of it was fashioned into a noose. One of the vigilantes climbed a big elm tree to tie the other end of the rope to a limb. Isbel was mounted on a horse, and the animal and its rider were led beneath the overhanging limb. Peter Christian, the aggrieved husband, got on the horse behind Isbel, looped the noose over his head, and quickly dismounted. When the horse was led away, Isbel dropped so far that his feet hit the ground. As he choked and writhed in anguish, "a feeling of intense horror" was felt by those in the crowd "capable in their heart of feeling one pulse of pity," but most bystanders just looked on coolly. Finally, Christian took hold of Isbel, and several other members of the mob helped him lift the man back up, while still others shortened the rope. Isbel was then dropped again and left "swinging between heaven and earth, a quivering, horrible sight to mortal eyes."[14]

But the thirst for vengeance was not yet slaked, said the *Leader*. After two or three minutes, "while the dark form was still vibrating with the last pulsations of ebbing life," Christian stepped up with a handgun and shot Isbel in the head near the right ear. Isbel was now just "a hanging mass of lifeless flesh and bone."[15]

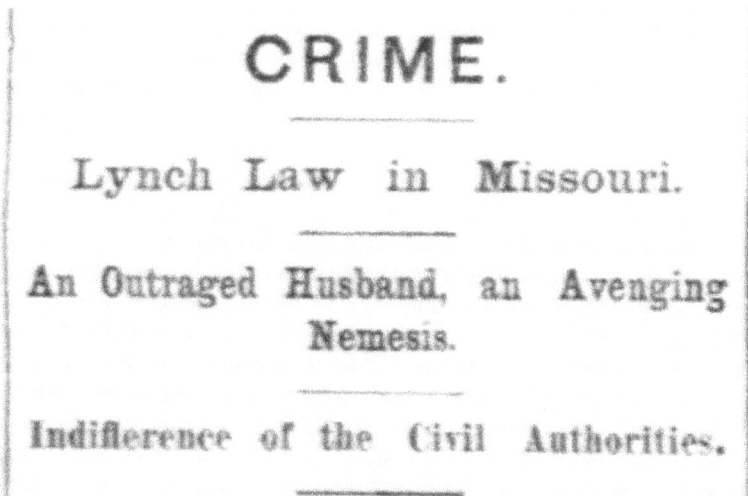

CRIME.

Lynch Law in Missouri.

An Outraged Husband, an Avenging Nemesis.

Indifference of the Civil Authorities.

Headline in the *St. Louis Missouri Republican* announces the lynching of Isbel.

After Isbel was dead and the thirst for blood had been quenched, "the satiated crowd" began to withdraw, but a stream of fresh curiosity-seekers arrived to gaze upon the corpse. Several of the new onlookers were African American, and one of the black women burst into anguished cries upon seeing the dead young man. "The sound touched the heart of another, and the infection flew from mouth to mouth until the place resounded with notes of grief. The sight was too agonizing for them to gaze on without feeling, and they gave vent to their sorrow in floods of tears." Isbel, who just moments before had "no friend to counsel or console" him, now had a host of mourners weeping "over his untimely death."[16]

The body was left hanging, though, until the county coroner, Dr. Peter Burns, summoned a jury and arrived to cut the corpse down. After viewing the body, the jury removed to the courthouse, where they rendered a verdict that Isbel had come to his death by hanging and shooting at the hands of Peter Christian, James Chadwick, and a third man named Piper, "assisted and encouraged" by "two to five hundred other persons, white and black, unknown to the jury."[17]

It was obviously important to the jury to point out that the mob that lynched Isbel was not composed entirely of white people, as if by so doing they could deflect some of the blame for the atrocity onto Isbel's own race. It seems highly unlikely, however, that more than a handful of black people were present at the hanging, and those that were present were probably no more than bystanders.

As dictated by the law, the verdict of the coroner's jury was placed in the hands of the proper authorities so that the guilty parties named by the jury could be arrested. "Whether anything will be done in that direction," said the *Springfield Missouri Weekly Patriot*, "we do not know; though we think the matter will be dropped without further agitation."[18]

And apparently it was. Both the *Leader* and the *Patriot* voiced obligatory outrage that the citizens of Springfield had seen fit to take the law into their own hands, but the newspapers stopped short of openly condemning the lynching. The consensus seemed to be, as the *Patriot* said, that "no punishment was too severe for the outrageous crime that had been committed; and that if Mr. Christian had promptly shot Isbel as an act of personal vengeance, at the time his wife recognized him as the villain who had outraged her, no regrets would have been felt."[19]

Chapter 7
Quite an Excitement at Walnut Grove
The Lynching of Greenberry Buis

When eighteen-year-old Martha Brinn of Walnut Grove married twenty-one-year-old Greenberry Buis about 1869, her father, James Brinn, opposed the match. Nevertheless, Brinn, who was considered "a respectable citizen of the county," allowed the newlyweds to live briefly with his family. Later, Buis and his wife moved across the line into Polk County, where he had relatives.[1]

Around the first part of 1872, Buis and his wife moved again, this time to Cass County, and Buis promptly got into trouble for stealing horses in neighboring Jackson County. He was arrested, tried, and convicted of grand larceny at the May term of the Jackson County court. Sentenced to three years in the state penitentiary, Buis was received at the Jefferson City facility in early July 1872. His wife, Martha, returned to Greene County and moved back in with her father.[2]

Buis was discharged from the state prison under a pardon from Governor Silas Woodson in late April 1873 after serving less than ten months of his three-year sentence. Upon his release, he came back to the vicinity of Walnut Grove, and he and his wife got back together.[3]

Apparently Buis's brief stint in the big house did little to cure him of his larcenous ways, because he'd been back home only about a month when he and a brother-in-law named Wood were accused of stealing sheep and selling them to butchers in Springfield and Polk County. They were arrested, but Buis escaped, while Wood was lodged in the Hickory County Jail at Hermitage.[4]

Buis was captured in Barry County during the first week of July 1873, and a posse started back with him to Polk County, where he would face prosecution. When the party approached the Walnut Grove area on Sunday afternoon July 6, Buis asked his escorts to let him spend the night at home with his family before taking him on to Bolivar and turning him over to Polk County authorities the next day. The posse agreed, and the party stopped south of Walnut Grove at the home of Mary Buis. She was the prisoner's widowed mother, but his wife, Martha, was also staying there.[5]

Buis went inside the home, and at least five men were detailed to guard him. About nine o'clock that night, five or six horsemen rode up to a fence in front of the Buis property and hollered to the guards outside the house that they wanted to talk. Two of the guards went out to the fence, and the riders asked whether the widow Buis lived there. The guards confirmed that she did. The horsemen then asked whether her son Greenberry was there, and the guards again answered in the affirmative. The riders wanted the guards to bring the prisoner out, but the guards said they couldn't do that because they were authorized to watch Buis in the house and nowhere else. The horsemen assured the guards they could take care of that matter, but the guards still balked, saying they wanted to "keep (their) skirts clear," or, in other words, to stay clear of any wrongdoing.[6]

One of the horseman rode off and came back promptly with at least twenty additional men. Most of the mob dismounted and marched into the yard, telling the guards that they needed to stand back if they wanted to keep their skirts clear. Three of the vigilantes went inside, and one of them demanded to know whether there was a sick man in the house. Mary Buis said that there was a man in bed but that he wasn't sick. As the three started toward the bed where Greenberry was resting, Mary pleaded with them not to hurt her son. One of the men took hold of Greenberry and told him to get up because they wanted to talk to him. Martha Buis rushed over and told the man he could talk to her husband in her presence. "Hold on, young lady," the man replied. "We want to talk to him some other place."[7]

Buis pleaded with the men to "reason the case" and to give him a trial, but the men only became more unyielding and started "using bitter oaths." They called Buis a "damned son of a bitch" and started dragging him from the house. Near the doorway, one of the guards stepped forward with his revolver in hand, demanding to know what was going on, but the vigilantes shoved him aside and told all the guards to stand back. "You who have been guarding him," they announced, "we take charge of him now."[8]

The mob took Buis about a quarter of a mile from his home and strung him up to a tree. The guards, according to the *Springfield Missouri Weekly Patriot,* were "powerless to prevent the terrible deed."[9]

The body was left hanging until about four o'clock the next afternoon when a coroner's jury arrived to hold an inquest. The guards were all called to testify before the jury, and all of them denied knowing any of the vigilantes. The only other person to testify at the inquest was Dr. A. C. Sloan, the same A. C. Sloan who'd been a member of the Regulators seven years earlier. He said he'd examined Buis's body after he was dead.[10]

Greenberry Buis Hung by a Mob!

Quite an excitement prevailed at Walnut Grove last Monday, caused by the announcement that Greenberry Buis had been hung by a body of armed men the night previous.

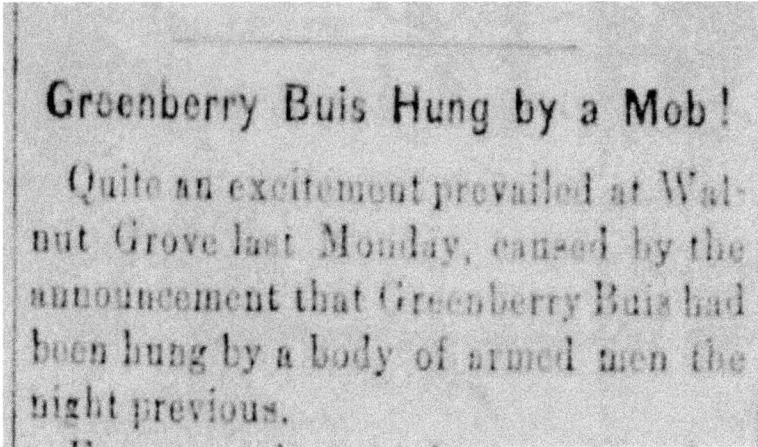

Headline in the *Springfield Missouri Weekly Patriot* heralding the Buis lynching.

The *Weekly Patriot* reported that Buis had been lynched because he had allegedly threatened the lives of a number of men. To comment further on the "horrible deed and do justice" was a difficult task, the newspaper allowed, before proceeding to offer just such comment:

> The poor people of Missouri suffered many hardships during the war, and hoped when peace dawned on the land that it would be such a peace as would insure "life, liberty and the pursuit of happiness," as well as the peaceable possession...of property. That there has been a large amount of stealing, bushwhacking and hellishness generally, throughout the country, since the war, none will deny. How to abolish the outrages entirely, is not easy. It can be done by abolishing the perpetrators, but law-abiding people would prefer to suffer much indignity rather than enforce this principle. The law is able, if it was enforced. The good people of Missouri have elected a Governor who sends the horse-thieves and robbers back among them, to take their hard-earnings, or take their lives even if they seek justice through the law, and what can they do to help themselves? We oppose mobs, but have great sympathy for honest, hard-working men, who have their property stolen and their lives in peril. We also add that we have but little

pity for men who make their living in this way, even if they get their necks in a rope.[11]

Chapter 8
The Murder of Sarah Graham and the Most Spectacular Court Procedure in the Entire Life of the County

On February 25, 1886, a search party went out from Brookline to the Emma Molloy farm about three miles northeast of the village intent on searching the premises for any sign of Sarah Graham. a woman who'd been missing several months. The occupants of the farm had turned away previous attempts to search the property, giving one excuse after another, but this time the men meant to get to the bottom of the mystery. They were particularly intent on searching an abandoned well in a hollow northeast of the farmhouse, and they'd brought along a windlass to facilitate the search.[1]

Using the windlass, the rest of the men lowered Isaac Hite into the well. At the bottom of the well, Hite looked around and saw the nude, decomposing body of woman lying on the muddy floor of a chamber that forked off to the north from the horizontal shaft of the main well, or cave.

Hite called up to the other men that he'd found a woman's body. The men didn't have to be told her identity, although a coroner's inquest would have to make it official. Emma

Molloy's foster daughter Cora Lee, the only adult on the premises when the men arrived to conduct their search, grew very distraught when they announced their discovery and would not let Sarah's sons go near the scene. While Hite and the other men were still devising a way to hoist the woman's body out of the well, John Potter, Brookline postmaster who'd been involved in the search for Sarah Graham since Christmas, set out for Springfield to report the discovery of the body. Just as the coroner would have to officially identify the victim, so, too, would he have to determine an official cause of death. But Potter thought he knew the answer to that question as well. George Graham, recently arrested on a bigamy charge, had never given anybody a straight answer anytime he was questioned about his first wife's whereabouts. And now Potter knew why. The smooth-talking Graham would soon be facing a much more serious charge.

Small trees in middle of this recent photo mark the approximate spot where Sarah Graham's body was found at the bottom of an old well. *Photo by Author.*

Emma Molloy was already a well-known newspaper woman in northern Indiana when she rose to regional fame in the early 1870s as an orator and an advocate of women's rights. By the latter seventies she had adopted temperance as her principal cause, and her prominence had spread throughout

Emma Molloy was already a famous temperance revivalist when the photo upon which this etching is based was taken circa 1877. *Author's collection.*

the country. Also a supporter of prison reform, she was at the height of her fame when she met George E. Graham at the Indiana State Prison North in 1880. Graham was serving his second term in the Indiana prison and had also served a previous term in the Illinois State Penitentiary, although, not surprisingly, he failed to reveal to Mrs. Molloy the full extent of his criminal background. In fact, the twenty-nine-year-old Graham had first run afoul of the law when he was just a ten-year-old lad, and he'd been in and out of trouble ever since. His conniving intelligence had helped him weasel out of a number of serious scrapes for which he'd never done time. But Mrs. Molloy was struck by his literary bent and articulate manner, and she thought she could save him.

Sketches of George and Sarah Graham from *The Graham Tragedy and the Molloy-Lee Examination.*

Taking George under her wing when he got out of prison, Mrs. Molloy made him manager of her temperance newspaper, and the Graham family and the Molloy family lived together in the same home for several months in Washington, Kansas. But Sarah and George had a falling out near the beginning of 1885, and Sarah returned to Indiana with the couple's two boys. Mrs. Molloy had to sell the financially struggling newspaper in the early spring of 1885, and she returned to the speaker's trail. Judge James Baker and other Springfield prohibitionists engaged her to come to Springfield for a series of lectures in May at the First Congregationalist Church at the corner of Jefferson and Locust streets. The lectures were very successful and were praised in newspapers as far away as St. Louis, and when the revival ended, Judge Baker arranged for Mrs. Molloy to purchase a farm southwest of Springfield near Brookline.

Near the first of June, about the time the deal on the farm was to close, George Graham, who'd gone back to Indiana about the same time Mrs. Molloy came to Springfield, showed up to declare his love for Cora Lee and to ask for her hand in marriage. A romance between the couple had been smoldering since Sarah had left Kansas, if not before, and now it burst into flame. George "confessed" he and Sarah had been living in sin in Kansas because she had divorced him while he was serving his first term in the Indiana prison, but if Cora and Mrs. Molloy

Cora Lee, whose romance with George Graham ultimately led to Sarah Graham's murder. From *The Graham Tragedy and the Molloy-Lee Examination.*

could find it in their hearts to forgive him for that transgression, it meant there was no legal impediment to his proposal. Cora Lee seemed truly in love with Graham; so, Mrs. Molloy gave her blessing to the match after confirming that a divorce between Sarah and George had indeed taken place. No one thought to ask about a remarriage. Mrs. Molloy and her family moved onto the farm in mid-June, and Cora Lee and George Graham were united in matrimony there a month later by the Reverend J. C. Plumb of the First Congregationalist Church. Leaving Graham to manage the farm, Mrs. Molloy returned to the lecture circuit.

Things seemed to go smoothly at the farm at first, but in late summer Sarah learned of George's marriage to Cora and started writing to George threatening to come to Springfield and expose him for the bigamist he was. They both knew his recent marriage to Cora was a sham, because they had rewed between his Indiana prison stints and were still legally married. George tried to talk Sarah out of coming to Springfield, even offering monetary inducements, but she insisted.

Graham finally arranged to meet her in St. Louis in late September. According to his later story, Sarah had agreed to let him take one or both of the boys back to the farm, while she returned to Indiana, but when they met in St. Louis, she insisted on going on to Springfield to reclaim her rightful place as his wife. Graham tried to get her to stay in St. Louis with relatives or go back to Indiana, but she wouldn't be dissuaded. When they reached Springfield on the evening of September 30, Graham arranged for his sons to stay overnight in a boarding house, assuring them that he and their mother would come back for them in the morning. It was a dark, rainy night, and according to Graham's story, he started for the Brookline farm on foot, thinking Sarah surely wouldn't try to follow on such a dank, dreary night, but she came right along with him.

When they reached the gate of the farm, it was the wee hours of October 1. Graham made one last attempt to talk Sarah out of "ruining him," but she insisted on going up to the farmhouse and "clearing Cora out." They got into a heated argument, and Graham killed her with a knife during the ensuing struggle. Then he stripped off her clothes, dumped her body in the abandoned well, and went on up to the house as if nothing was wrong.

But keeping his terrible secret proved difficult. As inquiries from Sarah's family back in Indiana became more and more persistent, he began to panic. About January 9, 1886, he passed three bad checks on Springfield banks and fled to Kansas City. He wrote Mrs. Molloy explaining that he needed the money to go looking for Sarah because she was missing and her family was blaming him for her disappearance. Convinced by his latest sob story, Mrs. Molloy persuaded him to return to Springfield, and she made his bad checks good. But Mrs. Molloy had scarcely gotten the wayward Graham out of one scrape before he found himself in another. In late January, Sarah's sister Abigail and her husband, Timothy Breese, arrived in Springfield to press charges against Graham for bigamy, swearing that Sarah had legally remarried George in 1878. He was arrested and lodged in the Greene County Jail in lieu of bond.

Now, less than a month later, with the discovery of the woman's body on the Molloy farm, the irrepressible Graham faced an even graver charge. Still in custody on the bigamy charge, he was also charged with first-degree murder. Cora Lee was arrested as an accessory before the fact to the murder, as it was thought she was an actual participant in the crime. Since Mrs. Molloy was away from home at the time of the murder, she was arrested as an accessory after the fact for allegedly helping conceal the crime.

The women's preliminary hearing got underway in mid-March 1886, while Graham was still awaiting his. Later called "the most spectacular court procedure in the entire life of the county" by local historians Jonathan Fairbanks and Clyde Edwin Tuck, the preliminary examination turned into a sensation that packed the courtroom with curious onlookers for almost every session and drew nationwide newspaper coverage. George and Sarah's thirteen-year-old son, Charlie, offered the most startling testimony when he swore he had seen his father in bed with Mrs. Molloy on more than one occasion while they lived in Kansas and had even seen him in bed with both Cora and Mrs. Molloy at the same time on at least one occasion. The defense countered that Charlie had been coached to lie and that any instances of physical contact he might have witnessed between his father and Mrs. Molloy were innocent expressions of affection such as between a mother and son.

Graham had defended Mrs. Molloy at first, but he'd turned against her when she refused to bail him out after he was arrested for bigamy. Two-thirds of the way through the preliminary hearing, he tossed another explosive charge into the proceedings when a long letter he had written detailing the torrid affairs he'd allegedly carried on simultaneously with Cora Lee and Mrs. Molloy over the past few years was published in various newspapers. In his account, he named towns throughout the Midwest where he had allegedly spent the night with Mrs. Molloy, giving the dates and the names of the hotels.

The scandalous charges so distressed Mrs. Molloy that the hearing was briefly interrupted. When it concluded in late March, Cora Lee was bound over for trial on a charge of accessory to murder before the fact and Mrs. Molloy was bound over on a charge of accessory to murder after the fact.

Graham was still awaiting action on his case when a mounted and disguised mob rode into Springfield during the wee hours of April 27, 1886, and took the prisoner forcibly from his jail cell at the rear of the Greene County Courthouse at College Street and the public square. He was loaded onto a spring wagon, taken to a spot north of the woolen mill (where Grant Beach Park is today), and strung up to a tree on or near the property of present-day Weaver Elementary School. The mob left a note on the body identifying themselves as "the three hundred" and warning that anybody who tried to discover their identity beyond that would be "speedily dispatched to hell."[2]

A couple of weeks later, a Springfield newspaper published a letter from Mrs. Molloy in which she categorically denied the scandalous charges of immorality George Graham had leveled against her. She offered corroborating statements from various individuals attesting that she could not possibly have been with Graham at some of the times and places he alleged, since she was with them. Mrs. Molloy's critics pointed out that she had conveniently waited until her accuser was dead before forcefully answering his charges. She countered that she had done so only because she wanted to be able to offer evidence, not just denials, and because she feared any aspersions she cast on George Graham's character might incite mob action against him, something that ended up happening anyway.

Mrs. Molloy was released on bond shortly after her arrest, and Cora Lee was released on bond a few months later. Cora's trial took place in June 1887. The prosecution tried to show that Cora had met George and Sarah in Springfield on the night Sarah was killed, accompanied them back to the farm, and actively participated in the murder with George. Contrary to the confession George had given, the prosecution maintained that Sarah had been killed with a gunshot, not a knife wound, although the doctors who performed the autopsy had been unable to retrieve a bullet. The state even suggested that Cora might have been the one to fire the fatal shot. The defense called Cora's sister Emma Lee and Mrs. Molloy's adopted daughter, Etta Molloy, to testify that they had spent the night at the Molloy home on the night in question and that Cora had been with them the entire night. Cora testified in her own defense to the same facts. The trial ended in a hung jury in late June, with four jurors reportedly voting for acquittal and eight favoring conviction.

By the time of Cora Lee's second trial in early 1888, some of the fervor surrounding the Sarah Graham murder case had died down, and a new panel of jurors was selected, some of whom were newcomers to Greene County and were little influenced by the early excitement surrounding the case. At the end of the trial, the jury came back after just seven minutes with a unanimous verdict of not guilty on the first vote.

After Cora was acquitted, Mrs. Molloy's case was dismissed, but the damage to her reputation had been done. As Mrs. Molloy herself noted, "There are no two classes of people whom the world...so readily believe a scandal about" as "a minister of the gospel and a woman." And when, as in Mrs. Molloy's case, "the two characteristics are combined, and a scandal can be concocted sufficiently ingenious for the public to swallow, however nauseating and polluting it may be, it is devoured with an ecstasy of delight."

After the charges against her were dropped, Mrs. Molloy moved to the West Coast and resumed her temperance work with moderate success, but she never again achieved the national and even international acclaim she had once enjoyed. She died in 1907 in northern California during a revival tour.

Meanwhile, Cora married Ed Juel in 1889, but he lived only five years. She then lived with her mother and later her sister. Cora died in 1943.

Charlie Graham went back to Indiana, where he grew to adulthood and apparently became a law-abiding citizen.

In 2004, Clifford Gorham, a collateral descendant of Sarah's family, placed a headstone in Maple Park Cemetery in Springfield to mark her gravesite in the southwest quadrant of the cemetery. The stone was meant not only to honor Sarah's memory but also as a tribute to the citizens of Springfield who had shown kindness to Sarah's sister and other Gorham family members during Sarah's murder investigation.

Chapter 9
Insane or Just an "Insanity Artist"?
Pea Ridge Hayes and the
Murder of Frank Keller

When George "Pea Ridge" Hayes went on trial in 1895 for the murder of Greene County deputy Frank Keller, several witnesses testified that he was an imbecile who didn't know right from wrong, but others claimed he was an "insanity artist" who only pretended to be crazy when he thought it would help his cause. One thing was certain, though—Hayes had been known throughout southwest Missouri as a pathetic, incorrigible character for a number of years before he killed Keller.[1]

Hayes was born about 1868 in Arkansas and grew up in the Pea Ridge area. He appeared on the scene in southwest Missouri in the late 1880s, and, traveling from town to town, he quickly developed a reputation throughout the whole area as a troublesome character because of his strange behavior. Often called "Pea Ridge" because of where he was from, he was continually "cutting up" or throwing "sham fits," either to amuse or perplex those around him. His antics earned him more ridicule than applause, and he often ended up in jail for vagrancy, disturbing the peace, or some similar offense. Occasionally he was whipped, run out of town, and told not to come back, but he usually did anyway.[2]

Pea Ridge could be belligerent, too, especially if he had been drinking. In July 1887, he was arrested in Springfield on a charge of disturbing the peace for brandishing a razor and threatening to cut another man. Hayes was fined fifty dollars and sentenced to three months in jail. In early April 1888, Pea Ridge was again arrested in Springfield, this time for vagrancy. He was ordered to leave town, but if he left, he came right back. On April 18, he was arrested in Springfield yet again, on an assault charge, but the case was dismissed when he appeared before a justice of the peace.[3]

Hayes finally got into serious trouble in late 1890 or early 1891 when he shot a man at Aurora. Although details of the incident are sketchy, he was convicted of assault with intent to kill in February of 1891 and was sentenced to two years in the state penitentiary. He was pardoned by Governor David R. Francis, though, after only nine months.[4]

Upon his release, Hayes came back to Lawrence County, where he showed up briefly in Mount Vernon before making his way to Aurora. On January 16, 1892, Pea Ridge boarded a train in Aurora and came to Pierce City. One of his fellow travelers was a man named Guinney, and when they disembarked at Pierce City, Hayes followed Guinney to the post office, where the latter set his valise down outside the door and went inside. Pea Ridge picked up the grip and carried it off down the street. Later that evening, the valise was recovered from under a foot-bridge where George had hidden it, and he was arrested and lodged in the Pierce City jail. A few days later, the city marshal escorted him to the fairgrounds on the edge of town and told him to "keep rollin.'" After the marshal left him, Pea Ridge wandered back into town, but, according to the *Pierce City*

Empire, he "finally rolled out and it is hoped he may not roll in this direction again soon."[5]

Leaving Pierce City, Hayes went to Springfield, where, on January 23, he got up on a makeshift platform on the public square and delivered a spontaneous oration on the evils of the Missouri penal system. The *Springfield Democrat* reported the incident as follows:

> Between twelve and one o'clock yesterday a rather short, fat young man placed a dry goods box on the northwest corner of the square and began to deliver a harangue about barbarous practice being indulged in by officials of the Missouri penitentiary. "When a prisoner fails to do a certain amount of work," said he, "they tie his hands above his head, strip the clothes from his back and a big nigger beats him on the back with a raw-hide until the blood pours forth in torrents." He was proceeding in this strain, growing eloquent at times and collecting a large crowd about him, when Officer Hayes stopped his discourse short. The man gave the name of Hayes, and says he was sent up for felonious assault from Mt. Vernon, and his term expired two weeks ago. He says he has been trying in vain to secure employment, and will be thankful for anything to do to earn money. He claims to be innocent of the crime of which he was convicted, and would like to secure a hall to lecture in.[6]

The *Mount Vernon Lawrence Chieftain* reprinted the *Democrat*'s story under the facetious headline, "Springfield Thought She Had a Distinguished Visitor."[7]

In April, Hayes turned back up in Pierce City, where a nightwatchman gave him to understand that it "might be injudicious" for him "to remain longer in the corporate limits" and that he should "find a more genial clime." The watchman suggested that Pea Ridge might want to go to "Oklahoma or thereabouts," and Hayes did make his way in that direction but stopped in Jasper County. One evening in mid-June, some men went into the engine house at a Carterville mine and heard a voice calling from the depths of the shaft. The man trapped at the bottom of the mine proved to be Pea Ridge. After he was placed in a tub and hoisted out, he claimed he'd been pushed into the shaft, but few people believed him. Most thought he'd probably been trespassing at the property, had gone up on the derrick in an attempt to shinny down a rope into the locked engine house, and had fallen into the shaft. He was taken to a local boarding house where he'd been staying, but he was refused admission. In reporting the incident, a Carterville newspaper noted that Hayes had "been in the pen and every jail and city prison in Northern Arkansas and Southwest Missouri."[8]

By September, Hayes was back in Lawrence County, where he was arrested for breaking into a store at Aurora. He was taken to Mount Vernon and lodged in the county jail to await the action of a grand jury. Still in jail a month later awaiting legal action against him, Pea Ridge procured a razor on the pretense of needing to shave and threatened a fellow prisoner with it. Then, turning the weapon on himself, he tugged on the skin of his neck and cut his own throat. The wound appeared to be serious at first, but he had mainly cut just the loose skin he'd pulled out.[9]

When Hayes appeared in the Lawrence County Circuit Court in mid-February 1893 to plead not guilty to burglary, "he attracted a great deal of attention and considerable mirth by his actions." If Pea Ridge's initial appearance in court provided a dose of amusement for those in attendance, his trial on March 2 turned into an outright spectacle. Labeling Hayes "'Pea Ridge' the invincible," the *Mount Vernon Lawrence Chieftain* opined that a more remarkable proceeding had never taken place in a Lawrence County courtroom "than the trial of this poor unfortunate, debased being." Although his behavior during the morning session was "disgusting," it was eclipsed in the afternoon when Pea Ridge "passed into a fit, foamed at the mouth with other terrible contortions." Court officials and spectators alike were "appalled," and the prosecutor at once "desisted from further action," dismissed the case, and turned Pea loose. Several physicians had previously testified that Hayes was "an irresponsible being," but the question, said the *Chieftain*, was what to do with him. "His general cussedness cannot be excused by the people where he locates. He is a pest to be dreaded like the cholera or small pox.... The penitentiary officials have decided that he cannot be confined there and the insane asylums are not intended for such as he.... It seems the county jail is the only place for him, and there he will doubtless spend the greater part of his life."[10]

Upon his release, Hayes went back to Aurora. One night in late March, he went into a saloon to buy some cigarettes and got into an argument with another customer. The other man pulled out a gun and fired into the wall above Pea Ridge's head. Both men were taken into custody, but Hayes was quickly turned loose when it was determined that he was "doing nothing more than minding his own business."[11]

From Aurora, Pea traveled to Jasper County and wasted little time getting into trouble there. Charged with larceny at the June 1893 term of circuit court, he pleaded not guilty at first but changed his plea to guilty and was sentenced to two years in the state penitentiary. He was received at the Jefferson City facility in mid-July and discharged in January 1895 under the three-fourths law, which provided for early release at the governor's discretion.[12]

Shortly after his release, Hayes returned to Jasper County, and by early April 1895 he was facing a judge again, this time on a minor offense in the Joplin police court. The *Joplin News* observed at the time that Pea Ridge was "an individual that should be chucked bodily into a sewer, for when a human being becomes so low and despicable that they turn him out of the penitentiary before he has even served his time, just to get rid of him, there is no punishment too severe." The *News* suggested that Hayes either be given a hundred lashes or run out of town. "It does no good to fine him as he never has a cent only what he begs, and he feels more at home in jail than anywhere else."[13]

Perhaps Hayes *was* run out of Joplin in early April, because he soon showed up in Springfield. Shortly after his arrival, he started making a nuisance of himself, and Greene County officers schemed to get rid of him. After lodging Pea Ridge in jail for some minor offense, Jailer Ben Alsup left the jail in charge of Deputy Frank Keller, and shortly after Alsup had departed, Keller told Hayes he had the keys and would let him loose if he would run away. Hayes agreed to the bargain and started running north, but he ran right into the path of Jailer Alsup, who was trying to avoid him. Alsup made a feint for his gun and ordered Hayes to stop, which made Pea run all the harder, as the jailer hoped. Hayes wasn't heard from again for thirty days or more, but he turned back up in Springfield in June and was again delivered to the jail on a minor charge.[14]

On June 22, while still in jail, Hayes made what the *Springfield Democrat* called "a very strong bluff at suicide." In a re-enactment of the scene he had orchestrated at Mount Vernon almost three years earlier, Pea Ridge procured a razor from another inmate and drew the blade across his neck, cutting a gash about three inches long and a half inch deep. The doctor who treated him said he didn't think Hayes had made an earnest attempt to kill himself but instead was just trying to avoid having to work on the rock pile, as he had "managed to do most of the time since his incarceration by having fake fits and keeping his name on the sick list." Jailer Alsup had threatened to throw Hayes in the dungeon if he kept throwing fits, which had caused Pea Ridge to resort to a more desperate shirking stratagem.[15]

Shortly after the suicide attempt, Hayes, while working on a chain gang, tried to escape by ducking into a saloon. When Deputy Keller, one of the overseers, followed Hayes into the bar, Pea Ridge picked up a chair and tried to hit the officer with it. Keller grabbed hold of the chair with one hand and with the other "played a lively tune around Pea Ridge's ears" with a billy club. Jailer Alsup also assisted in subduing the prisoner, and Hayes afterwards swore revenge, saying he would kill both Keller and Alsup.[16]

The opportunity to carry out the first part of his threat presented itself on July 9. Hayes was again on a work gang overseen by Keller about a mile north of the zoo on North Grant Street Road. When Keller bent over to inspect the work of some of the prisoners who were drilling into a limestone rock, Pea Ridge struck him a severe blow in the head with a pick, knocking the deputy down and out. Hayes took a pistol off the unconscious lawman and tried to shoot the other overseer, A. J. Bettisworth. He couldn't get the weapon to fire, and Bettisworth shot Hayes in the face with a shotgun. The shot did little damage, since the gun was loaded with bird shot, but it stunned Pea long enough for some of the other prisoners to corral him and disarm him.[17]

Keller died later that night, and Hayes was charged with first-degree murder. The prisoner was unremorseful, saying he only wanted to kill Jailer Alsup and then he would be ready to hang. "The worthless, thieving, murderous George Hayes," said the *Springfield Leader*, "is ready for the halter at last. He has been in all the jails of southwest Missouri, in the penitentiary and at last has reached his climax and should go through the trap door." Indeed, there was talk on the streets of Springfield of sending Hayes through to eternity without the ceremony of a trial, but the threats of mob violence proved idle.[18]

Sketches of Officer Frank Keller, left, and George "Pea Ridge" Hayes, the man who killed him. *From the Springfield Daily Republican.*

Pea Ridge spent two or three weeks in the dungeon at the jail after Keller's murder. Shortly after he was released back into the general population in mid-August, he tried to carry out his longstanding threat to kill Jailer Alsup. Hayes was in the exercise "bull pen" with other inmates when Alsup ordered them back into their individual cells. Refusing to obey, Hayes picked up a shovel and raised it above his head. When he started toward Alsup with it as though to strike him, the jailer fired a shot, and Pea immediately dropped the shovel and feigned injury. He was again consigned to the dungeon.[19]

Hayes was tried in late September 1895 at a special term of the Greene County Criminal Court. A. J. Bettisworth, the other overseer of the work gang, was the primary prosecution witness. During cross-examination, the defense tried to suggest that Keller had used abusive language toward Hayes in the moments leading up to the murder and that the deputy often abused Hayes by striking him with a whip, a tool handle, or other weapons. Bettisworth denied that such was the case. Some of the prisoners who had been on the work gang also testified to the facts surrounding the murder, and they were in general agreement with Bettisworth.[20]

Although S. P. Smith, Hayes's lead attorney, sought to show that Keller had mistreated his client, the primary defense strategy was insanity, not provocation. George's mother, seventy-year-old Martha Hayes, took the stand to testify that her son had been lazy, dull-witted, restless, and subject to fits ever since he was a small child. She said he never bothered anybody as long he was left alone but that the other boys were always picking on him and calling him "crazy Hayes." George left home when he was about thirteen and had been rambling around ever since. Mrs. Hayes said George had two brothers and an uncle who were also subject to fits. As if to explain the streak of insanity in her family, she admitted that she and George's father, who'd been dead several years, were first cousins. Contradicting his mother's testimony to a certain extent, one of George's brothers testified that George "acted just like an idiot" and was always fighting with his siblings. Several other witnesses testified as to George's bizarre behavior, and a few said they didn't think he knew right from wrong. One man testified that several years previously, when he was a conductor on a passenger train through northern Arkansas, George would stand on his head for the amusement of other passengers and solicit money to pay his fare. Two doctors who had been prison physicians while Hayes was in the penitentiary testified as to his imbecility. Hayes had spent much of his time in the insane ward, and, during his first term in the early nineties, he'd been pardoned out and sent back to Lawrence County because the prison officials were ill equipped to handle him.[21]

The prosecution countered during rebuttal that Hayes was just an eccentric who was good at playing the insanity card. Prosecutor A. H. Wear trotted a number of witnesses, including at least four doctors, to the stand to testify that the defendant knew right from wrong and that his supposed insanity was a sham.[22]

The jury was given the case at the conclusion of closing arguments on the evening of September 30. After deliberating several hours, the jury was split almost evenly between conviction and acquittal. Deliberations resumed the next day, and at one point eleven jurors stood for conviction. However, the twelfth would not budge, and he even managed to persuade one of the other jurors back to his side. The jury finally announced on the afternoon of October 1 that they were hopelessly deadlocked. Rather than undertake a new trial, however, the prosecution and the defense reached an agreement allowing Hayes to plead guilty to a lesser charge. The next day, he pleaded guilty to second-degree murder and was allowed to make a statement before sentence was pronounced. He explained that he'd killed Keller because the deputy abused him. He wanted to show all the scars on his back that he said Keller had given him, but Judge James J. Gideon told him such a demonstration was unnecessary. Gideon then pronounced sentence of ninety-nine years imprisonment in the state penitentiary, and Hayes said, "Much obliged, Judge" in a sincere voice. Gideon later remarked that it was the first time he'd been made to feel he'd done a prisoner a kindness by giving him ninety-nine years.[23]

Hayes was transported to Jefferson City late on the night of October 2, 1895, and he was received the next day at the state prison. He was transferred to the insane asylum at Fulton on June 21, 1901, and he was discharged on May 3, 1904, under a pardon from Governor A. M. Dockery. About three weeks later, Pea Ridge turned up in Fort Smith, Arkansas, and started preaching on the streets. On May 30, he caused a scene when he commenced praying in a loud voice for a young woman who had fainted in front of a drugstore. A short time after this, Hayes fell as he was trying to jump on a train near Springfield and was ground to death beneath the wheels. A contrary report years later claimed that all trace of Hayes was lost not long after he returned to Arkansas from the penitentiary.[24]

10
Anna McMahan and The Prettiest Boy
in the World
Murder, Suicide, or Something Else?

About 4:30 on Sunday afternoon, December 7, 1902, four shots rang out in an upstairs room of the Watson building at the corner of Walnut and Campbell streets in Springfield. Immediately afterward, nineteen-year-old William Pittman raced down the stairs, emerged from the building, and ran a half block north on Campbell to the Waddle Hotel, yelling for someone to summon a doctor. Pittman was seriously injured with a gunshot wound to the head, but he was fully conscious and talked freely to doctors, officers, and others arriving on the scene. He said a young woman named Anna McMahan had shot him without provocation as he stood before a mirror and that she then turned the gun on herself. Investigators hurried to the Watson building and found the twenty-three-year-old Miss McMahan dead in her room, but the circumstantial evidence they discovered was at direct odds with the story Pittman had told.[1]

The woman had been shot twice, once in the back of the head and once directly between the shoulder blades. As the

Springfield Republican observed two days after the shooting, this "leads nearly everyone to believe that she did not shoot herself." Many people, the newspaper added, thought it would have been "a physical impossibility" for Anna to have fired the shots.[2]

No kidding! One wonders why the skepticism wasn't unanimous. Just who were these devotees of the marvelous, few though they might have been, who thought the young woman could have pulled off such an unlikely feat of contortion as to shoot herself in the back of the head and then, failing in her first attempt to kill herself, been so determined to end her miserable life as to manage the even more difficult stunt of shooting herself between the shoulder blades?

Not only did the number and the location of the wounds Anna had suffered argue against a suicide attempt on her part, the location and trajectory of Pittman's wound suggested that it, in fact, was self-inflicted. The bullet had entered his right temple and come out of his head near the right eye, destroying his vision in that eye.[3]

So, investigators did not believe that Miss McMahan had shot Pittman without provocation, as he claimed. Instead, they believed he had killed her in a fit of jealous rage. He had apparently fired three shots at her, but one had missed and hit an iron bed post. The ball was found flattened and lying on the bed. After shooting Anna, Pittman had then tried to kill himself. Although he had known Anna only a few days, officers thought he was infatuated with her and had come to her room on Sunday afternoon expecting to rekindle their newfound intimacy. Instead, he discovered that she had entertained another man on Saturday night while he was out of town, and they got into a heated argument. As evidence of this theory, investigators found an empty pint whiskey bottle and an empty quart beer bottle in Anna's room that they thought she and the other man had shared.

Pittman denied this charge, claiming that he had shared the whiskey with Anna himself, although he admitted he knew nothing about the beer bottle. Investigators also found a note they thought Anna had written to the unidentified man.[4]

A JEALOUS LOVER

WILL PITTMAN MURDERED ANNA M'MAHAN.

HE THEN SHOT HIMSELF

Headline in the *Springfield Leader and Democrat* captures the initial public assessment of the McMahan murder case.

Pittman, who lived on a farm outside Springfield with his parents, had come to town about the first of December, which was a Monday, and taken a room at the Waddle Hotel (also called the Afflack Hotel after its owner), because he had been summoned to testify before a grand jury that was convening throughout the week to investigate a number of cases in which the defendants were charged with selling liquor to minors. Early in the week, Pittman made the acquaintance of Anna McMahan, who worked at the hotel as a dining room girl, and by Thursday she started entertaining him in her room at the Watson building. The pair spent much of their time together over the next couple of days until Pittman left on Saturday to return home for his brother's birthday.[5]

If Pittman had known what awaited him when he got back to Springfield, he might have stayed home, but he came back to town on Sunday. His confrontation with Anna occurred shortly after he got back, and now he was under arrest for her murder. In serious condition but still conscious, he was taken to his hotel room and placed under guard there.[6]

The day after the shooting, Coroner J. C. Matthews convened a jury to hold an inquest into Anna's death. Pittman, who was the chief witness, repeated essentially the same story he'd told when he first ran from the Watson building, but the jury didn't buy it. They concluded that "Anna McMahan came to her death as the result of a pistol shot fired by William Pittman."[7]

Because of Pittman's serious condition, his pre-liminary hearing was postponed until early 1903, when he was indicted for first-degree murder and bound over for trial in Greene County Criminal Court. Jury selection for his trial got underway the second week of April, and testimony began on the 9th with the courtroom "crowded to the doors with eager spectators." Three witnesses who lived in the Watson building or were visiting at the time of the shooting testified that they heard four shots. One remembered that he heard three shots in quick succession followed by a pause before the fourth shot. However, another witness said the pause occurred between the second and third shots, while the third witness recalled more than one pause. All three witnesses went to Miss McMahan's door after they heard the shots and saw her lying on the floor. One of the three witnesses, Shirley Doherty, said that she saw Pittman hurrying from the building after the shooting. She then went to Anna's door, asked what was wrong, and got only a groan from the dying woman in response.[8]

Perhaps the most important witness for the prosecution was Coroner Matthews. He said that when he was called to the Watson building about 4:30 p.m. the afternoon of the shooting, he found Miss McMahan lying dead in the floor and a .38 caliber pistol two and a half feet away from her body. He found a bullet hole in the young woman's back, and the next day during the post mortem he also found a bullet wound to the back of the head. When he found the pistol, it had blood smears on it, but there was no blood on Anna's hands. Also, her skin was not powder burned around either of her wounds, as it likely would have been if the wounds had been inflicted from a very close distance. Matthews said he thought it was impossible for the girl to have inflicted both wounds. In support of the coroner's opinion, Dr. J. E. Taft, who had also examined the dead woman, agreed that it was impossible for Miss McMahan to have inflicted both wounds, and he thought it hardly possible for her to have inflicted either one.[9]

Four witnesses testified as to Pittman's behavior and statements when he first appeared on the street yelling for help or immediately after he was taken to his room at the Waddle Hotel. Two of the witnesses said Pittman told them that the girl had shot him, another testified that the defendant said he wasn't sure what had happened or who'd shot him, and the fourth said Pittman made no answer when asked how he got shot.[10]

Pittman got a chance to tell his side of the story on April 10, the second day of testimony, and the defense strategy was considerably different from the story Pittman had told in the immediate aftermath of the shooting. Taking the stand in his own defense, he still said that Anna McMahan had shot him first, but he now claimed that he wrested the gun from her and shot her in retaliation. It had all happened during a jealous quarrel as the prosecution said, but Miss McMahan was the jealous one, not Pittman.[11]

Pittman explained that, although he'd seen Anna McMahan, around the hotel throughout the week preceding the shooting, he did not talk to her until Thursday. That evening, he went to her room at her invitation and she told him he was "the very fellow that she had been looking for" and "the prettiest boy in the world." She declared her love for Pittman and said she wanted to marry him. When he protested that his folks would be against such a marriage, Anna suggested running away together. Over the next two days, Anna continued to pledge her love for him and to urge marriage, and when he prepared to leave on Saturday to go home, she asked him to bring back a pistol for her to keep in her room.[12]

When be arrived back in Springfield on Sunday afternoon, he went directly to Anna's room, where she took the pistol from him. After they talked a while, she again asked him about marrying her, and he finally told her, "I wouldn't marry you or any woman like you, on my mother's account."[13]

"Then you will die right here," Anna declared, as Pittman stood in front of the mirror, and before he could turn around, she fired. Seriously injured but still on his feet, he turned and grabbed the gun away from Anna, who was standing very close to him. "Hurt, mad, and bewildered," he "fired just as fast as (he) could," and then dropped the gun and ran down the stairs to the street.[14]

The prosecution subjected Pittman to a grueling cross-examination, forcing him to deny statements that, according to other witnesses, he'd made in the immediate aftermath of the shooting. The state also tried to recall Coroner Matthews to review the testimony Pittman had given before the coroner's jury. However, the defense objected that, since Pittman was

already under arrest at the time of the coroner's jury, the
introduction of such testimony would be equivalent to forcing
the defendant to incriminate himself, and the judge sustained the
objection.[15]

The defense called two young women who were co-
workers of Miss McMahan to corroborate the defendant's
testimony that Anna, not Pittman, was the aggressor in their
relationship. A Miss Peak testified that Anna had told her she
was "struck on" Pittman and that the other girls had better leave
him alone. Ella Much said Anna appeared hung over on the
Sunday morning before the shooting and that she had told Ella
that same morning that, if she saw Pittman, to tell him not to
come to her room or he "would be liable to be killed." A third
woman partially confirmed the testimony of the first two.[16]

The defense then offered to show through six different
witnesses that Anna McMahan's reputation for chastity was not
good, but the judge sustained the prosecution's objection to the
introduction of such testimony. Perhaps the fact that Anna had
been previously married but had left her husband and reassumed
her maiden name contributed to her dubious reputation, and it is
true that the lessee of the Watson building was under indictment
in the criminal court at the time of the murder for "keeping a
disorderly house." However, Anna had taken her room in the
building only a couple of weeks before she was killed, and her
mother had rented the room for her. In addition, before going to
work at the Waddle Hotel, Anna had worked at a number of
other places in Springfield, where she was considered a "very
neat and industrious" young woman who always "did the best of
work." She also was devoted to her mother and helped support
"the old woman." So, whether she was indeed a woman of easy
virtue is uncertain.[17]

The Pittman case was given to the jury on Saturday
evening, April 11, and when they came back on Monday

morning, after deliberating throughout the weekend, they announced that were unable to reach a verdict. The vote stood eleven to one in favor of conviction on a charge of second-degree murder. A few of the jurors had originally favored a first-degree murder conviction, while the majority favored second-degree. The first group agreed to the reduced charge as a concession in order to get a verdict. However, one holdout, identified as N. J. Pierce, originally favored acquittal, and he would agree only to a charge of manslaughter in the fourth degree. Pierce came under intense criticism for his stance. Many observers thought that he should not have been on the jury to begin with because he was biased, and some even suggested that he had perjured himself during jury selection. The judge declared a mistrial and set April 24 as the date for Pittman's new trial.[18]

Pittman, though, didn't want to take a chance on a second trial. After he learned about the overwhelming vote in favor of conviction at his first trial and the angry mood of the people after his acquittal, he decided to throw himself on the mercy of the court. On April 15, he pleaded guilty to second-degree murder, but his pleas for leniency fell on deaf ears. Judge James J. Gideon sentenced him to fifty years in the state prison.[19]

Pittman apparently found a more sympathetic listener in Missouri governor Alexander Dockery. The prisoner arrived in Jefferson City on May 6, 1903, to begin serving his fifty-year sentence, but he received a gubernatorial pardon on September 10, 1904, after serving only a year and a third.[20]

Chapter 11
A Scene Never Before Witnessed in Springfield
The 1906 Easter Weekend Lynchings of
Three Black Men

During the late 1880s and early 1900s, it was fairly common for black men accused of serious crimes to be summarily lynched even when there was little evidence they'd committed the alleged crimes. What made the Springfield lynchings of Horace Duncan, Fred Coker, and Will Allen on the late night of Saturday, April 14, and into the wee hours of Sunday, April 15, 1906, at least a little unusual was that they were lynched on virtually no evidence. In fact, the best evidence available pointed to their innocence, and many citizens of Springfield knew this at the time. Yet few people made any effort to stop the extralegal hangings, and no one made a firm effort. The angry, bigoted mob of three thousand men and boys who gathered on and near the square that Saturday night were so "feverish with a thirst for human blood" that no one dared oppose them.[1]

After seven years in a childless, unhappy marriage that was strained by ill feeling between her and her in-laws, twenty-two-year-old Mina "Minnie" May Edwards left her husband on his farm near Fair Play and came to Springfield in early to mid-March of 1906, looking for something different. Adopting the name Mabel Edmondson, she went to work as a domestic. Sometime in early April, she left Springfield and took a job at the Harvey House in Monett. She quickly decided the work was too hard and, on Friday, April 13, she came back to Springfield, where she secured a job in the home of Henry J. Fox, superintendent of the city's electric light plant. That evening, she met an acquaintance, twenty-two-year-old Charles Cooper, on Boonville Street, and he went with her to the St. James Hotel to retrieve a valise she'd previously left there. At the hotel he offered to take her to her new place of employment on North Campbell, but the couple decided it was a nice night for a buggy ride and didn't go straight to the Fox residence.[2]

About 10:00 p.m., the two were traveling in Cooper's buggy on West Phelps Avenue near its intersection with Franklin, when, according to their later story, they were accosted by two masked black men. One of the assailants took hold of the horse's reins to halt it while the other covered Cooper and his companion with a revolver. After they'd relieved Cooper of his watch and $15 and taken Mina's purse, the pair knocked Cooper unconscious with a blow from the revolver and dragged Mina from the buggy. They took her through a gate into a pasture, held her down by the throat, and, according to the following day's *Springfield Daily Republican*, "abused her in turn."[3]

When Cooper came to, Mina was nowhere to be seen, and he drove quickly to Boonville Street, where he reported what had happened to two Springfield police officers, Trantham and Wimberly. Together, the three men returned to the scene and found Mina, "in a weak and fainting condition," wandering in their direction as they approached. Giving her name as Miss Mabel Edmondson, she said one of the black men who attacked her was tall and wearing an overcoat, while the other was short and heavyset. Officer Wimberly took the young woman to his residence on nearby Main Street so she could receive proper attention. Her condition was described as serious. Her throat and chest showed hand prints where her assailants had held her, and her clothes were badly torn. Wimberly and Trantham searched the vicinity where the attack had taken place but turned up no likely suspects.[4]

Mina Edwards, fifth from left, poses with her sisters several years before she was allegedly attacked in Springfield by two black men. *Courtesy Rob Schroeder and Springfield Police Museum.*

The next day, Saturday, April 14, several young black men, including twenty-year-old Horace Duncan and twenty-one-year-old Fred Coker, were arrested, and Mina was brought to the police station to see if she could identify her attackers. Finally admitting that she was not Miss Mabel Edmondson but was, instead, a married woman, Mina was unable to name any of the suspects as her assailants. All the men were released. Cooper, however, insisted he recognized Duncan and Coker as the two men who had robbed him, even though they were masked at the time, and they were re-arrested late Saturday afternoon. Tom Morrow, Duncan and Coker's white employer, told police that the two men had been working at the Baldwin Theatre on St. Louis Street setting up for a new production until ten o'clock on Friday night and, therefore, could not have been at the corner of Phelps and Franklin at the same time, but the two young black men were held nonetheless.[5]

Throughout the day on Saturday, men and boys milled around the public square discussing the attack on "Mabel Edmondson" and the possibility of extralegal retribution. As darkness descended on Springfield, those talking lynching grew more earnest, and at shortly after 9:00 p.m., a crowd of about a thousand men and boys formed on the south side of the square. Suddenly the horde started down College Street, picking up curiosity seekers and would-be vigilantes as they went. At Campbell Avenue, the procession turned south and passed within half a block of police headquarters and the city jail, but no law officers came out to oppose the throng. Learning that Duncan and Coker were not at the city jail (the present day Calaboose Museum), the gang turned east on Walnut Street and then took South Avenue back to the square.[6]

Here the mob paused as if to formulate definite plans. After a brief parley, the leaders started across the square with "whoops and yells" and headed down the Boonville Avenue hill "at a rapid pace," with many recruits and hangers-on tagging along. Near Phelps Avenue, a streetcar crossing Boonville forced its way through the crowd, and some of the mob fired shots at the vehicle, breaking several windows. Others in the disorderly throng threw rocks at the streetcar until almost every window in the vehicle was knocked out.[7]

When the mob reached the Greene County Jail at the northeast corner of Boonville and Center (now Central), Sheriff Everett Horner quickly turned out the lights in the building and then stepped out to meet the vigilante horde. He told the men to go away and threatened to fire into the crowd if they didn't disperse, but the mob answered the sheriff's bluff with cries of derision and started firing shots, some into the air but a few into the walls and windows of the jail.[8]

Greene County Jail and adjoining sheriff's quarters as they appeared at the time they were stormed by vigilantes in 1906. *Courtesy Rob Schroeder and Springfield Police Museum.*

Horner ducked back inside the jail and, fearing innocent people would get killed, told his deputies not to return fire. He telephoned the police department and asked for reinforcements, but only a few officers were dispatched to the jail and they arrived too late to help. The leaders of the mob secured a battering ram from a nearby house and started battering a side door of the jail but to little effect. Some of the men then broke into the sheriff's private residence adjoining the jail. They destroyed furniture, terrorized the sheriff's wife, and began battering an interior door that led to the jail. Meanwhile, the sheriff and his deputies retreated to the second floor of the jail, where many of the cells were located, and they took positions above the cell cages.[9]

Sheriff Everett Horner, who offered at least a token resistance to the angry mob. *Courtesy Rob Schroeder and Springfield Police Museum.*

The vigilantes finally succeeded in forcing open the inner door, and they rushed into the sheriff's office until the whole place was "filled with shouting, screaming, frenzied men and boys." Berserk with anger and excitement, they smashed the sheriff's telephone and started demolishing furniture and breaking windows. Turning their attention to the door that led to the second floor cells, they attacked the steel locks with sledgehammers, axes, and chisels. When one man would tire, another would take over, and finally the door was forced open.[10]

Stampeding upstairs, the horde surrounded the cell room, peering in to try to locate Duncan and Coker, and then they began working on the cell room door. The sheriff, from his perch above the cells, tried to dissuade the angry mob. "Men, you are doing wrong," he said. "These Negroes are merely suspected men and it is possible they are not guilty." The bloodthirsty mob responded with racial epithets, demanding that the sheriff turn over the prisoners.[11]

When the vigilantes started demanding the keys, Jailer E. C. King went down to the sheriff's office and retrieved a key, which he turned over to the mob. However, it was the wrong key, as another officer had accompanied King downstairs and left the building with the real key. When the vigilantes discovered the ruse, they grew incensed, breaking everything in sight they hadn't already broken and vowing vengeance on the law officers. The men with the tools went back to work with renewed energy, and within a few minutes, they broke the lock and forced the cell door open. This news was relayed to the large crowd that had remained outside the jail, and they let out an exultant cry that could be heard for blocks around.[12]

Rushing into the cells, the mob herded out all the African-American prisoners. The vigilantes looked the inmates over, picked out Duncan and Coker, and dragged them downstairs. After closing the steel door to keep the rest of the crowd out, the leaders of the mob, numbering about twenty, bound Duncan and Coker and took them out through a side window, where the bars had been knocked out. Both prisoners screamed and struggled mightily, proclaiming that they were innocent, as they were half dragged, half carried along. By the time they reached the street, their strength was sapped almost to the point of fainting.[13]

The mob leaders briefly debated where to take the prisoners, but the issue was quickly decided when cries went up from the crowd of 2,000 urging, "Take 'em to the square." With a cluster of mob leaders surrounding each prisoner, the march uptown began. "The procession filled Boonville Street from side to side, and was two blocks long," said the *Daily Republican*. "Men were singing, shouting and cursing, and intermittently, shots were fired." Duncan and Coker fainted along the way and had to be carried.[14]

Entering the square about 11:30 p.m., the mob headed straight for the Gottfried Tower near the center of the plaza. It was a tall, slender tower made of steel with a white statue of Lady Liberty sitting at its top and a bandstand about ten feet above its base. About half a dozen men scampered up the steps to the bandstand, and a couple of the men below tossed them two ropes that had seemingly appeared out of nowhere. The ropes were looped over the railing of the bandstand. Coker, already virtually unconscious and unable even to stand on his own power, was seized, and one end of one rope was placed around his neck. About a dozen members of the mob grabbed the other end of the rope and hoisted him up. He was already so close to death, if not already dead, that his body did not even convulse when he was swung into the air. The rope was tied, and he was left dangling.[15]

Punctuating their work with frenzied shouts, the leaders of the mob then grabbed Duncan and placed the other rope around his neck. Unlike Coker, Duncan fought desperately to the point that his clothes were virtually torn off and he was naked from the waist up when he was finally jerked into the air. His body convulsed and jerked about violently for several minutes before he finally died of strangulation.[16]

Onlookers gather at the Gottfried Tower on the Springfield Public Square, the morning after the lynchings. *Courtesy History Museum on the Square.*

Several thousand people witnessed the double lynching. "The entire square was filled with men and boys, as tightly packed as they could stand," said the *Springfield. Daily Republican.* "The side walks were crowded, and in all the shop doors and windows were crowds of people. The *Republican* reporter thought it noteworthy to add that, among the horde of men and boys, "many women were seen interestingly watching the spectacle," and a number of them "hurrahed with the men" when the horrible deed was accomplished. "Such a scene as attended the capture and execution of Coker and Duncan," concluded the newspaperman, "was never before witnessed in Springfield."[17]

When Coker and Duncan showed no signs of life, the mob leaders doused their bodies with coal oil and lit a fire of sticks and wooden boxes beneath the bodies, which were hanging with their feet barely off the ground. "The blaze shot up, enveloping the two forms," said the *Kansas City Star*. The ropes burned, and the bodies fell into the pyre. Twice Duncan's body rolled away and quit burning, but the maddened crowd, using sticks, pushed and prodded the charred flesh back onto the fire.[18]

As soon as the bodies were virtually consumed, shouts of approval and cries of "Let's get the others," went up. "Overcome with their orgy and filled with exultant frenzy over their success, their nostrils filled with the fumes of the burning victims," the mob turned their attention once again to the jail. At least one report claimed some of the leaders of the original mob drifted away, while only the "rabble part" headed back to the jail intent on lynching Bus Cain and Will Allen, two black men who had been accused of killing an old man named Rouark on the Drury College campus two months earlier.[19]

Cain was not at the jail, as he and thirteen other prisoners had escaped after the mob forced open the cells in removing Duncan and Coker. However, the frenzied horde found Allen cowering in a dark corner of his cell. They battered down the door with sledges, surged into the cell, and beat him almost senseless with sticks and stones when he showed fight. They pulled him out, bound his hands with rope, and half dragged, half carried him to the street, where he quit fighting and said he could walk on his own. The mob then started with him toward the square, punctuating the march with shouts, curses, and an almost constant fusillade of random gunfire.[20]

At the square, Allen "exhibited remarkable courage," walking up the steps of the tower and mounting the rail of the bandstand on his own. As he stood on the railing, he was given "a sort of mock trial." One of the leaders of mob shoved a lantern in his face so that the crowd below could see him. The leader identified him as Will Allen, murderer of Old Man Rouark, and asked what should be done with him. "Hang him!" cried the crowd. Asked whether he had anything to say for himself, Allen admitted his identity, but he said Bus Cain killed Rouark and he had nothing to do with it.[21]

Even as a noose was looped around his neck and the other end of the rope tied to a yardarm of the electric tower, Allen retained his extraordinary composure in the face of the shrieking, howling crowd. Staring down at the embers where Duncan and Coker had been incinerated about two hours earlier, he did not quake as he continued to maintain his innocence in a firm voice. Someone in the crowd challenged him to jump off and "show (his) gameness," and when he didn't immediately accept the dare, someone else shoved him from behind. It was exactly two o'clock in the morning as he plunged through air. The fall broke his neck, but it also broke the rope. Allen's body jerked into a somersault and fell into the embers. His body tossed about and convulsed for a moment and then lay still. The rope was tied back together and the body lifted into the air, but Allen was apparently already dead, as he gave no signs of life. After letting the body hang for about five minutes, the mob lowered him into the embers again and burned his body on the same spot where Duncan and Coker had been roasted. "The lights had been put out all around the square," said the *Republican*, "but the ruddy glow of the fire shed a ghastly light over the surroundings."[22]

As the flames died down, Springfield mayor-elect James L. Blain appeared on the scene and addressed the crowd, telling them that they had done enough and that they should go home. Although some in the crowd urged a return to the jail in search of more black prisoners to lynch, most heeded Blain's advice and began to disperse. Some observers later suggested that if someone in a position of authority had addressed the nascent mob in a similar manner when it was first getting organized, the lawless outbreak might have been avoided. But no one had, and the mob had grown into a frenzied horde that would forever "cast a stain on the fair name of Springfield."[23]

By daylight on Easter Sunday, the mob had largely dispersed, replaced now by curious onlookers and souvenir seekers. "This morning the church bells rang as cheerily as if the night before had nothing to hide," said the *Kansas City Star and Times*. "Children on their way to Sunday school stopped and prodded with older folks among the ashes for relics. A trousers button sold for five cents. A piece of the hangman's rope brought twenty-five cents and all day the town square was filled; all day there were muttered threats against the negroes."[24]

Fearing more violence against their race, many black citizens of Springfield fled the city on Sunday or went into hiding. Others took up arms, prepared to defend themselves should an attack come. To prevent another outbreak of lawlessness, Sheriff Horner and other prominent Springfieldians petitioned Governor Joseph Folk to call out the Missouri National Guard. Volunteer posses, deputized by Sheriff Horner and Mayor B. E. Meyer, helped maintain order until the first troops arrived late Sunday evening.[25]

On Monday, April 16, Greene County circuit judge A. W. Lincoln, urged by prosecutor Roscoe Patterson, ordered a grand

Fred Coker gravesite at Springfield's Hazelwood Cemetery. *Photo by the author.*

jury to investigate the lynchings. Patterson promised to vigorously prosecute all the mob members that could be identified, and Gov. Folk sent Missouri's assistant attorney general to Springfield to help in the prosecution. Although Mina Edwards had initially been unable to identify her attackers, she had changed her tune by Monday. She was now sure that Coker was one of them, and she thought he got what he deserved. She did not know whether Duncan was one of the men who assaulted her or not, she said, because he was not brought before her when she was taken to the police station.[26]

Several men suspected of being members of the mob were arrested and released on bond even before the grand jury began its work on Tuesday, April 17. Having learned of Mina's plight, her father, Robert J. Reeves, and her estranged husband, William J. Edwards, arrived in Springfield from Polk County on Tuesday. Edwards left early the next morning, but he and his wife had reportedly reconciled before he departed. Later the same morning, Reeves left Springfield with his daughter, but, in an effort to protect her from the harassment and threats she'd begun to receive, he would not disclose their destination. In the immediate wake of the Saturday night lynchings, rumor had it that many of the leaders of the mob were men who'd come to Springfield from Polk County, where Mina Edwards was from, but by Tuesday the 17th, it was generally admitted that almost all of the vigilantes were homegrown Springfieldians.[27]

After more than a month of investigation, the grand jury delivered its report to the circuit judge on the evening of May 23, 1906. The jury returned fourteen true bills containing indictments against twenty-two people, as one of the bills named multiple individuals. The report read in part, "We find that the lynching of the negroes on the night of April 14 was not only unjustifiable and unlawful, but was without reason or excuse." The jury concluded not only that Coker and Duncan were innocent of the attack on Mina Edwards but also that it was questionable whether such an attack even occurred. The fact that Mina was in good physical condition the morning after the alleged attack and the fact that her "reputation for virtue and chastity" was not good made it "at least doubtful whether her story is worthy of belief." It did not help that both Mina and her male companion, Charles Cooper, had disappeared shortly after the lynchings and could not be found in Greene or Polk County so that they could be brought before the grand jury to testify. The jury's report was highly critical of the Springfield Police

Department for making almost no effort to prevent the lynchings. It found no fault with Sheriff Horner's actions at the jail on the night of the tragedy but did suggest that he might have taken better steps to have prevented the mob's formation in the first place. The names of the persons indicted by the grand jury were not disclosed at first, but it was known that four of the indictments were for first-degree murder, several for second-degree murder, and the rest for burglary, jail-breaking, and perjury.[28]

The grand jury was not without its own critics. The *Springfield Leader* lambasted the jury's report as practically worthless. The jury was made up of ten Republicans and only two Democrats, and the *Leader* charged that the report was colored by partisan politics. As an example, the newspaper cited the fact the jury praised Sheriff Horner, a Republican, while roundly criticizing the police force, "part of a Democratic administration." The *Leader* also faulted the jury for attacking the character of various people, including Mina Edwards. The newspaper even wondered sarcastically whether the jury might indict her. In retrospect, it does seem that Mrs. Edwards suffered a good dose of what today might be called victim blaming. For instance, one of the people called before the grand jury was Rosa Cameron, madam of Springfield's most notorious house of ill repute, the Plainview Hotel, located on North Franklin near the scene of the alleged attack on Mrs. Edwards. Although Rosa testified that no man came to her place bringing a woman on the night of the attack, just the fact that she was called to testify and asked such a question suggests the dubious opinion some of the jury members must have held of Mina Edwards.[29]

Two Springfield residents, thirty-three-year-old Daniel "Doss" Galbraith and twenty-nine-year-old J. Hill Gooch, were arrested on June 5 on charges of first-degree murder in connection with the lynchings, and another man, Harry Hacker, was arrested for perjury. Court officials had difficulty qualifying a jury when Galbraith's trial got underway in August, and the prosecution reduced the charge from first-degree murder to second-degree murder, at least partly because of this difficulty, since a smaller jury pool was required for the lesser charge.[30]

In his opening statement, Prosecutor Patterson charged specifically that Galbraith had placed the rope around Duncan's neck and also ignited the fire that consumed Duncan's and Coker's bodies. The defense, on the other hand, claimed Galbraith was not even on the square at the time Duncan was hanged but only appeared afterward and took a piece of rope as a souvenir. The climax of the trial came on August 22 when Galbraith took the stand in his own defense and told what the *Springfield Daily Leader* claimed was a "flawless story." The case went to the jury on the evening of August 23, and the jurymen reported back the next day that they were split ten to two in favor of acquittal. After deliberating throughout the day on August 24, the jury was still deadlocked, and the judge declared a mistrial. Speaking of the verdict, Missouri attorney general Herbert S. Hadley observed that Galbraith had the largest portion of the Springfield community behind him "not because they believed he was innocent but because they believed he was guilty."[31]

Galbraith was shot on the Springfield square on the night of October 6 by a young man who had testified against him at his trial, but he was not seriously hurt. After a series of continuances, Galbraith's new trial and Gooch's first trial were docketed for the August 1907 term of Greene County Circuit Court. On August 24, however, the new prosecutor, W. R. Self, announced that he was dismissing all charges against both defendants because it was "impossible to get witnesses."[32]

Thus ended what was perhaps the most notorious episode in the criminal history of Greene County. And one hundred fifteen years later, the stain that the *Republican* newspaper reporter said the event cast "on the fair name of Springfield" has never been completely cleansed.

12

One of the Most Cold Blooded Crimes
in Greene County History
The Murder of Joshua and Elizabeth Ellis

After Eugene Tucker murdered sixty-three-year-old
Joshua Ellis and his fifty-eight-year-old wife, Elizabeth, on the
northwest outskirts of Springfield in February of 1909, Tucker
claimed he'd killed Ellis in self-defense and that he'd shot the
woman accidentally. But the old couple's seventeen-year-old
granddaughter Mary, an eyewitness to the incident, told a
different story. It didn't help Tucker's case either that he'd told
two law officers just minutes before the shooting that "the
damned old son of a bitch" Ellis had his cows and that, if he
couldn't get them back one way, he'd do it another way. Nor did
it help that, just minutes after the shooting, Tucker bragged to a
neighbor he met on the road that he'd "killed two of the sons of
bitches" and meant to kill the third one, referring to the Ellises'
forty-one-year-old son, George.

Convicted of first-degree murder in the death of Elizabeth
Ellis, Tucker was sentenced to hang, but he never paid the full
price for his heinous crime. Nowhere near![1]

The thirty-five-year-old Tucker had previously run a
restaurant in St. Louis, but a year or so before the shooting, he'd

moved to Springfield. He'd worked briefly in a downtown lunchroom before taking up farming in the Ellis neighborhood north of West Nichols Street and east of the present-day West Bypass. Tucker and Ellis had scarcely spoken to each other until sometime around the first of the year 1909, when a horse and cow belonging to Tucker got into a corn field on the adjoining Ellis farm and damaged some of Ellis's fodder. Ellis and his son George impounded the animals until Tucker paid for the damages, as the Missouri stock law provided for, and Tucker paid $3.25 to regain possession of his horse and cow. The transaction, though, left Tucker bitter.[2]

Six weeks later, shortly after noon on February 22, Ellis and his son found two of Tucker's cows in this same corn field destroying their fodder. George went to Tucker's nearby home to tell him two of his cows had gotten into the Ellis field again, but, not finding Tucker at home, he explained the situation to Tucker's brother-in-law Arthur Kittrell. The two men argued, and Kittrell assaulted George with a stick of firewood.[3]

The *Springfield Missouri Republican* claimed Kittrell nearly beat George Ellis to death, but George was well enough to go back home and help his father herd the two Tucker cows out of the field and into their barn. The men then came to Springfield to swear out a warrant against Kittrell for assault. A doctor examined the younger Ellis and pronounced him in serious condition. George remained in Springfield for treatment, while his father started for home, accompanied by a constable and his deputy. As the three men passed the Tucker house, which lay about a half mile northeast of the Ellis home, Joshua Ellis pointed it out to the lawmen, but they stayed with the old man until he turned south down the lane toward his own house.[4]

It was sometime after four o'clock when the officers started back the way they'd come and met Tucker on the road. Tucker, who had just gotten back from Springfield and learned about the impoundment of his stock and the confrontation between Kittrell and George Ellis, was visibly angry. When the lawmen inquired about Kittrell's whereabouts, Tucker denied he even knew such a person. He finally admitted that he did know him and promised to deliver him to authorities in Springfield the next day. But he was still mad. He cursed Joshua Ellis, saying "the damned old son of a bitch has got my cows," and he said he was on his way to get them back. Tucker asked the officers to go look at the corn field his cows had allegedly disturbed and they would see there was nothing in there that the animals could hurt. The lawmen advised Tucker that Ellis had told them he could have his cows back if he would come after them. Tucker replied that he had no gun and was not armed, but "I am going to get my cows, and if I can't get them one way I will get them another."[5]

The officers then returned to Springfield, and Tucker started west toward the Ellis farm. He must have gone back to his house, though, because when he showed up at the Ellis place between 5:00 p.m. and 5:30 p.m., he was accompanied by a seventeen-year-old lad named Charlie Dubel, his wife's stepbrother. Tucker demanded that Joshua Ellis give his cows back, but Ellis refused to do so until Tucker paid the damages. Tucker refused to pay, and as he turned to leave, he warned that he would be back and that he would "come prepared."[6]

Tucker and young Dubel returned about six o'clock and found Joshua Ellis, his wife, their granddaughter Mary, and a five-year-old child on the premises. Tucker called Ellis outside, and the two men walked toward the barn, where the cows were impounded. Elizabeth Ellis followed close behind, and Mary came outside and stood on the porch. The two men were still talking when Tucker suddenly pulled out a revolver from his overcoat and opened fire. Old Man Ellis seemed to stoop or duck downward at the first shot, but the second one caused him to stagger back and fall to the ground. Tucker fired several more shots, but Mary didn't know exactly how many. The next thing she knew her grandmother came onto the porch and collapsed in the kitchen doorway.[7]

After the shooting, Tucker went up to Mary and demanded that she retrieve the key to the barn for him so he could get his cows out. She got the key and threw it at him as he stood in the yard reloading his pistol. Tucker and the Dubel boy then got the cows out of the barn and herded them toward the Tucker place. Neighbors who'd heard the shots quickly arrived and helped Mary and her mother, who had just returned from Springfield, carry Joshua and Elizabeth Ellis into the house. Joshua died in about half an hour, and his wife died fifteen minutes later. Neither was able to talk or give any statement before dying.[8]

Meanwhile, a man named Luke Wallace met Tucker and Dubel on the road as they were driving the cows home just minutes after the shooting. As Wallace approached, Tucker drew his revolver and yelled out, demanding to know whether Wallace was "the other son of a bitch." Wallace asked what was the matter, and Tucker said he'd already killed two SOBs and planned to kill the other one (i.e. George Ellis). Wallace asked what two people he was talking about, and Tucker said, "The old man and the old woman."[9]

The coroner arrived at the Ellis home about 7:30 that evening and found both Joshua and Elizabeth Ellis dead. He summoned a jury to view the bodies but postponed an inquest. Meanwhile, Tucker, after taking his cows home, walked to Springfield and turned himself into authorities. He also gave up the murder weapon, a .32 caliber Smith and Wesson revolver. Authorities learned that he had purchased it a couple of years earlier after a smaller caliber pistol he owned failed to fire when he tried to shoot a black man at his St. Louis lunchroom. Tucker was taken before justice of the peace C. A. Hubbard, who committed him to the Greene County Jail, charged with what the

Republican called "one of the most cold blooded (crimes) ever committed in Greene County." Later that night, officers went out to the Tucker place and arrested Kittrell for his assault on George Ellis.[10]

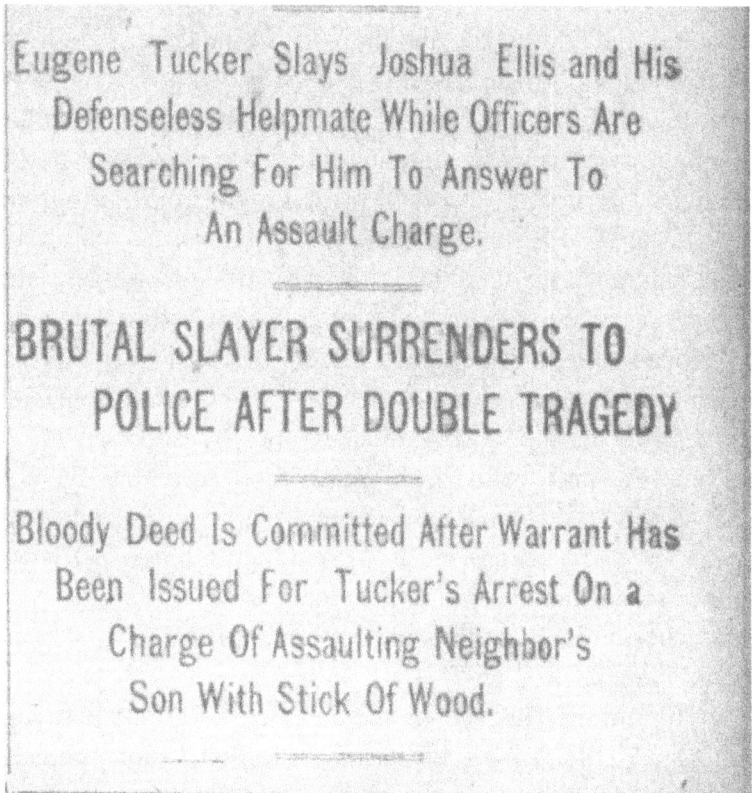

Eugene Tucker Slays Joshua Ellis and His Defenseless Helpmate While Officers Are Searching For Him To Answer To An Assault Charge.

BRUTAL SLAYER SURRENDERS TO POLICE AFTER DOUBLE TRAGEDY

Bloody Deed Is Committed After Warrant Has Been Issued For Tucker's Arrest On a Charge Of Assaulting Neighbor's Son With Stick Of Wood.

Headlines in the *Springfield Missouri Republican* tell the story of the Ellis murders.

The inquest into the deaths of the Ellises was held on February 25. The coroner determined that Joshua Ellis had been shot twice. One shot entered his side, passed through the abdominal cavity, and came out the other side. The other entered his mouth and went out the back of his head. Elizabeth had been shot four times. Three of her wounds were minor, but a fourth bullet, which had passed through her chest, proved fatal.[11]

Fearing mob violence, authorities held Tucker's preliminary hearing at the jail on February 27 rather than risk moving him to Justice Hubbard's office. The prisoner was charged with two counts of first-degree murder and bound over for trial in circuit court. Tucker deeded over his farm so he could hire a lawyer to represent him.[12]

The prosecution decided to try Tucker for the murder of Elizabeth Ellis first. The trial got underway with jury selection in late April, and testimony began on May 3. The primary witness for the prosecution was the Ellises' granddaughter Mary, who had recently married and was now Mary Hawkins. She said she was standing on the porch at the Ellis home and saw Tucker shoot her grandfather and grandmother, who were both unarmed. Luke Wallace was also called to the stand to relate the conversation he'd had with the defendant almost immediately after the shooting in which Tucker admitting killing "the old woman and the old man" and vowed to kill George Ellis.[13]

The next day, Tucker took the stand in his own defense. He claimed to have shot Joshua Ellis in self-defense. He said that the old man was mad and that he'd been told he had a reputation as a quarrelsome and dangerous man. He added that Ellis had his hand on his hip as though ready to reach for a weapon and that he opened fire when the old man made a threatening move toward him. He said he shot the woman accidentally as he was shooting at her husband and didn't even know he'd shot her until young Dubel told him as they were driving the cows away. Tucker sobbed as he told his story, and even a couple of the jurymen were moved to tears. According to the *Springfield Missouri Republican*, the courtroom was "crowded to its limits" on both days of testimony.[14]

The case was given to the jury on the late afternoon of May 4. They came back after several hours of deliberation and told the judge they unanimously favored conviction but could not agree on punishment. Eight reportedly favored hanging while the remaining four favored a ninety-nine-year prison sentence. Two of the four recalcitrant jurors changed their minds late that night, and shortly after deliberations resumed the next morning, a third man decided to go with the majority. The fourth, though, held out for life imprisonment until shortly before noon, when he finally gave in, and a verdict of death was announced. Tucker was the fourth man given the death sentence in Greene County and the first whose death sentence was assessed by a jury, as sentence was pronounced by the court prior to 1907.[15]

Tucker's attorney made a motion for a new trial. Judge Alfred Page denied the motion and set the execution date for July 9. However the case was then appealed to the Missouri Supreme Court, automatically staying the execution.[16]

The high court took up the case at its October 1910 term and handed down its ruling in December. One of the main contentions in the defense's bill of exceptions was that Judge Page erred in not allowing the jury to consider a second-degree murder verdict since Tucker acted in the heat of passion after Joshua Ellis cursed and verbally abused him. However, the supreme court sided with the judge, saying the heat of passion defense did not apply in Elizabeth Ellis's case, since she had done nothing to provoke Tucker and the evidence showed that she had not been killed accidentally as he claimed. The position of Elizabeth, her husband, and Tucker at the time of the shooting formed a triangle, so that Tucker could not have shot her by accident while shooting at her husband. Instead, he must have turned the gun on her after shooting her husband. This scenario was supported not only by Mary Ellis's eyewitness testimony but also by neighbors who reported hearing a pause between two distinct sets of gunshots. The high court thus sustained the lower court's verdict and reset the execution date for January 26, 1911.[17]

Tucker's lawyer made a motion that the supreme court reconsider its decision, and a Springfield newspaper noted at the time that, whether the motion was rejected or not, there was at least a fair chance that Tucker might not have to pay the ultimate penalty. Reportedly, the local Women's Christian Temperance Union had taken an interest in Tucker's case, and the WCTU and other friends of Tucker were already planning to appeal to Governor Herbert S. Hadley for clemency, should the high court not reverse itself. However, the WCTU denied the assertion, explaining that a member of its jail visitation committee had visited Tucker but that the organization as a group was taking no interest in the Tucker case.[18]

In late December, the high court denied the defense request for a new hearing, and Tucker's fate was now squarely in the hands of Governor Hadley. The defense filed a petition for clemency, and the request was supported, according to the *Republican*, by "many of the most influential people of the city." They thought Tucker had "conducted himself creditably prior to the crime" and that he had been an "excellent prisoner" since his confinement almost two years ago. Acting on the petition, Hadley granted a sixty-day stay of execution in mid January 1911. The hanging was rescheduled for March 24.[19]

After the governor's stay of execution, Tucker's lawyers continued their efforts on their client's behalf, asking that the sentence be commuted to life imprisonment. On the evening of March 4, two inmates of the Greene County Jail overpowered a deputy, got his keys, and locked him in a cell. They offered to open Tucker's cell door and let him escape with them, but he declined. Tucker told the escapees, as later recounted by the deputy, that the sheriff and his deputies had always treated him well and that he planned to face whatever punishment he had coming. The *Republican* commented that Tucker's waiver of the opportunity to escape elevated him in the eyes of many people, and the *Republican* speculated that his decision to remain in jail would probably go a long way in securing the commutation his lawyers sought.[20]

On March 14, Governor Hadley commuted Tucker's sentence from death to life imprisonment, and the governor did indeed cite the prisoner's passing on a chance to escape as one factor in his decision. Hadley also mentioned Tucker's excellent reputation prior to the crime, his apparent lack of premeditation in committing the crime, his turning himself in immediately after the crime, and his good behavior since his arrest. The governor's decision was generally met with relief and approbation in Springfield.[21]

Tucker was taken to Jefferson City on the night of March 14, just hours after word of the commutation reached Springfield. Twenty-seven-year-old Cora May Tucker, the convict's wife, expressed joy and relief upon learning her husband had been spared the death penalty, and she sobbed pitifully as she saw him off to the penitentiary; but it didn't take her long to seek the affection of another man. On July 1, 1911, reportedly with Tucker's blessing, she filed for divorce. The decree was granted a few days later, and in mid-July she was united in marriage to J. R. Hughes, a young man who had been her childhood sweetheart.[22]

In March 1918, Tucker was paroled after serving only seven years in prison. He was released into the custody of Mrs. Sallie A. Moore, a wealthy Los Angeles woman and a leader in the Christian Science Church, and he was supposed to work on her ranch. In January 1919, Tucker married Ida Kittrell, Cora's stepmother, in Los Angeles, and they were living there at the time of the 1920 census with three of Ida's children. One was a younger brother of Charles Dubel, the lad who'd been with Tucker when he killed the Ellises, and the other two were children by Ida's second husband, F. M. Kittrell, who was Cora's father.[23]

Chapter 13
The Death of Mollie Bass
Accident or "One of the Blackest Crimes in the History of Greene County"?

About five o'clock on the morning of January 24, 1911, twenty-seven-year-old Andrew Jackson Bass ran up and down the road near his rural Bassville, Missouri, home hallooing to his neighbors that his house was on fire and that he needed help. When the first of the neighbors arrived on the scene, they found Bass back home standing beside a wagon or hack containing his two small children, who were covered up with bedclothes. A. J., or Jack as he was often called, appeared to be in great distress, and when asked where his wife was, he said he feared she was in the burning building. The second story of the two-story frame house was engulfed in flames to the point that it was impossible to get upstairs, but a few of the neighbors were able to go into the downstairs part of the house and retrieve some furniture and household articles. According to an initial report, "It was with difficulty that neighbors restrained Bass from rushing into the burned and falling building in search of his wife."[1]

As soon as the flue in the house collapsed, bystanders saw portions of the woman's burned and charred body lying on or near the ruins of the flue. As the fire raged, the onlookers kept hearing loud, periodic reports that sounded like gunfire coming from the burning house.[2]

Bass explained that when the fire first started, he and his wife, twenty-three-year-old Mollie, roused from sleep and rescued their two little girls, Ruby, 4, and Lucille, 2. The couple then began fighting the fire, with Mollie pumping water and Jack throwing it on the burning building. After the pair had the blaze somewhat under control, they went back into the house and were upstairs continuing to douse the fire when it flared back up around the flue, blocking the stairway and trapping them on the second floor. Commanding Mollie to follow, Jack jumped from a second story window, planning, he said, to position a cart full of hay below the window so that his pregnant wife could also jump to safety. However, the leap to the ground stunned Bass, momentarily knocking him unconscious, and when he awoke, he saw no sign of his wife at the window. Uncertain where she was, he raced to alert his neighbors rather than pull the cart over to the window.[3]

An inquest held by a justice of the peace later in the day on January 24 concluded that Mollie Bass died from a fire of unknown origin, although it was conjectured by many that a defective flue caused the blaze. However, Mollie's father, William Goodwin, was not satisfied with the verdict. His daughter and Bass had had a rocky marriage, having only recently gotten back together after a period of separation, and Goodwin suspected foul play. He insisted that Greene County coroner A. H. Nichols conduct a second inquest, and on January 26, Nichols and county prosecutor J. R. Mason trekked to Bassville to carry out the requested investigation.[4]

One of main witnesses at the second inquest was A. J. Bass. He repeated basically what he'd said on the day of the fire—that he and his wife had gotten trapped on the second floor while trying to extinguish the blaze and that he'd jumped from the window expecting his wife to follow him but that she apparently was overcome by smoke and never made it to the window. Although some people thought Bass had acted in a cowardly manner by leaving his wife in the burning building, none of the witnesses who'd been present on the day of the fire introduced evidence to suggest foul play. Two doctors were summoned to the inquest, but they arrived near the end of the inquiry just as Mollie Bass's body was being readied for burial. The doctors gave the charred body a cursory glance, and, seeing no obvious wounds to suggest a cause of death other than burning or suffocation, allowed it to be lowered into the grave. Thus, the coroner's jury concluded that Mollie had died as a result of her failure to escape from the burning building, and, according to a Springfield newspaper, "all suspicions that foul play might have been the underlying cause of the death of Mrs. A. J. Bass...were found to be groundless."[5]

But William Goodwin was still not satisfied that justice had been served in Mollie's case. His suspicions no doubt intensified when A. J. Bass dropped his little daughters off at a sister's house a few days after the second inquest and absconded to parts unknown. Goodwin beseeched Prosecutor Mason to re-open an investigation into his daughter's death, and Mason obliged, ordering that Mrs. Bass's body be exhumed and re-examined on February 6.[6]

Two doctors from Fair Grove conducted the examination. While carefully inspecting the body, they found several small shots or pellets in the heart and also a larger hole that they thought was made by a shotgun blast. They concluded that Mollie Bass had come to her death from one or more gunshot wounds rather than as a result of the fire. This information was conveyed to Prosecutor Mason, who immediately issued a warrant for the arrest of A. J. Bass, now charged with "one of the blackest crimes known in the history of Greene County."[7]

The warrant was placed in the hands of Greene County sheriff W. E. Freeman, whose investigation led him to believe Bass was holed up in Stuttgart, Arkansas. At Freeman's request, the Stuttgart city marshal located and arrested the fugitive in Stuttgart on February 11 and held him for Greene County authorities. Armed with extradition papers, Freeman trekked to Arkansas a few days later and brought Bass back to Springfield, where he was lodged in the Greene County Jail. At his preliminary hearing on February 24, Bass was formally charged with first degree murder and bound over for trial.[8]

Bass's trial began in late April in Greene County Circuit Court. During opening arguments on April 26, Prosecutor Mason reviewed the evidence in the case, including the third inquest showing that gunshot wounds had been the cause of death. Mason also introduced a circumstance leading up to the fatal day that had not been previously revealed. Some three months before the fire, Bass had allegedly taken his wife to a Springfield doctor and asked him to perform "an illegal operation" on her in order to end her pregnancy. Saying he already had more kids than he could take care of, Bass supposedly urged the operation even after he was told it might endanger his wife's life.[9]

Because of Bass's reported "peculiar actions and remarks" during his incarceration in the Greene County Jail after his arrest, some observers expected his attorneys to pursue an insanity defense, but Bass's lawyers made it clear during opening arguments that they intended to show that the defendant was entirely innocent of the charge against him. He and his wife were on good terms at the time of the fateful fire, and he did all he could to save her. Bass had previously been an agent of an ammunition company, and he had hundreds of shells stored on the stairway of his house. Many of them had exploded during the fire, causing the sounds like gunfire that the neighbors had heard as they watched the house burn. The shots found in Mollie's body were caused not by the discharge of a gun but by the exploding shells inside the building. Although their client was "not perhaps possessed of any too much intelligence," he was always a loving husband except when her family brewed trouble between the couple. The defense lawyers said Bass's decision to alert his neighbors rather than attempt to rescue his wife after his jump from the second-story window was a result of temporary disorientation caused by the jolt he received when he landed. They pointed out that, after he later returned to the scene, he had to be restrained from re-entering the blazing house in search of his wife.[10]

During testimony, the prosecution called several witnesses to the stand to testify that exploding shells which were not confined lacked the necessary force to have caused Mollie Bass's death, as the defense theory held. The state also introduced testimony that the defendant had purchased coal oil in Bassville not far from his home on the evening before the fire and that the can containing the coal oil was virtually empty when investigators located it after the fire. The implication was that Bass had used the coal oil to purposely start and spread the fire as a means of covering up the shooting death of his wife. In addition, the prosecution also pointed out that Bass's shotgun was found outside in the hack. This, the prosecutors suggested, was further evidence that Bass had used the gun to kill his wife. Otherwise, he likely would have left it in the house, where it would have been destroyed by the fire. Finally, prosecutors called William Goodwin to the stand to refute the notion that his daughter was on good terms with the defendant at the time of her death.[11]

Despite the suggestion by Bass's lawyers during opening arguments that Mollie Bass was likely killed by exploding shells, they sprung a surprise when it came time for them to present their case. They suggested instead that the woman had suffocated from smoke inhalation. She had died neither from flames nor from shot propelled in any manner. The defense attorneys called several physicians who testified that the condition of Mrs. Bass's heart as revealed by the autopsy was very similar to what one might expect from suffocation. Although the defense lawyers now claimed that the victim's death resulted from suffocation, they nonetheless called one or two expert witnesses to counter the state's contention that exploding shot had to be confined in a tightly enclosed space in order to carry lethal force.[12]

When Bass took the stand in his own defense on the last day of testimony, the courtroom was "filled to overflowing with an eager crowd of curious persons." Explaining the empty coal oil can, the defendant said Mollie had filled three lamps almost immediately after he'd brought the oil home. He also said it was not an unusual circumstance that his gun was found in the wagon because he often kept it there or in an outbuilding rather than in the house. He accounted for the numerous shells being in his house by the fact that he had for some time been an agent for an ammunition company. Bass ended his testimony with a strong denial of the allegation that he'd killed his wife. "Of course, I didn't!" he said in response to a direct question from one of his attorneys. "I wouldn't shoot the mother of my children!"[13]

On cross-examination, the most damning statement the prosecution elicited from Bass was an admission that he failed to take his wife out with him when he jumped from the window because he "was excited and didn't think of her." Prosecutors also got Bass to admit that he might have told one of his neighbors when he first gave the alarm that he'd left his wife carrying out items from the burning house when he knew that not to be the case.[14]

Closing arguments in what the *Springfield Missouri Republican* called "one of the most sensational and peculiar murder trials in the history of this county" came on Monday, May 1. In reviewing the facts of the case, the state's attorneys paid much attention to what they considered a major inconsistency in Bass's story. Although he had insisted that he jumped to safety through a second story window, the window in question was found to be closed and with its panes unbroken after the blaze was finally extinguished. Prosecutors reminded jurors that Bass had not only behaved dishonorably in deserting his wife in the burning house but that he had also abandoned his kids and fled to Arkansas in the wake of his wife's death. Although he had not been charged with any crime at that point, his flight, the state contended, was the act of a man with a guilty conscience. And why had Jack Bass not mentioned at the inquest the many shells he stored in his home but instead had waited until he'd been charged with murder?[15]

Bass's lawyers countered that the whole case against their client was a flimsy thread of purely circumstantial evidence and that he would not even have been brought to trial were it not for the fact that his former father-in-law had such an irrational dislike for him. The defense pointed out that their client came from a well-respected family, the Basses being "among the best residents of Greene County." (Jack Bass's grandfather, Andrew Jackson Bass, after whom the defendant was named, was one of the very first white settlers in Greene County.) The defense attorneys said it was unthinkable that a member of the Bass family would commit such a black crime as their client had been accused of. They understandably neglected to mention that William Goodwin and his family were also long established and well respected in the county. The defense urged that jurors not let Bass's dubious behavior in deserting his wife prejudice them against him in rendering a decision as to whether he was guilty of murder but that they instead consider only the facts in the case, which they felt clearly favored their client.[15]

The case was handed to the jury during the mid-afternoon of Monday, May 1. The jurors were given three options: finding the defendant guilty with a sentence of death, finding him guilty with a sentence of life imprisonment, or finding him not guilty. After deliberating overnight and taking eight ballots, the jurors filed into the courtroom at nine o'clock the next morning and announced that they had reached a verdict finding Bass guilty of murder and assessing him a sentence of life imprisonment. Bass scarcely reacted to the verdict, only commenting to his guard, "Well, they hit me rather hard, didn't they?"[17]

Bass's attorneys immediately announced their intention of filing a motion for a new trial, and they filed such a motion two days later, on May 4. Judge Alfred Page denied the motion on May 6, and the defense then appealed the case to the Missouri Supreme Court, thus postponing implementation of the sentence. Bass was retained in the Greene County jail pending the outcome of the appeal. Division Two of the supreme court finally took up the case in November 1912, and the justices affirmed the verdict of the lower court. Bass was then transported from Springfield to Jefferson City on November 21. However, Bass's attorneys once again appealed, asking that the full supreme court consider the case. On December 10, the full court handed down the same ruling that Division Two had, affirming the verdict of the Greene County court.[18]

All hope for Bass appeared to be lost, but his attorneys still did not give up. Their petition for a rehearing was granted, and in the late spring of 1913, the full Missouri Supreme Court once again took up the case. This time the justices concluded that Bass's abandonment of his wife to the fire had indeed prejudiced the jury against him and that the circumstantial evidence did not logically lead, beyond a reasonable doubt, to a verdict of murder. Thus, the high court reversed the verdict of the lower court and ordered that Bass be released. He was discharged on June 5, 1913 after serving only a little over six months in the state penitentiary.[19]

A. J. Bass's headstone in Larimer County, Colorado. *Courtesy Derald Johnson and Find A Grave.*

A. J. Bass returned to Greene County, where he regained custody of his two little girls. He then moved to Colorado and remarried there in 1917. At the time of the 1920 census, he and his new wife, Anna, were living in Larimer County, Colorado, with Bass's two daughters by his first marriage, Ruby and Lucille, living with them. Bass died in Larimer County in 1968 at the age of 84.[20]

14
The Kidnapping and Murder of Baby Keet
One of the Most Sensational Criminal Cases
in Springfield History

About ten o'clock on the evening of May 30, 1917, the live-in nurse for fourteen-month-old Lloyd "Buddy" Keet checked on the baby in his room at the Keet residence near Pickwick and Meadowmere in the exclusive Meadowmere Place neighborhood of Springfield, Missouri. She then retired to an adjoining or nearby room for the night. A maid also lived on the premises, and neither she nor the nurse saw or heard anything unusual after bedtime. But about midnight the baby's parents, James Holland and May Keet, returned home from a dance at the Springfield Country Club (located on Glenstone where the Country Club Shopping Center is today) and found the child gone. Kidnapped! Apparently someone had sneaked into the child's room on the east side of the home and handed the baby to an accomplice through an open window.[1]

The next morning, thirty-three-year-old J. Holland Keet, a prominent and wealthy Springfield businessman, received a letter through the mail demanding $6,000 in ransom for return of the baby and giving detailed instructions for Keet to follow to

Photo of home from which Baby Keet was kidnapped, taken near the time of the crime. *Courtesy Rob Schroeder and the Springfield Police Museum.*

effect the exchange. Although Keet would not reveal the details of the letter at first, he left alone in his car late on the night of the 31st in the midst of a violent storm. "Deep rumbles of thunder" echoed in the distance, "staccato flashes of light from the sky" added to the "terror of the night," and "a blinding torrent of rain" pelted Keet as he crept along in an open convertible. Following a circuitous route that had been laid out for him by the kidnappers, he drove south of town on National Avenue through Galloway and on to Ozark. From there he went west to Nixa, back to Springfield, and west toward Republic, maintaining his speed at twelve miles an hour as he'd been instructed to do. But no one appeared to flag him down or give him additional instructions as the letter had promised, and he arrived back in Springfield after 4:00 a.m. on the morning of June 1, exhausted and frightened for the safety of his child.

Apparently someone had followed Keet against his wishes, and the kidnappers had spotted the tail and declined to carry through with the promised exchange. Hundreds of citizens who'd been patrolling the streets of Springfield and awaiting word from Keet reluctantly abandoned the search for the night.[2]

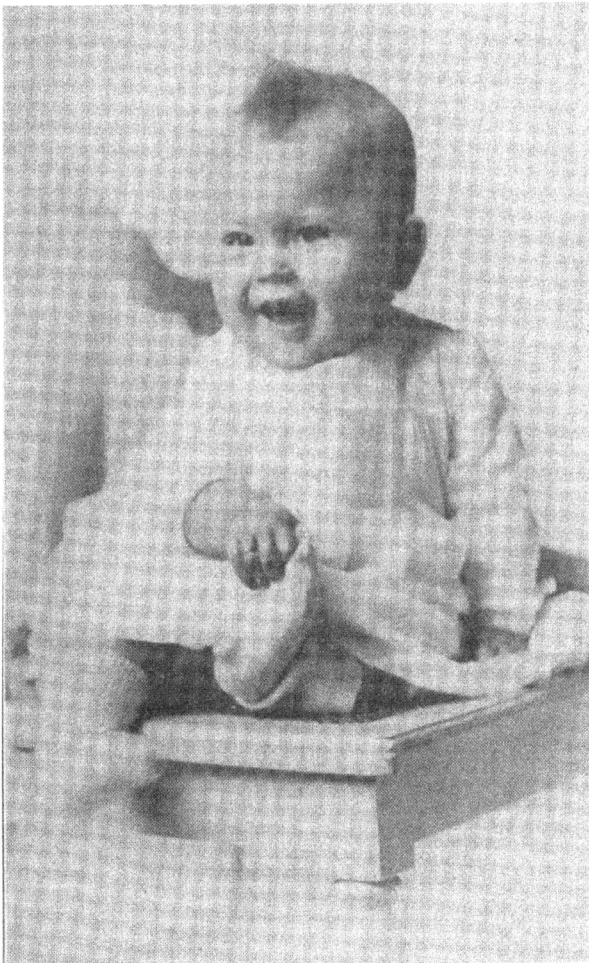

Baby Lloyd Keet. *Courtesy Rob Schroeder and the Springfield Police Museum.*

News of the Baby Keet kidnapping made headlines across the nation, drew reporters to Springfield from all over the

Midwest, and had the people of Springfield and surrounding vicinities in a stir for days. It was suspected that the little boy was being held south of Springfield, and "dozens of the caves in the hill country" were searched. "Residents...devoted practically their entire time to a hunt for little Lloyd Keet. Every character of transient is suspicioned and examined. Automobiles constantly provide a thrill for the searchers at the thought that some clue be secured."[3]

As the days dragged on with no definite clues into Buddy Keet's disappearance, authorities began to criticize the boy's father for not cooperating more closely with them and for keeping certain details of the letter he'd received right after the kidnapping secret. It was thought by some that Keet had been in further contact with the kidnappers since the initial letter but that he would not divulge the communications. One rumor even suggested that the child had already been returned but that the Keet family, in accordance with the demands of the kidnappers, was keeping it secret until a specified time. Meanwhile, officers and volunteers continued to roam the countryside around Springfield in search of the little boy, and Keet himself was out looking for his son much of the time. On the evening of June 3, a messenger reportedly delivered a note to the Keet home assuring the family that little Lloyd was safe and being held less than an hour's drive from Springfield but that, if the Keets did not call off the "detective bloodhounds," they would "never see the baby again" because it would be killed if any of the detectives got too close to the hideout.[4]

On June 4, another communication was delivered to the Keet home that was rumored to have come from the kidnappers. It was purported to be the fourth such communication the Keets had received from the kidnappers of their son. J. Holland Keet gave a statement that morning intimating, without definitely confirming, that he had, indeed, been in communication with the kidnappers. He suggested that he was trying to meet all the kidnappers demands so that his son would not be harmed. After giving the statement, Keet was nowhere to be found throughout the rest of the day, again giving rise to speculation that he was on a clandestine errand to deliver the ransom in exchange for his baby boy. In the meantime, a man driving a car generally matching the description of one seen near the Keet home on the night of the kidnapping was arrested on suspicion and interrogated for over an hour before being released.[5]

About this same time, a break in the case came when a Springfield taxi driver, George Walker, told officers investigating the Keet kidnapping that he had been approached several months earlier about participating in a plot to kidnap Springfield jeweler C. A. Clement. Although the Clement plot had not been carried out, authorities thought there might be a connection between the Clement plot and the Keet kidnapping because of similarities in the two cases. On the strength of Walker's statement, six people were targeted for arrest. They were Claude Piersol, Taylor Adams, his wife (Allie), their two sons, and Sam McGinnis. Walker was also later arrested, either as a suspect or a material witness. The Adams home at 731 Delmar Avenue, about a mile from the Keet home in Meadowmere Place, was searched, and a baby bed was found that appeared to have been recently slept in, even though no small children lived at the residence. Investigators speculated that Baby Keet might have been held at the Adams home for a few days after the kidnapping before being moved elsewhere. During the search, Mrs. Adams gave officers a "scorching tongue lashing," although no physical resistance was offered. After the six suspects were arrested, all but McGinnis confessed to involvement in the Clement plot but denied any knowledge of the Keet kidnapping. The Crenshaw mansion, a large home south of Springfield and west of Campbell Street Road where the conspirators had planned to hold Clement, was searched in hope that the Keet baby might be found there, but to no avail. The home of Piersol's grandfather near Billings was also searched as a possible hiding place, but nothing out of the ordinary was found there. The only real tidbit of evidence officers had at this point to suggest the involvement of Piersol and his pals in the Keet kidnapping was Piersol's statement to Walker on the morning after the kidnapping that he'd been up nearly all night and had gotten very little sleep.[6]

Newspapers reported on June 6, before the arrest of the six suspects was widely known, that J. Holland Keet had been in negotiations with the kidnappers and they had repeatedly assured him that his child was safe. However, Keet had made two night trips into the countryside, following instructions from the kidnappers, in an effort to pay the ransom in exchange for the return of his little boy, but for some reason the kidnappers had decided not to carry through with their end of the bargain. Observers speculated that either the kidnappers felt conditions were not right for the exchange or they were simply testing Keet's good faith. About this same time, authorities agreed to give Keet free rein in his dealings with the kidnappers, as he'd been requesting, rather than interfere in any way with his efforts to bring his child home safely the best way he saw fit. Shortly after this, the Keet family, who had thus far remained hopeful, became confused and bewildered when they learned of the arrest of the six suspects, but they were still unconvinced the people in custody were the kidnappers of their little boy.[7]

After her arrest, Allie Adams became less defiant. Still denying knowledge of the Keet kidnapping, she tried to blame her family's involvement in the Clement plot on Claude Piersol. Declaring that she knew Piersol was bad news, she said, "We didn't have anything to do with the kidnapping plot and my two sons are innocent. We were all living happily and making money and now our home is broken up."[8]

As the one-week anniversary of Baby Keet's kidnapping passed with still no clue as to the infant's whereabouts, the search for the child went nationwide. Four people were arrested in Pennsylvania on suspicion but quickly released. "Scarface" Riley, an underworld figure that Springfield authorities thought might be a link between the Clement case and the Keet case, was arrested in Chicago, but he proved an alibi. A Springfield newspaperman observed, "The father of the missing baby is anxious to pay the ransom but apparently the kidnappers are afraid to attempt further negotiations with him." Did it not occur to the newsman that the reason the kidnappers weren't attempting further communication with the Keet family might be that they were already in custody?[9]

Detectives did make such a connection, and they continued to grill the suspects who were under arrest, particularly Claude Piersol, whom they thought might be the ringleader of the gang. Piersol's grandfather was questioned again, and a letter Piersol had written to Taylor Adams asking, "Are you still in on it?" was closely examined to see whether it might have been written by the same person who wrote the ransom note to J. Holland Keet.[10]

Shortly before noon on June 9, about a week and a half after Baby Keet had been kidnapped, his body was found floating on the water at the bottom of an old well or cistern on the Crenshaw property (current site of the Hy-Vee Market near the intersection of Battlefield Road and Kansas Expressway). He was still wrapped in the blanket in which he had been sleeping when he was taken from the Keet home. Mode of death was apparently drowning, as a coil of old wire had been tied around the body before it was thrown into the well. Baby Keet had been dead about three or four days. The little boy's body was brought back to Springfield, and mob fever swept through the town when citizens learned of his death. The suspects being held in the case were whisked out of town for fear the gathering mob would take the law into their own hands. About the same time that Lloyd Keet's body was found, local officials announced that federal authorities had joined the investigation and were working on the theory that both the Keet kidnapping and the Clement kidnapping plot were part of a sinister kidnapping ring that did indeed involve "Scarface Riley" and that was instigated by German operatives as part of the Kaiser's covert World War 1 effort against the United States.[11]

When the lawmen took the suspects out of Springfield, part of the mob gathered on the public square pursued the officers in an attempt to overtake them and either wrest the prisoners from their custody or force them to return the suspects to Springfield. Sheriff Will Webb's original intent was to take the prisoners to the state penitentiary at Jefferson City. However, word had been telephoned ahead to residents north of Springfield that the sheriff might be coming their way, and small mobs formed all along the way, forcing the lawmen to take a circuitous route in order to dodge the would-be vigilantes. Approaching Humansville, Webb and his deputies turned west to avoid an encounter with a mob of about two-hundred men that awaited them in the small town, and several miles west of Humansville the lawmen were forced to take to the woods with their prisoners.[12]

A posse of about thirty-five or forty men, including some of the most prominent citizens of Springfield, finally overtook the sheriff late Saturday night near Stockton. They took Piersol and Cletus Adams, the oldest Adams son, from the sheriff and his deputies, assuring the lawmen that they would not kill the prisoners but merely try to get information from them. The posse took the two men to a nearby lodge, where they grilled them repeatedly. Piersol remained calm throughout the interrogation, while Adams grew very agitated, but neither would confess or say anything more than they'd already said back in Springfield. The vigilantes then took Piersol off into the woods, put a rope around his neck, and lifted him off the ground three different times until he was blue in the face. Someone also fired a bullet that whizzed past his ear, but the young man remained resolute in his refusal to talk. In fact, he seemed so composed that some in the posse began to doubt that he knew as much about the Keet kidnapping as they had thought, and the two prisoners were returned to the sheriff. Some observers speculated that the reason Piersol was able to maintain his composure is that he'd overheard the men assure the sheriff that the prisoners would not be seriously hurt. Piersol and Cletus Adams were taken to Kansas City for safekeeping, while the other four suspected kidnappers were jailed at Stockton.[13]

Meanwhile, thousands of people milled on and near the Springfield square throughout the afternoon of June 9 and into the morning hours of June 10, awaiting word of the fate of the prisoners with many hoping they would be returned to Springfield so that they could be summarily dealt with in the city where they had committed their crime.[14]

On June 10, the number of letters the kidnappers had written to J. Holland Keet was confirmed at three, and their contents were published for the first time. The first, received by Keet on the morning after the kidnapping, began, "We sure got your kid. Don't say anything to police or put it in the papers. There are three of us, and we want $2,000 apiece; so it will cost you $6,000 (six thousand) to get him. We got another one picked out, so if we don't get this from you, we can tell them to see what we did to yours." The second letter, which Keet received the next day, said that the exchange had not been made because Keet had failed to abide by their instruction not to have anybody else interfere. It gave him a stern warning that this was his last chance and said he would soon be receiving new instructions for the exchange. The third letter outlined those instructions, but for some reason the kidnappers chose again not to effect an exchange when Keet attempted to carry out the new instructions. A comparison of the letters to samples of Piersol's handwriting prompted authorities to conclude tentatively that Piersol had written the letters.[15]

The funeral service for Baby Keet was held on June 11 at the Keet home. Only family and close friends were admitted inside, but hundreds of people milled around on the grounds outside. After the service, the little boy was buried at Maple Park Cemetery.[16]

The twenty-year-old Piersol reportedly admitted that he was a member of a gang directed by Scarface Riley at the behest of the German government. It was also learned that Piersol was an avid reader of German war books. However, he continued to deny any involvement in the kidnapping and killing of Lloyd Keet. A twenty-six-year-old Springfield man named Dick Carter, who had first been implicated by Cletus Adams's confession, was identified as the baby's likely killer. Carter was charged with murder, and a nationwide hunt for him was instituted.[17]

On Monday, June 18, Piersol and Cletus Adams were formally charged with murder to keep them from being released on writs of habeus corpus. Sheriff Webb traveled to Kansas City to serve the warrants, and the prisoners were released into his custody. He took them to St. Louis and lodged them in the city jail there. The next day, Dick Carter was arrested at Hutchinson, Kansas, and a Springfield detective was dispatched to Hutchinson to bring him back to Missouri. For fear of mob violence, he was taken to Kansas City instead of Springfield. A grand jury inquiry into the Keet case was scheduled to begin in Springfield later in the week. After their arrival in St. Louis,

Piersol and Cletus Adams underwent a severe grilling, but they still refused to implicate themselves in the Keet kidnapping and murder. It was learned, however, that Piersol was an admirer of little children and liked to collect photos of babies.[18]

SHERIFF MACKEY - DICK CARTER - T. ADAMS - SAM McGINNIS,
C. ADAMS - MRS ADAMS - M. ADAMS - CLAUDE PIERSOL.
Accused Members of Gang Who Were Arrested

Webster County sheriff G. W. Mackey, back row left, and the seven suspects arrested in the Keet baby kidnapping-murder case. *Courtesy Rob Schroeder and Springfield Police Museum.*

Carter was brought to St. Louis on June 21, and he, Piersol, and Adams were questioned the next day in the St. Louis chief of detectives office. Although none of the suspects made a specific confession, Greene County prosecutor Paul O'Day, who was present for the interrogation, said he thought, because of general admissions Piersol made, that he knew more than he was saying. One of the admissions Piersol made was that he had visited the Crenshaw mansion in December of 1916 or January of 1917. He had previously mentioned visiting the place but said the visit took place much earlier.[19]

Late on the night of June 22, Taylor Adams and Sam McGinnis were brought to St. Louis from Stockton, and the next day they were questioned as the previous three suspects had been. Afterwards, the other three were questioned again, and Carter, who'd previously denied involvement in either the Clement kidnapping plot or the Keet abduction, admitted he had been involved the Clement plot. Piersol, however, bore the brunt of the grilling. When the clothes that Baby Keet was wearing when he was found in the well were tossed in front of the suspect with a demand that he confess, Piersol still refused to admit involvement in the Keet case.[20]

Allie Adams and her youngest son, Maxie, were still being held at Stockton. When a Cedar County assistant prosecuting attorney tried to interrogate Mrs. Adams on or about June 30, she proved to be even more uncooperative than the suspects who'd been questioned at St. Louis. She denied any knowledge of a kidnapping ring, and the prosecutor responded that he knew she was lying, because Claude Piersol's grandfather, who'd recently been hit by a train and killed, had made a full confession to his involvement in the Keet crime before he died. Allie laughed at the interrogator and told him he was the one who was lying.[21]

In mid-July the charges of murder against Piersol, Cletus Adams, and Dick Carter were dropped and charges of conspiracy to kidnap Lloyd Keet were filed instead. The other suspects were charged with conspiring to kidnap C. A. Clement. When all the suspects were brought to Springfield in late July for preliminary examination, Taylor Adams was added to those charged in the Keet case, while Carter, now charged only in the Clement case, was no longer named in the Keet case. All the defendants were granted changes of venue to Webster County.[22]

As the suspected ringleader of the gang, Piersol went on trial first, in October 1917. One of the main pieces of evidence the prosecution presented against him was the testimony of handwriting experts who said the defendant almost certainly wrote the ransom letters. The rest of the state's case amounted mostly to a strong interweaving of circumstantial evidence. When Piersol took the stand in his own defense, he remained unshakeable in his denial of involvement in the Keet case throughout an intense grilling by prosecutors. Nevertheless, on

Claude Piersol was considered the ringleader of the kidnapping gang. *Courtesy Rob Schroeder and the Springfield Police Museum.*

the evening of October 15, the jury came back with a guilty verdict after six hours of deliberation. Sentence was set at thirty-five years in the state penitentiary. A series of appeals delayed imposition of sentence, and in December, Piersol gave an elaborate statement to Webster County sheriff G. W. Mackey detailing the entire Keet kidnapping plot. How much of his confession was true is, of course, unknown, but he said the baby died accidentally after being dosed with laudanum to keep it quiet. Piersol was eventually taken to Jefferson City in April of 1919. He was discharged in May of 1938 after serving twenty and a half years of his thirty-five year term.[23]

After Piersol's trial, Taylor Adams pleaded guilty and was sentenced to fifteen years in prison, but he was discharged under the state's merit time rule after serving only eight. Cletus Adams also pleaded guilty. He was sentenced to ten years in the penitentiary and served slightly over five before having the sentence commuted by the governor. Charges against all the other suspects were eventually dropped.[24]

15
"Don't Hit Her No More"
A Murder at Percy's Cave

On the evening of Monday, August 14, 1922, a group of young adults drove out from Springfield in three cars to Percy's Cave (now Fantastic Caverns) northwest of town. The caravan included Ernest Cameron and his wife, Eva; John Yancy and his wife, Aline; and George Aurentz and his date, Della Armstrong. Yancy was an uncle of Ernest Cameron, and Aurentz was a brother of Eva Cameron. All the members of the group knew each other and were on friendly terms, or so it seemed. But strained relations lay just beneath the surface, and the tension was about to reach the breaking point.[1]

Upon arrival at the cave property, all of the group except for the thirty-seven-year-old Yancy walked down a hill to a pavilion, where a dance was in progress. Yancy stayed in his car near the road with a bottle of liquor. Some of the others besides Yancy had also been drinking, or soon would be. It was about 9:00 p.m.

At the entrance to the pavilion, Aurentz, a thirty-three-year-old World War I veteran, checked a pistol he was carrying at a concession stand run by Willard Crow, nineteen-year-old son of the property owner, J. W. Crow. Aurentz, Della, Ernest, Eva, and Aline then started dancing on a platform built for that purpose beneath the pavilion. Exactly what happened after this was disputed during subsequent legal proceedings, but we can reconstruct, in a general fashion, the most likely sequence of events. Not long after the group arrived at the dance, twenty-five-year-old Ernest Cameron, accompanied by his wife, brought some food back to John Yancy at the cars, where Ernest and Eva got into a minor dispute. However, they temporarily resolved the matter and returned to the dance pavilion. About an hour later, Eva, who was thirty-two years old and had been previously married, danced with a man named John Hedgpath, and after the dance, he remarked, "That little black haired woman is a good dancer." He added that, if he could dance with her a few times more times, she would teach him how to dance. Overhearing the remark, Ernest replied, "That woman is my wife." To defuse the situation, another man, who knew both parties, promptly interceded. He introduced Cameron and Hedgpath, but Hedgpath, realizing Cameron was still angry, soon ambled away to avoid trouble. Ernest then took up the matter with Eva, and they got into another argument. The dispute grew so heated that Eva struck at Ernest, and he retaliated by hitting her and, by some accounts, knocking her down. Getting to her feet, she appealed to her brother for help, but George told Eva he didn't want to have anything to do with the matter.[2]

Shortly afterward, Eva and Ernest, still quarreling, started back toward the cars. They hadn't gone far when Eva started cursing her husband and throwing rocks at him. "Run, you son of a bitch!" she yelled.[3]

Eva retreated to the pavilion, and Ernest soon came back as well. Eva again complained to her brother of Ernest's mistreatment of her, and George remarked to nobody in particular that he was going to kill Cameron if he didn't stop fighting with his sister. Aline Yancy, who overheard Aurentz's threat, went to where the cars were parked and told her husband, John, he needed to get Ernest away from the dance before a serious fight happened between him and George. But what neither Aline nor John Yancy knew was that it was already too late to prevent what would prove to be a deadly confrontation.[4]

About the time Aline left the pavilion, J. W. Crow announced that the dance was over and he was getting ready to shut the place down. Ernest started back toward the cars, pushing or dragging his wife along. As the couple neared the cars, according to Eva, her husband struck her in the face with a pop bottle. She stumbled back down the hill and saw her brother, who had retrieved his pistol from Willard Crow, leaving the dance with Della. Eva again called to George for help, and he hurried past her to where Cameron was standing near Yancy's car smoking a cigarette and where Aline was still talking to her husband through the car window.[5]

Stopping a few feet in front of Cameron, Aurentz said, "You damned little son of a bitch, I'm going to shoot you." Yancy yelled from his car for George not to shoot, but he drew his pistol and fired three shots in quick succession as Cameron turned away as if to retreat. Struck by two of the shots, Cameron stumbled back, collapsed, and died almost instantly. Eva Cameron rushed up just after the third shot was fired and yelled to her brother, "Oh, George, you've killed him! You've killed him in cold-blooded murder." Yancy started to get out of his car, but Aurentz challenged him, daring anybody who was kin to Cameron and wanted to take up the matter to step out. Aurentz then retreated into the woods, and one or more bystanders were immediately dispatched to summon authorities. John Yancy went to where his nephew lay on the ground and realized Ernest was dead. Other people also started gathering around, some suggesting that the body be moved to the pavilion or taken to

Springfield. Yancy, who didn't want the body moved until the sheriff or coroner arrived, went back to his car to retrieve a pistol. He then stepped back out and, brandishing the weapon, warned everyone not to move the body until authorities arrived. Yancy was heard to say, as he guarded the body, that he was going to see to it that Aurentz was prosecuted for murder, even if he had to spend $20,000, or words to that effect.[6]

CAMERON, IS MURDERED AT PERCY'S CAVE

Police Search for George Aurentz, Who Is Alleged to Have Killed a Relative During Argument.

Headline in the *Springfield Missouri Republican* the morning after tells the story of the Percy Cave murder.

Greene County coroner Ellis Paxson showed up about an hour after the shooting and transported the body to Springfield.

Meanwhile, Aurentz hid out in a barn on the Crow property that night and then called the sheriff's office the next morning to turn himself in. The sheriff drove out and brought him back to Springfield, lodging him in the Greene County Jail. After his arrest, the prisoner gave a statement claiming that Cameron threatened him and reached toward his pocket, as though going for a weapon, before Aurentz shot him. However, the only weapon Paxson had found on Cameron's body when he reached the scene was an unopened pocket knife.[7]

The next day, August 16, Paxson held an inquest into Cameron's death. The principal witnesses included John Yancy, Aline Yancy, and Eva Cameron. John and Aline Yancy both testified that Aurentz came up to Cameron and started shooting without provocation other than the fact that Cameron had hit Eva earlier in the evening. However, Eva said that Ernest was still hitting her when her brother walked up, that George said, "Don't hit her no more," and that Ernest then cursed and taunted her brother, daring George to shoot him. She said Ernest then turned away and jerked his hand back before George opened fire. Eva also said she did not remember saying that George had killed Ernest in cold-blood, despite the fact that several witnesses testified to that effect.[8]

In addition to giving damning testimony against Aurentz in the Cameron killing, Yancy also implicated Aurentz as an accomplice in an armed robbery in Springfield three months earlier and one or two other crimes. He added that the quarrel between Aurentz and Cameron actually started several weeks before the dance when Cameron refused to join Aurentz in one of his criminal enterprises. Aline Yancy confirmed parts of her husband's incriminating testimony. After hearing all the witnesses, the coroner's jury was out only five minutes before coming back with a verdict of death "from gunshot wound fired by George Aurentz with intent to kill."[9]

The conflicting statements given by Mr. and Mrs. Yancy versus those given by Aurentz and his sister foreshadowed the separate lines of argument the prosecution and defense would pursue in subsequent legal proceedings.

John Yancy was a star witness for the prosecution at Aurentz's preliminary examination in early September, where he repeated much the same testimony he'd given at the coroner's inquest. The defense sought to impugn Yancy's testimony by showing his prejudice in favor of his nephew and his determination to see Aurentz pay for Cameron's death. Yancy admitted that he'd said Aurentz ought to be arrested, but he denied the defense accusation that he'd said he would pay $20,000 to "get" Aurentz. The defense further suggested that Cameron was, indeed, armed with a pistol when he was shot but that Yancy had taken it off his body as he knelt over him immediately after the shooting. Eva Cameron testified for the defense, claiming she'd seen Yancy kneel over her husband emptyhanded and then stand back up with a gun in his hand. She added that Yancy had also tried to bribe her into testifying against her brother. Another defense witness, Mike Patterson, said he'd heard Yancy's offer to pay $20,000 to get Aurentz, but he contradicted Eva's suggestion that Yancy had taken a gun off her husband's body. At the conclusion of the hearing, Justice J. O. Kerr ruled that Aurentz should be held for trial without bond.[10]

Aurentz's trial for first degree murder got underway in early December 1922. The courtroom was filled with spectators for nearly all sessions of the trial. Medical experts testified that the cause of Cameron's death was a bullet wound near the base of the neck that entered from the back and ranged upward severing the spinal cord. Another wound to the shoulder was superficial.[11]

John and Aline Yancy were again important witnesses for the prosecution, largely repeating what they'd said at previous proceedings. Other state witnesses were called to back up John's and Aline's testimony and to establish that Yancy had not taken a pistol off Cameron's body. Instead, he'd retrieved a pistol from his car immediately after the shooting, briefly laid it on the ground when he knelt beside the body, and then picked it back up as he rose. One of the state witnesses was John Hedgpath, the man who'd danced with Eva Cameron just prior of her violent argument with her husband. He told of the dance and also said he'd later witnessed the shooting. Aurentz had come directly up to Cameron near the cars, threatened to shoot him, and then immediately did so. Eva came hurrying up after her husband had already fallen and accused her brother of killing Ernest in cold-blood. Although Eva had since changed her tune, the prosecution said she was not a credible witness because she was the sister of the defendant and, therefore, not objective. As Hedgpath pointed out, she was not even present at the immediate scene during the confrontation between her brother and her husband but instead came rushing up about the time the last shot was fired.[12]

While the state sought to undercut Eva Cameron's credibility, attacking opposing witnesses was an even more vital part of the defense's strategy. Aurentz's attorneys went after John Yancy in particular, both during rebuttal and during questioning of its own witnesses. The lawyers sought to show not only that Yancy was out to get their client but that he was a man of low character who had been involved in several criminal enterprises. Hedgpath, too, was a man whose "reputation...for truth and veracity and general citizenship" was bad. At least one defense witness, in addition to Eva Cameron, stated that he'd seen Ernest Cameron make a move as if to reach for a weapon before Aurentz shot him. In addition, the defense called several witnesses to testify that there was a longstanding feud between Aurentz and Cameron and that Cameron had threatened to kill the defendant on one or more occasions prior to August 14. Part of the reason for the feud was that Cameron had been habitually abusive not only toward his wife but also toward George and Eva's mother, with whom he and Eva lived. On rebuttal, the prosecution was able to elicit from at least a couple of the defense witnesses an admission that they were acquainted with the defendant and had visited him in jail since his incarceration.[13]

Near the end of the trial, Aurentz took the stand in his own defense. He testified that Cameron had made threats against him and was abusive to both his sister and his mother, reinforcing what previous defense witnesses had already said. The mother, Ida Aurentz, later took the stand to also confirm these details. In questioning their client, the defense tried to highlight his military service during World War I, but on rebuttal the prosecution pointed out that the defendant was facing a vagrancy charge in Greene County at the time of his enlistment and that he'd gone into service to avoid jail time and to get the charge dismissed. The state's attorneys also suggested that Aurentz had done little except loiter around Springfield since his discharge.[14]

Arguments ended on the late afternoon of December 7. Although Aurentz had been charged with first degree murder, the judge gave instructions allowing for a lesser degree of guilt. The case was then given to the jury, and the jurors deliberated only about two hours before coming back at nine p.m. with a verdict of second degree murder. Sentence was set at twenty-five years in prison. A Springfield newspaper noted at the time that the Aurentz case had been "the most noted case to be tried in the Greene County criminal court in many years." At every session, said the reporter, the courtroom had been "crowded to capacity" with even standing room at a premium.[15]

In mid-December 1922, Aurentz was released on $10,000 bond pending the outcome of a defense motion for a new trial, but he was returned to the county jail when the appeal was denied later the same month. The defense then appealed the verdict to the Missouri Supreme Court, and Aurentz remained in the Springfield jail pending the high court's decision.[16]

On June 5, 1924, the supreme court overruled the lower court's decision largely on the grounds that Eva Cameron's statement that George had killed her husband in cold-blood should not have been admitted, either as evidence tending to show George's guilt or to contradict and impeach Eva's later testimony. Since she was not at the immediate scene when the shooting started and did not witness the confrontation leading up to it, her initial reaction was no more than an uninformed opinion. The case was, therefore, remanded to Greene County for retrial.[17]

The new trial took place in early January 1925. Although there were a few new witnesses called, only a minimal amount of new evidence was introduced, and the proceeding was largely a rehash of the first trial. Interest in the case and attendance in the courtroom was not as great as they had been at the 1922 trial. On the evening of January 9, the jury, after less than two hours of deliberation, came back with the same verdict as the first jury—murder in the second degree—but with a sentence of twenty years rather than twenty-five. A defense motion for a new trial was quickly overruled, and the case was again appealed to the Missouri Supreme Court. Aurentz was allowed to go free on $10,000 bond pending the high court's ruling.[18]

His freedom lasted a year and a half. The supreme court took up Aurentz's case at its April 1926 term, and this time the decision went against him. In late May, the justices affirmed the verdict of the Greene County court, and Aurentz was returned to the county jail almost immediately. He was transported to the state prison in Jefferson City on June 6 to begin serving his twenty-year sentence.[19]

Aurentz didn't exactly do hard time, though. He was "given much freedom from the start," according to the *Springfield Leader*, and was "permitted to go and come almost at will." He was made a 'trusty' and, as an expert on dogs, had charge of the prison bloodhounds. Several times he was given furloughs to visit his mother and other family members in Springfield. He had just returned to Jefferson City from attending his mother's funeral in Springfield on October 30, 1930, when he learned the next day that Governor Henry Caulfield had granted him a parole. According to a Jefferson City newspaper, many citizens in both Cole and Greene counties had urged the parole and were gratified by it. The prisoner was released on November 3, having served less than four and a half years at the big house. Aurentz died in Ray County, Missouri, on May 16, 1939, at the age of forty-six, and his body was returned to Springfield for burial in Eastlawn Cemetery.[20]

Chapter 16
Newell "Dobb" Adams Goes on a Rampage
One of the Most Atrocious Crimes
in Greene County

By 1928, Springfield resident Newell "Dobb" Adams had served a few jail sentences on minor charges, and he was known to city policeman as a "bootlegger and liquor runner." But few people could have foreseen the violent rampage Adams would go on in mid-June of that year, killing two people and seriously injuring two others. Perhaps only his twenty-three-year-old wife, Meada, could have predicted such an explosion of rage, because Adams had also been convicted several times in municipal court of beating her.[1]

In fact, Adams had been beating his wife regularly during the six months prior to his violent outburst. He threatened to kill her if she left him and then beat her when she stayed. One time he pushed her head back against the seat of a car and drew a knife across her throat several times as he threatened her. Another time, when Meada did leave him, he spotted her on the street in downtown Springfield, jumped out his car with a gun, and told her to "get in the car and be damn quick about it" or he'd shoot her. He took her home, and she tried to live with him again, but he kept beating her. Finally, sometime in mid-June,

Meada left again and went to stay with her sister Lona in Kansas City.[2]

No one would tell Adams where his estranged wife had gone, but he meant to find out. Tanked up on liquor, he summoned a taxi to 551 West Pine Street in Springfield during the early afternoon of June 18. A cabbie named Roy Wells picked him up and, after taking him first to 817 Weaver, drove him to the edge of town on West Division to the home of twenty-three-year-old Zella Sinclair, one of Meada's best friends. Adams sent Wells to the door to tell Miss Sinclair that Adams had an old friend of hers downtown who wanted to see her, and she agreed to go with the them. As soon as she got in the car, however, Adams became abusive, demanding to know where his wife was. When Zella said she didn't know, Adams pulled out a revolver and angrily ordered Wells to drive out of town on North Grant Avenue Road.[3]

After they'd gone about five or six miles, Adams forced Wells to stop, get out of the car, and walk on up the road. The infuriated Adams then dragged Zella from the vehicle and again demanded to know where his wife was. Although Adams had been drinking, he didn't look drunk, according to Zella's later recollection. He just "looked wild" and had a glassy-eyed stare. When Zella refused to say where Meada was, Adams shot her in the stomach, gravely wounding her. Wells, hearing the gunshot and the young woman's screams, hurried to a nearby farmhouse to call police and an ambulance.[4]

Meanwhile, Adams left the scene on foot but quickly hitched a ride in a truck driven by a farmer boy, and he forced the lad to take him back into Springfield. The crazed Adams then went to the home of his mother-in-law, Sarah Whalin, at 1701 West Webster, where he found Sarah and her sixteen-year-old daughter, Edith McCrary. Another sister of Meada, Edith was a pregnant newlywed.[5]

Appearing peaceful at first, Dobb asked for a drink of water, which he was given. But he soon brought up the subject of the trouble between him and Meada and asked where she was. When the two women refused to tell him, he flew into a rage. Cursing and flourishing his pistol, he forced the two women to accompany him as he started searching the house from room to room. They searched downstairs and then went upstairs. When Adams still saw no sign of Meada, he pointed his pistol at Sarah and threatened, "You tell me where she is or I'll shoot the hell out of you."[6]

Sarah insisted she didn't know where Meada was, but Adams either didn't believe her or didn't care. He shot her twice in the stomach, and she cried out in agony as she fell to the floor.[7]

The madman then made a dash toward Edith. The young woman begged him not to shoot her as she jumped into a nearby closet and closed the door. She tried to hold it closed, but Adams got it open and attacked the expectant mother with a knife, stabbing her on her back and left side. Edith was able to grab the knife away from her brother-in-law, but then he struck her in the head with the butt of his revolver. Sarah was crying and begging for a drink of water, but Adams wouldn't let Edith get it for her and wouldn't let her call an ambulance. "You can call all the damn doctors and ambulances and police you want to when I get out of here, but you'll call me a taxi first."[8]

Edith called a cab, and after it picked Adams up, she ran to a neighbor's house for help. She fainted and woke up in an ambulance, as both she and her mother were being rushed to a hospital.[9]

Meanwhile, Adams sought refuge at 907 College Street, the home of a distant cousin named Allen Hull. A manhunt was organized for the fugitive, and police officers, acting on a tip, finally located him at the College Street address about seven

o'clock that evening. Hull told the lawmen that Adams wasn't
there, but they insisted on searching the place for themselves.
Officers Francis "Ted" DeArmond and W. K. Webb entered the
house by the back door while Officer Tony Oliver led a posse of
other policemen at the front door. When DeArmond reached to
switch on a light in a darkened rear room, a gunshot rang out
from inside the room, striking the officer. As he staggered back,
a second bullet struck him, and he fell dead to the floor.[10]

Officer Francis "Ted" DeArmond, who was killed by Dobb Adams. *Courtesy Rob
Schroeder and the Springfield Police Museum.*

At the first sound of gunfire, the team of officers who were trailing Oliver declined to follow him into the house, and they were later accused of cowardice. Webb and Oliver, though, engaged the gunman in a furious exchange of lead. After the two sides had traded about twenty-five shots with no injuries on either side, a lull ensued, and Adams offered to give up. He emerged from the room with his hands held high, but, as he drew close to the two officers, he physically attacked them and was only subdued after Webb struck him in the head with his revolver. After being taken into custody, Adams expressed no remorse for his rampage. On the way to the police station, Webb remarked that he should have shot Adams, and the captive taunted, "Well, go ahead and shoot. I don't care." Later, Adams told Sheriff Alfred Owen that he "would have gotten several more of those cops if (his) revolver had not jammed" and that the malfunction was the only reason he gave up. He said he was glad he'd shot DeArmond, although he made no mention of the women he'd shot.[11]

Adams was taken from the police station to the Greene County Jail, but when a threatening mob began gathering around the jail, lawmen whisked him away in an automobile. The lawmen were followed by the mob, but south of town, Sheriff Owen gave the vigilantes the slip by taking to the woods with the prisoner while the driver of the vehicle continued on. Owen then summoned another car and took Adams to the Taney County Jail in Forsyth. The prisoner was brought back the next day as emotions began to subside.[12]

Early on the morning of June 19, Meada Adams arrived in Springfield from Kansas City, and she was interviewed at the Springfield Baptist Hospital, where she was visiting her mother, her sister, and her friend. Referring to her husband, Meada said, "He is the most brutal person I can imagine.... Sometimes I think he's crazy and sometimes I think it's just downright meanness....

I wish the mob had got him last night, and I don't care if they string him up. He deserves it."[13]

Newspaper photo of Newell "Dobb" Adams, from the Springfield Sunday News and Leader

In the early afternoon of June 19, Mrs.Whalin died from her wounds, less than twenty-four hours after she'd been shot. Meanwhile, Zella Sinclair remained in critical condition, and it was questionable whether she would survive. Edith McCrary was expected to make a full recovery from the stab wounds and beating she'd taken at the hands of Adams.[14]

Urging that Adams had authored "one of the most atrocious crimes ever committed in Greene County" and that he deserved to die, Greene County prosecutor W. W. Hamlin filed charges of first degree murder against the prisoner in the deaths of both Officer DeArmond and Sarah Whalin. However, the Whalin case was deferred, pending the outcome of the DeArmond case. The preliminary hearing in the first case was held on June 20, and Adams was bound over to the circuit court without bond to await trial.[15]

Adams was granted a change of venue to Polk County, and his trial got underway at Bolivar in mid-July. The two main witnesses for the state were Tony Oliver, one of the officers involved in the shootout in which Officer DeArmond was killed, and Edith McCrary, the defendant's young sister-in-law. Their stories varied very little from the way they'd told them in the immediate aftermath of the crime.[16]

Lawyers for Adams pursued an insanity defense, and they called Meada Adams to the stand as the star witness. Torn between love and hate for her husband, she said he had not been in his right mind the past nine months. Up until then, Dobb had been the "life of the party" and easy to get along with. Then he began beating her, threatening to kill her, and otherwise abusing her. Other witnesses who'd known Adams for some time testified as to the change that had come over him in recent months, causing him to go from a friendly person to a moody one who alternated between violent anger and suicidal depression. The prosecution countered that Adams well knew the difference between right and wrong and that only a sane man could have planned the crimes against the three women the way he did.[17]

On July 19, the jury came back twice during their three and a half hours of deliberation to report that they agreed on a first-degree murder verdict but were unable to agree on punishment, and each time Judge C. H. Skinker sent them back for further deliberation. When they came back a third time to say they were still split, reportedly ten for the death sentence and two for life imprisonment, Skinker gave the jury the option of leaving the assessment of punishment to him, and that's what they did. Skinker condemned Adams to die by hanging in late August, but a defense appeal to the Missouri Supreme Court automatically delayed the execution.[18]

On August 11, while Adams awaited the outcome of his appeal, Zella Sinclair died of the wounds he had inflicted on

Zella Sinclair, one of Adams's victims, from the *Springfield Leader and Press*.

her almost two months earlier, and he was indicted on a third charge of first-degree murder. A few days later, Meada attempted suicide by taking a drug overdose, but she survived and was released from the hospital after a brief stay.[19]

In late May 1929, the Missouri Supreme Court, ruling that Judge Skinker errored in imposing the death penalty after the jury couldn't agree, overturned Adams's verdict and remanded the case for retrial. Adams had been returned to the Greene County Jail after his conviction in Polk County, and the high court's action caused such an uproar in Springfield that lawmen had to once again spirit the prisoner away to avoid mob violence.[20]

Adams's reprieve proved brief. The state appealed the supreme court decision and won a rehearing in early June, less than two weeks after the ruling had been handed down. In mid-August, the supreme court reversed itself and reset Adams's execution for late September. Adams had claimed all along, "They'll never hang me," but now there seemed to be no way for him to escape such a fate. About noon on September 9, 1929, however, he found a way to cheat the hangman by taking a large does of poison in his cell at the Greene County Jail. A doctor tried to save him but to no avail. He spent several agonizing hours but remained conscious into the evening. He kept repeating that he never meant to kill the women and didn't even remember doing it, but he expressed no remorse for shooting DeArmond, claiming that the officer had shot at him first. As death approached, Meada was summoned to the jail, and she was by her estranged husband's side at the end. After he died, she saw to his burial arrangements.[21]

In late October 1929, Meada was found near her West Pine Street home suffering from a gunshot wound to the knee, but she refused to give much information about the incident, saying only, "Take it from me, it doesn't pay to trifle." Meada was said at the time to have taken up with a man named Hobart Dean, who like her ex-husband, was thought to be a bootlegger.[22]

Meada Adams got into trouble of her own after her notorious husband died. Pictured here when she was received at the state prison in 1930. Courtesy Missouri State Archives.

In January 1930, Meada was arrested, along with an ex-con named Nate Faulkner, on an armed robbery charge. With a cigarette in her mouth and a tattoo that said "To Mother" on her left arm, Meada presented a hard appearance, but she was subdued and youthful in her manner and "considerably prettier" than she'd been at time of her late husband's rampage. Meada said that she'd only met Faulkner about the time she suffered the gunshot wound to her knee. She still wouldn't provide details about the knee injury except to say it was an accident. Meada had been keeping company with Faulkner since the injury, but she didn't know he was an ex-convict until the day they were arrested, and she denied having robbed anybody. After Meada had already been arrested and taken to the station, the police found a ring in her room that had been taken during the robbery, but she suggested they might have planted it. She said the only time she'd ever been previously arrested was once on a drunkenness charge, and all the trouble she'd ever had was due to "the wrong sort of companions."[23]

At Meada and Faulkner's trial in mid-February 1930, the victims of the holdup positively identified the pair as the robbers, and they were convicted of armed robbery. Meada was sentenced to thirteen years in the state prison and transported to Jefferson City. She was given an early release in 1937 because of merit time.[24]

Chapter 17
The Young Brothers Massacre
The Deadliest Shootout in US Police History

On Saturday afternoon, January 2, 1932, the Springfield Police learned that brothers Harry and Jennings Young, both career criminals, were likely holed up on the Young family farm near Brookline. Since the farm was located in a rural section of the county, Sheriff Marcel Hendrix was notified, and a posse of ten officers, composed of men from both the sheriff's office and the police department, set out in three vehicles to bring the desperadoes in. The officers knew the Young brothers might be dangerous. Twenty-seven-year-old Harry was wanted for killing a lawman in Republic, and thirty-five-year-old Jennings was an ex-con with a record of crime longer than his younger brother's. But as the lightly-armed lawmen approached the farm about seven miles west-southwest of downtown Springfield, they assumed their sheer numbers would be sufficient to deter any violence or to outgun the brothers if necessary. It would prove a fatal miscalculation.[1]

Jennings Young and another brother, Paul, had been convicted of burglary and grand larceny in Christian County in 1919, and they served three years in prison before their ten-year sentences were commuted by the governor. In early 1924, Jennings was charged with burglarizing a store in Billings, but

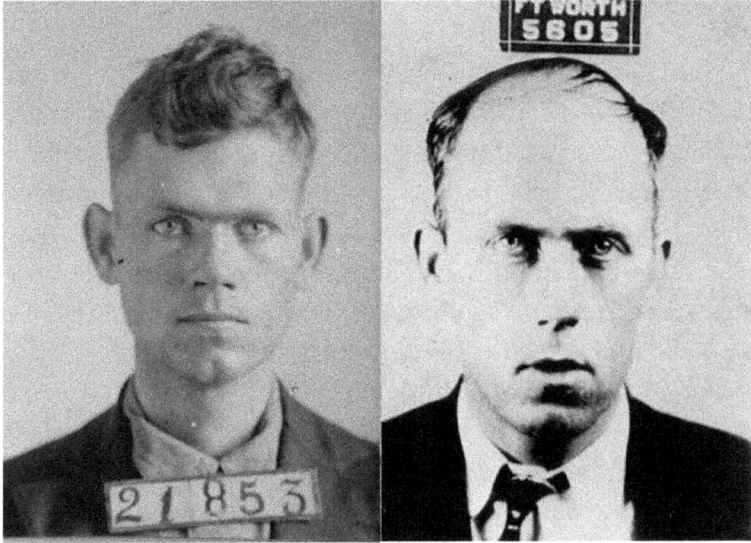

By 1932, both Jennings Young (left) and his brother Harry had long criminal histories. *Courtesy Rob Schroeder and the Springfield Police Museum.*

before the case could be resolved, he was charged in federal court with breaking into and robbing a freight car at Nichols Junction on the west edge of Springfield. His mother, his brother Harry, and two other brothers were also implicated in the crime, but the charges against them were dropped when Jennings pleaded guilty in December 1924 and was sentenced to three years in the federal penitentiary at Leavenworth. Released after a couple of years, Jennings returned to Greene County and promptly resumed his life of petty crime. Meanwhile, Harry Young embarked on his own criminal spree. From late 1925 to early 1927, he was implicated in a series of escalating crimes that culminated with his conviction in Greene County in March 1927 of burglarizing a Springfield filling station. He was sentenced to three years in prison, and he served a year and a half before being discharged under a merit-time rule in late September 1928. Eight months after his release he graduated to murder when he killed Republic town marshal Mark Noe on June 2, 1929.[2]

Sometime in the late 1920s, Jennings joined his brother Paul in Texas, where Paul had already established a criminal headquarters. Jennings quickly became involved in a car theft ring, and in early 1930 he was indicted at Fort Worth on three counts of violating the Dyer Act against stealing and transporting automobiles for interstate commerce. He was convicted in April and again sent to Leavenworth, this time for a two-year stint. Whether the fugitive Harry was involved with Jennings in the car theft ring is not certain, although it seems likely. What is known for sure is that, after Jennings was released from federal prison in early November 1931, the two brothers rendezvoused in Texas.[3]

But on Wednesday, December 30, 1931, less than two months after Jennings was discharged from Leavenworth, he and Harry drove back to Missouri from Texas in two separate stolen cars and arrived at the Young place late that evening. The next morning they went to Aurora to try to sell one of the vehicles but were turned away. Jennings enlisted the help of his sister, Lorena Young Conley, who, along with her husband and child, had also just arrived from Texas. On Thursday afternoon, Lorena drove to Clyde Medley's used car lot on McDaniel Street in Springfield in one of the stolen vehicles, an almost-new Ford sedan, while Jennings and another sister, Vinita, stayed behind in a second car. Medley offered Lorena $250 but told her he needed a clear title to the vehicle, which was registered under the name J. P. Young. Lorena and her brother went to a notary public to get the automobile signed over to her, but when she returned on Friday, Medley put her off again, telling her he didn't have $250 in cash and couldn't get it until the next day, since the banks were closed for New Year's Day.[4]

The Young sisters, Vinita and Lorena, were taken into custody when they tried to sell a stolen car for their brothers. *Courtesy Rob Schroeder and the Springfield Police Museum.*

Lorena and Vinita returned to the car lot early Saturday afternoon, January 2, 1932, but in the meantime Medley had gotten suspicious and reported the previous attempted transactions to the police. Springfield officers were waiting to arrest the young women, and they were taken to the police station for questioning. They denied knowing anything about the whereabouts of their brothers, but the interrogators grew suspicious that they weren't telling the truth. Sixty-five-year-old Willie Florence Young, widowed mother of the Young siblings, was in Springfield and went to see her daughters upon learning of their arrest. According to some reports, when she heard that the police suspected her sons were at the farm, she promptly telephoned to warn them. Although this assertion is unlikely, one thing seems certain—the officers hardly took the Young brothers by surprise.[5]

Far from it.

Willie Florence Young, mother of Jennings and Harry. *Courtesy Rob Schroeder and the Springfield Police Museum.*

When the ten lawmen reached the Young farm, it was almost four o'clock in the afternoon, and already the early shadows of a winter evening were creeping across the countryside. The first police car to reach the scene parked northeast of the two-story farmhouse, while the other two pulled up directly in front of (or east of) the house. The men piled out of the vehicles, and gathered in front of the house from a safe distance to discuss strategy. As the officers approached the house, there was no sign of activity and no answer to their halloos when they knocked on the front door. There appeared to be nobody home. Even after police detective Virgil Johnson fired a cannister of tear gas at an upstairs window, all was quiet. But unbeknown to the officers, Harry and Jennings Young, "famous shots even among the squirrel hunters" of the Ozarks, lurked inside with shotguns and high-powered rifles, while the lawmen carried mostly handguns.[6]

The Young farmhouse as it appeared near the time of the shootout. *Courtesy Rob Schroeder and the Springfield Police Museum.*

Sheriff Hendrix, Deputy Wiley Mashburn, and Springfield detective Frank Pike circled around to a rear door at the southwest corner of the house, as most of the other lawmen took up tactical positions behind trees and other makeshift fortifications surrounding the house. Finding the door locked, Sheriff Hendrix resolved not to leave until he knew for sure whether the Youngs were on the premises. According to Pike's later account, he, Hendrix, and Mashburn got up a head of steam and rammed into the door simultaneously. When the door flew open, two blasts from a double-barrel shotgun exploded from inside the house. Hendrix fell dead in the doorway, and Mashburn fell backward mortally wounded, one side of his face almost completely torn off. Hit in the arm with buckshot, Pike staggered back and then raced to the front of the house to join his comrades. The sheriff and his deputy were either dead or seriously wounded, he hollered to the others, as he took up a position behind a tree.[7]

The officers still could not see anyone inside the house, but they started firing their pistols at the windows. The gunmen inside the house returned fire, chipping the bark off the trees that the officers stood behind. Springfield policeman Charley Houser, more exposed than his fellow officers, was standing behind a small tree northeast of the house. Chief of Detectives Tony Oliver ordered him to seek better shelter, but before he could obey, a bullet fired from an upstairs room of the house struck him in the head, killing him instantly.[8]

Oliver ordered detectives Virgil Johnson and Ben Bilyeu to go for help, and they ran to a police car parked just off Haseltine Road on the lane leading to the farmhouse. During the dash, Johnson received a flesh wound in the leg, and, as the men scrambled into the vehicle, another bullet fired from the house broke out the car's windshield. R. G. Wegman, a civilian who'd been allowed to ride along on the jaunt from Springfield, hopped into the car as well, having decided he'd had enough adventure. The car tore off toward Springfield with Johnson at the wheel.[9]

Out of ammunition, Springfield detective Ollie Crosswhite crawled toward the shelter of a cellar in the backyard, near the northwest corner of the farmhouse. One of the brothers fired a rifle at Crosswhite but missed before a shotgun blast from close range virtually blew his brains out. It is generally believed that Jennings Young, considered a better marksman than his brother, did most, if not all, of the deadly rifle work during the shootout, while Harry wielded the shotgun.[10]

Detective Sid Meadows was the next man to go down. When he peeked out from behind the tree where he was taking shelter, a rifle bullet struck him "right in the forehead," killing him instantly.[11]

The six victims of the Young Brothers Massacre. *Courtesy Rob Schroeder and the Springfield Police Museum.*

Shortly after Meadows was hit, Chief Oliver, the only lawmen left with a rifle, shouted "They got me." Pike glanced over and saw Oliver leaning down behind a tree, but he raised back up and resumed firing. "They got me," Oliver repeated. "They're going to get all of us!" He ordered the survivors to run for their lives, and just as he turned as if to obey his own order, another bullet struck him in the back. Then he just "kinda squatted down" and fell over dead.[12]

Pike and city detective Owen Brown, the only officers left on the scene who weren't dead or dying, fired a couple of more shots, all that was left of their ammunition, before deciding to take the chief's advice. Before leaving, though, they heard someone yell from the house, ordering them to throw down their guns and come inside. "We got the rest of them and we're going to get you, too."[13]

The four officers who survived the Young Brothers Massacre. Left to right: Owen Brown, Ben Bilyeu, Frank Pike, and Virgil Johnson. *Courtesy Rob Schroeder and the Springfield Police Museum.*

That was enough to convince Pike and Brown to make a run for it. Suffering only minor wounds, they struck out to the east toward Haseltine Road with bullets kicking up dirt all around them as they ran. Out on the road, they met the first of the reinforcements coming out from Springfield and warned them not to get closer to the house than a hundred yards or they would be picked off. After the passengers in the first car piled out, Pike and Brown got in, and the driver took them back to Springfield.[14]

Hundreds of lawmen and volunteers soon gathered near the farmhouse, but no one dared approach. As darkness settled in, two men were seen striking out across a field from the direction of the house, but they made their escape before they could be intercepted. At first, it was thought that at least three and perhaps as many as five gunmen were at the Young farmhouse and participated in the shootout with lawmen. One of them was thought to be Paul Young, and Charles "Pretty Boy" Floyd was rumored to be another. However, only two men were seen leaving the premises, and it was finally agreed that Harry and Jennings Young had been at the house alone and done all the shooting.[15]

Later that night, after escaping from the farmhouse, the Young brothers made their way to Springfield, where they stole a car and headed for Texas. The brothers wrecked the car the next afternoon, January 3, near Streetman, Texas, and the weapons they'd used in the Brookline shootout were found in the vehicle after they abandoned it.[16]

Harry and Jennings hitched a ride into Houston, about a hundred and seventy miles away, and rented a room in the private residence of J. F. Tomlinson. The owner grew suspicious and went to Houston police on Tuesday morning, January 5. A squad of heavily armed officers arrived and surrounded the Tomlinson cottage. This time the tables were turned. The Young brothers, armed only with pistols they'd taken off the dead and dying officers at the Missouri farmhouse, were the ones who were badly outgunned. After a brief exchange of gunfire between the two sides, Harry and Jennings Young shot and killed each other rather than risk being taken alive.[17]

Several members of the Young family were arrested in the aftermath of the massacre at their farm, but only Paul was prosecuted. Charged with transporting a stolen car, he was convicted and sent to Leavenworth, but he, like his remaining brothers and sisters, eventually went straight. The bodies of Harry and Jennings Young were brought back to Missouri for burial about January 9, but they were held at a Joplin funeral home until final arrangements could be made.

They were taken to Greene County on January 13 for identification, but the hearse was met at the Greene-Lawrence county line by a crowd, including a number of police officers, who protested the Young brothers being buried in Greene County. Because of fear of violence, the bodies were taken back to Joplin later on the 13th and buried in an unmarked grave at Fairview Cemetery. Some time afterward, Lorena and Vinita placed a headstone on their brothers' common grave.[18]

Young brothers gravestone at Fairview Cemetery, Joplin. *Photo by the author.*

Still today, after almost ninety years, the Young brothers massacre, during which six lawmen lost their lives on that fateful day in 1932, remains the deadliest shootout in US law enforcement history, and interest in the notorious event endures. It has been the subject of numerous magazine articles, a brochure, and at least two books; and Springfield newspapers still recall the infamous incident from time to time. The farmhouse where the deadly encounter occurred is still there, facing east near the intersection of Farm Road 148 and Haseltine Road, although the home has been remodeled.

18
Bonnie and Clyde Invade Greene County
The Kidnapping of Police Officer Tom Persell

Bonnie Parker and Clyde Barrow were from the Dallas, Texas, area, and that's where they got their start in criminal activity. At the height of their notoriety in the early 1930s, though, they spent much of their time crisscrossing the four states of Kansas, Oklahoma, Arkansas, and Missouri, often just one step ahead of the law. They favored the Ozarks with their presence on several occasions, including at least two forays into Greene County.

Bonnie and Clyde were not yet widely known when they made their first appearance in Springfield on Thursday, January 26, 1933. About six o'clock in the evening, the outlaw couple, along with seventeen-year-old sidekick W. D. Jones, were slowly circling the Shrine Mosque in a V-8 Ford coach with an Oklahoma license plate, as though they were scouting for a car to steal. Springfield motorcycle cop Tom Persell spotted their suspicious activity and decided to investigate. Pulling alongside the vehicle as it crossed the Benton Avenue viaduct, he motioned the driver to stop. The driver hollered that he had no brakes, but he turned the Ford onto Pine Street (now Tampa) and pulled to a halt.[1]

As Persell again came abreast of the automobile, he stopped his motorcycle, dismounted, and started toward the Ford. The driver (later identified as Clyde Barrow) immediately stepped out to meet him with an automatic sawed-off shotgun. He ordered Persell to throw up his hands or he'd "blow (his) damn head off." When Persell complied, Clyde jerked the officer's revolver from its holster. Barrow tossed the gun to his companion sitting on the passenger's side front seat (i.e. Jones), and Persell slid into the middle of the front seat. Bonnie, whom Persell knew at this point only as "the girl," sat in the back seat, covering the hostage with a .45 army automatic pistol in her hand. Still standing outside the vehicle, Clyde spotted a boy across the street looking curiously at what was going on, and he shouted, "Get the hell out of here!" The lad took off running as Clyde climbed in behind the steering wheel and roared away.[2]

According to Persell's later account, Clyde was the only one of the gang who talked initially, and he was "quite profane." He wondered why Persell didn't know better than to stop a car with an out-of-state tag, and the officer told him that was what he got paid for. Clyde then demanded that Persell guide them out of town, since the Barrow gang was not familiar with the streets of Springfield. Persell piloted them to North Glenstone, where they turned east on Highway 66. They had gone but a short distance when Clyde asked whether there was a back road to Joplin, and Persell said there was. With Bonnie consulting a map, the gang turned back to the west and took Highway 65 north. Clyde ordered Persell to climb into the back seat, and the officer obeyed. "Every time that man said do something, I did it, and I don't mean maybe," Persell recalled.[3]

Persell was covered up with a blanket, and Bonnie held a pistol on him as Clyde pulled into a filling station and bought gas in the vicinity of Greenlawn Cemetery. Shortly after leaving the station, Clyde told Persell to get back in the front seat. As the officer climbed over the backrest, he noticed what he called "a veritable arsenal" lying in the floorboard when he accidentally stepped on one of the gang's suitcases and broke it. The stockpile of arms included two rifles, two automatic shotguns, a Thompson submachine gun, and a number of pistols. Persell also noticed several sacks of coins in the back seat and a bag in the front seat that he thought contained money as well. In addition, Clyde carried a big wad of bills.[4]

Persell described the girl he sat beside in the back seat for a short time (i.e. Bonnie) as "not the least bit beautiful." She was red-haired and freckled and weighed, he estimated, about 110 pounds. She wore a dark coat and "a sort of turban-like hat on the side of her head." Persell described Clyde as "a

Persell considered Bonnie "not the least bit beautiful." *Author's collection.*

slim, dark-faced desperado," and W. D. Jones as "a chunky thug" who liked to caress his machine gun proudly.[5]

Persell called Clyde, left, a "dark-faced desperado" and W. D. Jones a "chunky thug." *Author's collection.*

When Bonnie and W. D. finally started talking, they, too, were profane. All three gang members "hardly said anything without cussing," according to Persell. When Clyde addressed Bonnie, he called her "Hon" or "Babe," and W. D. called her "Sis," while Bonnie called Jones "Bud." The gang told Persell about stealing a tan V-8 Ford in Springfield earlier in the day on Thursday, but they abandoned it southwest of town because they considered the color too conspicuous.[6]

Continuing north on Highway 65, Clyde turned off at Crystal Cave toward Pleasant Hope. He "batted along" at fifty miles an hour over the rough, curvy, muddy roads, even though his headlights were dim from a low battery. Persell assumed the low battery was why the gang had been looking to steal another car.[7]

After passing through Pleasant Hope, the gang came out on Highway 13 between Brighton and Bolivar. From there, they pursued a circuitous route that took them through the edge of Morrisville but also included a detour north toward Fair Play. Persell said he lost his bearings a time or two and wasn't exactly sure where they were. Bonnie repeatedly consulted a road map to help navigate, especially when Clyde wanted her to find a back road around a town so that he didn't have to drive straight through it.[8]

Resuming their westward flight, the gang passed through the edge of Greenfield, where Clyde almost hit another car, forcing it into a ditch. As the gang approached Golden City, they again made Persell get down in the back seat and covered him with a blanket so they could stop for gas. At the service station, a nightwatchman came by and flashed a light on the bandit car, but Clyde stepped out of the machine to exchange pleasantries with him and he went on his way.[9]

About this time, both Bonnie and W. D. ran out of cigarettes and began bumming from Persell, who had opened a pack shortly after getting in the car with the gang. Clyde didn't smoke, but Bonnie, "who was as profane as her companions, simply 'ate' fags." W. D. was also a chain smoker or close to it.[10]

Continuing west from Golden City, the gang emerged on Highway 71 between Jasper and Lamar, and Clyde was suddenly back in familiar territory. He headed south, dodging "from one country road to another," with no one providing directions, until he came out in a residential area of Carthage. He drove around a while looking for a car to steal until he finally suggested to Bonnie they might have better luck in Webb City. She agreed, and they struck out across country roads again until they came to Webb City. W. D. got out a couple of times and looked around, but the gang had no better luck in Webb City than they had in Carthage.[11]

Clyde then drove to Oronogo, and while in the town he kept talking about a gun battle he'd recently been involved in there. "Some monkey in the bank took a shot at us," he told Persell. (This was a reference to a holdup Clyde and two sidekicks had pulled at the Farmers and Miners Bank of Oronogo two months earlier, on November 30, 1932. Not only had Clyde and one of his partners traded lead with the cashier, but the gang had run a gauntlet of gunfire from local citizens as they sped away from the bank in their getaway car. Bonnie waited for the robbers outside town, where they switched cars, but W. D. was not involved in this caper.) Persell later recalled that, at one point while he was held hostage, Clyde also mentioned some trouble he'd had in Ash Grove. Some observers took this as a reference to the January 12, 1933, robbery of the Bank of Ash Grove, but whether Clyde was indeed involved in this heist has not been established.[12]

The gang left Oronogo and drove to Joplin, where they continued their unsuccessful search for a car to steal. They then went back to Oronogo, where Clyde parked the car and disappeared in the darkness. When he returned fifteen minutes later, he was carrying a car battery. After driving outside town, Clyde stopped again to put the new battery in, and Persell helped with the task. During the installation, Persell walked behind the car to try to get its license number, but he could only make out a partial number because the plate was so muddy.[13]

With the new battery installed, the gang headed southwest, passed through Stone's Corner intersection several miles north of Joplin, and headed toward Carl Junction. They called Persell's attention to the intersection, told him they were going to let him out down the road a ways, and said if he'd walk back to the intersection and turn south toward Joplin, he'd soon come to a motor court, where he could make a phone call for someone to come and get him. True to their word, they stopped and let him out about twelve miles northwest of Joplin. It was 12:30 a.m. on Friday, January 27. Showing more spunk than sense, the twenty-five-year-old Persell asked for his revolver back when they let him out, and Clyde told him no, "You're lucky as it is."[14]

Bonnie and Clyde released motorcycle cop Tom Persell unharmed after taking him on a pell-mell ride along backroads from Springfield to Joplin. *Courtesy Rob Schroeder and the Springfield Police Museum.*

Persell walked back to the motor court, a distance he estimated at about eight miles, and called the Joplin Police. They came and got him and took him to their station. From there, he called the Springfield Police, and two Springfield officers, accompanied by Persell's wife, drove to Joplin to pick him up in the early hours of Friday morning. When Persell got back to Springfield, he was greeted as a returning hero, and his story made front-page headlines in the Friday edition of all three city newspapers.[15]

The identity of Persell's captors remained a mystery. Their familiarity with the territory around Joplin caused some to speculate that they were from that area, while the Oklahoma license on the car they were driving suggested they might be from the Sooner State or thereabouts. Persell viewed a number of wanted posters, but none of them looked like his abductors. Late Saturday, January 28, an abandoned car matching the kidnappers' vehicle was found near Cherryvale, Kansas, and Persell traveled there the next day and positively identified it as the car in which he'd been held hostage.[16]

It was not until after the Barrow gang killed two law officers in a shootout at Joplin two and a half months later, on April 13, that the identity of Persell's kidnappers became known. The gang left behind, in the apartment where the shootout occurred, several rolls of film containing photos of themselves. From the photos, authorities quickly identified three of the five gang members: Clyde Barrow; Clyde's brother, Buck; and Buck's wife, Blanche. Persell viewed the photos and confirmed that Clyde was one of the three people who'd kidnapped him. He also pointed out the fourth and fifth members of the gang, later identified as Bonnie Parker and W. D. Jones.[17]

On February 12, 1934, Bonnie and Clyde again showed up in Springfield, where their theft of an automobile led to a shootout with law officers later the same day. That morning, the desperate duo and two other gang members stole a new car from the Walnut Street residence of George Thompson of Thompson Tire Company and then fled south. The two sidekicks were driving the Thompson auto, and Clyde and his "cigar-smoking sweetheart," as a Springfield newspaper called Bonnie, were in a separate vehicle. The bandits passed through Hurley at high speed, and law officers picked up their trail near Galena. The gang ran into a roadblock near Reeds Spring and, after taking a backroad to go around the blockade, ended up shooting it out with lawmen on the southwest outskirts of Reeds Spring until the officers ran out of ammunition.[18]

This playful pose of Bonnie and Clyde is one of many photos developed from film found in their Joplin hideout. *Courtesy of the FBI.*

Bonnie and Clyde were killed in a police ambush near Arcadia, Louisiana, on May 23, 1934, a little over three months after their last known foray into Greene County, but their infamy lived on and perhaps even grew after their death. Tom Persell, who lived to be over eighty years old, continued for the rest of his life to enjoy a certain celebrity because of his 1933 encounter with the infamous pair. Anytime Bonnie and Clyde were mentioned in local newspapers, the Persell kidnapping was sure to be part of the story, and Persell was interviewed at least a time or two over the years and asked to recount his close call with the notorious outlaws. He was featured in a 1968 story a few months after the *Bonnie and Clyde* movie starring Warren Beatty and Faye Dunaway came out. Persell resented the movie because he didn't like seeing his former captors portrayed in a romantic light. Even after Persell died in 1989, his story continued to be told in Springfield newspapers. In 1999, the *News-Leader* interviewed his son for a retelling of the kidnapping story, and as recently as the summer of 2020, columnist Steve Pokin recounted the episode for the same newspaper.[19]

Chapter 19
The Murder of Savilla Scott and the
Last Legal Hanging in Greene County

Within hours after twenty-one-year old Savilla "Billie" Scott's bullet-riddled body was found beside James River Club Road (present-day South Fremont) a few miles southeast of Springfield shortly after 6:00 a.m. on the morning of March 29, 1933, several people had been arrested for questioning, and authorities concluded that the motive for her killing was probably jealousy, because she was known to have had "a number of sweethearts in recent years." Savilla was "a comely young negro woman" and was considered "a girl of many admirers." The implication seemed almost to be that Savilla might have unwittingly contributed to her own demise by being too generous with her affections. Jealousy no doubt did play a part in the dispute that led to the young woman's murder, but later evidence suggests that Savilla had more reason to be jealous than the man who killed her, because it was he who had been playing the field, not Savilla.[1]

The victim's identity had not yet been established when Greene County sheriff Scott Curtis arrived about 8:00 a.m. at the Campbell Undertaking Company in Springfield, where Acting

Coroner W. A. Umbarger had taken the body. Shortly after Curtis got there, a young black man named Edward "Jeff" Warren, who worked for the undertaking firm, came into the room and said, "That's Savilla Scott." Under questioning, Warren told the sheriff that Savilla worked as an elevator girl at

Greene County sheriff Scott Curtis arrested Sonny McDaniel for the murder of Savilla Scott. *Courtesy of Rob Schroeder and the Springfield Police Museum.*

Turner's Department Store in Springfield and that she lived with
Frank "Sonny" McDaniel. Although Warren seemed reluctant to
cooperate, Curtis made the young man ride along in search of
McDaniel and point out where he lived. Nobody was home at
the McDaniel residence on North Forest Avenue, but the sheriff
spotted the twenty-eight-year-old McDaniel at Barney
Freeman's pool hall on Boonville Street and arrested him.
McDaniel claimed that he had not seen Savilla since she left his
house about 8:00 p.m. the previous evening and that he had
stayed home all night after that time. Nevertheless, McDaniel
was retained in custody, while Warren was soon released.[2]

Besides Warren and McDaniel, others arrested in the
immediate wake of Savilla's murder included Hilbert and
Thelma Crittenden, a married couple with whom Savilla often
kept company; Tom Scott, Savilla's former husband; and Bob
Ward, a former boyfriend. Found on Savilla's body was a note
that read, "Come over tonight—Thelma." However, Thelma
Crittenden said she had not written the note, and a comparison
of the handwriting to Mrs. Crittenden's proved inconclusive.
Like Warren, Thelma and her husband were released after
questioning, as were Scott and Ward.[3]

An inquest into Ms. Scott's death was held on March 30,
the day after her body was found. So many black residents of
Springfield wanted to attend the proceeding that it had to be
moved from Campbell's Undertaking to the courthouse. The
first witnesses were four farmers who told of finding the body,
but Frank McDaniel, described as "a giant young negro," was
the primary witness. Repeating the story he'd told the sheriff,
Sonny said Savilla had lived with him for the past nine months.
The last time he'd seen her was about 8:00 p.m. on the 28th when
she left his house without explanation. He said he didn't ask her
where she was going because it was none of his business. Savilla
had been shot with a large caliber weapon, and McDaniel said

the only gun he owned was a .25 caliber pistol. Contradicted on this point by other witnesses, he admitted he had previously owned a .38 caliber pistol but he'd sold it several months earlier. A white couple, Albert Jones and his wife, testified that they called at the McDaniel home shortly before 8:00 p.m. on the 28th and that they had observed no ill humor between "Villa and Sonny." Similarly, Oscar Greer, a close friend of McDaniel's, testified that, as far as he could tell, McDaniel was not jealous of Savilla. McDaniel's mother, Maude Lyles, caused a stir when she took the stand to testify that Savilla had once brandished a gun and threatened Sonny's life. Jeff Warren, the young man who'd first identified Savilla's body, said he had borrowed McDaniel's car on the night of the killing and had returned it about 10:00 p.m. Both Tom Scott, the ex-husband, and Bob Ward, the ex-boyfriend, said they'd never seen Savilla in the company of other men since she'd been living with McDaniel.[4]

After a day-long inquest, the jury concluded that Savilla Scott was shot to death by an unknown party, but, based on the evidence so far, the jurors recommended that Frank McDaniel be held for further examination. In addition to the incriminating circumstances surrounding the current crime, McDaniel's prior record no doubt contributed to the jury's suspicion. In April 1924, Sonny had been convicted of burglary and sentenced to two years in the state penitentiary. Discharged after fourteen months, McDaniel came back to Springfield. In August 1929, he shot and mortally wounded a black man named Tom Morley in a dispute that arose over Sonny's attentions to Morley's fifteen-year-old daughter. No charges were filed against McDaniel, as the shooting was ruled self-defense. In October 1930, Sonny was sentenced to a year and a day in federal prison at Leavenworth for illegally selling whiskey. In addition, McDaniel had been involved in a car wreck in which another black man was killed, and some people blamed Sonny for the accident.[5]

Frank "Sonny" McDaniel had served two prison terms and been in trouble with the law several other times before he was arrested for killing Savilla Scott. *Courtesy Rob Schroeder and the Springfield Police Museum.*

Jeff Warren was re-arrested after the coroner's inquest into Savilla's death, and on April 4 his mother visited him at the jail. Mrs. Warren, described as "a highly respected negro woman," realized her son was hiding something. She urged him to tell authorities what he knew about the murder case, and he finally agreed. In the presence of his mother, Sheriff Curtis, and Prosecutor Dan Nee, young Warren gave a statement that, in the words of the *Springfield Daily News*, lifted the "veil of mystery surrounding (the) Savilla Scott slaying." He said he had personally witnessed Frank McDaniel kill Savilla and that the only reason he hadn't come forward sooner was that McDaniel had threatened his life if he did.[6]

Prosecutor Nee had previously learned that McDaniel and Ms. Scott argued at a dance on the night of March 27 over McDaniel's attentions to other women. Sonny went home without Savilla, and she showed up sometime later, accompanied by her sister and her sister's husband. She was crying as she started taking down the curtains that she had installed in McDaniel's bedroom, saying she was moving out. McDaniel didn't try to stop her, because he "didn't give a damn."[7]

Jeff Warren took up the narrative from there in his statement to the prosecutor. He said he and McDaniel went to a show together at the Landers Theater in the early evening of March 28. They then went to McDaniel's house at the corner of Forest and Pythian, and Warren borrowed McDaniel's car. When Warren brought the car back, the two men went out for sandwiches at Graham's Rib Station. They met a couple of girls and drove them home, and then McDaniel started to drive Warren to his home on East Cherry Street. At the corner of Benton and Pine (now Tampa), they saw Savilla walking alone and stopped to pick her up. McDaniel said he was on the way to take Warren home, and she agreed to go along.[8]

They crossed the viaduct spanning Jordan Creek, but when they got to Cherry Street, McDaniel kept driving. "Don't you want to turn there if you're going to take me home?" Warren asked as they went through the intersection.

"I'll take you home when I get ready," McDaniel said. "You ain't liable to get home."

McDaniel drove west to Campbell Street Road and turned south. When Savilla asked him again about taking Warren home, he renewed his warning. "Both of you ain't liable to get home."

South of Springfield, McDaniel turned west off Campbell Street Road and stopped on a deserted, rural road. McDaniel shut off the engine, lit a cigarette, and asked whether either of his passengers knew why he'd come out to such an isolated spot. They both said no—that they thought he was going to take Warren home.

"I came out here to kill you," McDaniel threatened.

"I don't see why, Sonny, you want to kill me," Savilla said.

"Because you did me dirty." After a pause, though, he added, "I guess I won't." He started the engine and drove back toward the east.

After about two miles, he turned north on a road Warren did not identify (James River Club Road). A short distance north of the intersection, McDaniel pulled to the side of the road and stopped again. He ordered both passengers out of the car. He told Warren to walk to the front of the car and made Savilla come with him to the back of the car. Warren heard Savilla pleading with McDaniel for her life. Then she shouted, "Jeff, don't let him kill me!"

Responding to Savilla's plea for help, Warren ran to the rear of the car and told Sonny not to kill her. McDaniel threatened to kill Warren, too, if he didn't get back to the front of the car, and the younger man retreated to his previous position.

Warren heard McDaniel say, "Little girl, you're just another girl gone," and then he heard four shots ring out. Walking to the front of the car, McDaniel renewed his threat to kill Warren, too. Warren begged him not to, and Sonny finally agreed to let him live, but with a promise to kill him later if he ever said anything about what he'd witnessed.

McDaniel drove back to his house and told Warren to spend the night with him. Afraid to say no, Warren went to bed but didn't sleep a wink all night for fear that McDaniel might decide to kill him after all. The next morning, though, Sonny drove him south on National and dropped him off at the corner of Elm Street about 7:00 a.m. From there, Warren walked home and got ready for work.[9]

A charge of first-degree murder against McDaniel was prepared the same day Warren gave his statement, and it was filed the next day before Justice D. E. Holman. The courtroom was packed for McDaniel's preliminary hearing on April 14. Jeff Warren testified to the facts in the case as he'd previously related them to the prosecutor, and Holman ordered McDaniel bound over without bond for trial in the circuit court.[10]

At the beginning of McDaniel's trial on June 19, defense lawyers succeeded in getting the first-degree murder indictment against him quashed because the transcript of the testimony from the preliminary hearing had not been properly filed and certified. The defendant was a free man for about two seconds before Judge Warren White ordered him held for a new preliminary examination. Rather than pursue a new preliminary hearing, however, prosecutors came back after a noon recess and filed an amended transcript of the original hearing, which Judge White allowed over the strenuous objection of the defense.[11]

Testimony then began, with Jeff Warren again serving as the star witness for the prosecution. He repeated the story he'd told at the preliminary hearing of personally witnessing the murder. Oscar Greer also took the stand for the state. Contradicting what he'd said at the coroner's inquest, Greer admitted he'd witnessed "repeated quarrels" between McDaniel and Savilla Scott and that Savilla had often complained to Sonny about his attentions to other women. One time McDaniel had blacked Savilla's eye, and the couple had argued the night before the murder. Greer also testified that McDaniel did own a large caliber revolver, contrary to what he had claimed.[12]

The main defense strategy was to try to establish an alibi, and McDaniel's lawyers called several witnesses to back their client's story that he was home all evening on the night of the murder. The defense also attacked the credibility of the state's witnesses because several of them were either in jail at the time or had previously been convicted of petty crimes. In addition, the defense made repeated mention of the note found on Savilla's body, implying that it represented a line of investigation authorities had not adequately pursued.[13]

The jury got the case about 5:00 p.m. on the 20th and came back three hours later with a guilty verdict and a death penalty recommendation. The courtroom was packed, and McDaniel sat perfectly still with "the faintest trace of a smile" as Judge White read the verdict.[14]

A defense motion for a new trial was overruled, and Judge White formally pronounced sentence on June 26. He set July 28 as the date for McDaniel's hanging, but an appeal to the Missouri Supreme Court automatically stayed the execution. On June 28, the prisoner was taken to the Missouri State Penitentiary for safekeeping until the high court rendered its decision.[15]

Among the defense's contentions in its appeal to the Missouri Supreme Court were claims that McDaniel's testimony at the coroner's jury amounted to self-incrimination and that the amended transcript of the preliminary hearing testimony should not have been allowed. Rejecting these claims, the high court upheld the lower court's decision on March 5, 1935, and set McDaniel's new execution date for April 12.[16]

McDaniel was slated to hang from a scaffold surrounded by a stockade outside the jail, which was located behind the courthouse at the corner of Boonville and Central. Capacity of the stockade was limited to one hundred people, but as preparations for the execution got underway, Sheriff Curtis was overwhelmed with requests for passes to witness the spectacle. Several people even volunteered for the job of executioner. "Outstanding among those who wanted to spring the death trap" was a pretty twenty-year-old business student named Thelma

Newspaper photo of Thelma Rediger, who volunteered to serve as McDaniel's executioner. *From the Springfield Leader and Press.*

Rediger, who aspired to write mystery and detective stories and thought being a hangman might provide valuable experience for her chosen endeavor. After the story of her request, accompanied by her picture, was published in a Springfield newspaper, Thelma was so inundated with letters that she thought about hiring a private secretary. Some of the letters questioned why a beautiful young woman like Thelma would want to perform such an unpleasant task, but most came from kindred spirits who supported her, including a good number from men who wished to strike up a romance with her. Sheriff Curtis told Thelma and all the others who wanted to act as executioner that the job belonged to him and he meant to carry out his duty, as unpleasant as it might be.[17]

When construction of the gallows behind the jail finally got underway about the first of April, many curious onlookers gathered to inspect the work, and even after the stockade was complete, crowds continued to stream through the enclosure to view the gibbet. When it was announced on April 10, two days before the scheduled execution, that the stockade would be closed to the public that night, "the crowds grew in size until it looked like election day."[18]

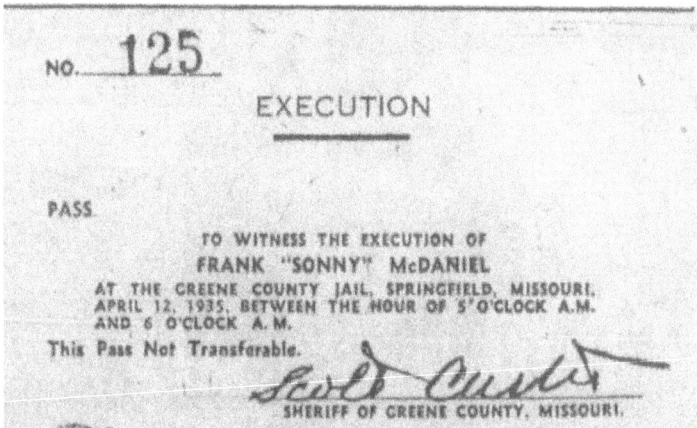

NO. **125**

EXECUTION

PASS

TO WITNESS THE EXECUTION OF
FRANK "SONNY" McDANIEL
AT THE GREENE COUNTY JAIL, SPRINGFIELD, MISSOURI,
APRIL 12, 1935, BETWEEN THE HOUR OF 5 O'CLOCK A.M.
AND 6 O'CLOCK A.M.
This Pass Not Transferable.

SHERIFF OF GREENE COUNTY, MISSOURI.

Facsimile of pass to witness McDaniel execution from the *Springfield Leader and Press.*

Sheriff Curtis drove to Jefferson City and brought McDaniel back to Springfield on April 11 so that his relatives could visit him during his last night on earth. Sonny still maintained that he did not kill Savilla Scott, telling the sheriff that he got railroaded because he was "a two-time loser" while Jeff Warren, the main witness against him, was "a Sunday school boy." Shortly after his arrival at the Greene County Jail in the late afternoon of the 11th, McDaniel was baptized by the Rev. H. W. James of the Pitts Chapel Methodist Church. Sonny's mother, Maude, was in attendance, and she continued visiting her son throughout the evening. They said their final farewells about midnight when Mrs. Lyles and all other visitors were asked to leave.[19]

This newspaper photo from the *Springfield Leader and Press* shows the scene at the gallows outside the Greene County Jail shortly after McDaniel dropped through the trap.

Shortly after midnight, Sheriff Curtis read the death warrant to McDaniel. The condemned man stayed up most of the night and ate a light breakfast early on the morning of April 12. He spent his last hour reading the Bible, religious tracts, and stories about himself in the Springfield newspapers. Already bound and shackled, McDaniel was led through a second-story window of the jail and up some steps onto the scaffold shortly after 5:00 a.m. With a cigarette dangling from his mouth, he bid the sheriff adieu and spoke to several other officers, as a crowd of about 200 ticket holders inside the stockade pressed in around the gallows to witness the spectacle of Greene County's first legal hanging since the pre-Civil War execution of Willis Washam. About a thousand other people milled around outside the stockade.[20]

"Take that cigaret out of my mouth," McDaniel said, as a deputy started to put the black hood over his head. Those were Sonny's last words. The deputy removed the cigarette, put the hood over the prisoner's head, and looped the rope around his neck. Sheriff Curtis immediately pulled the lever, and McDaniel dropped through the trap door at 5:20 a.m. The fall did not break his neck, and he hung for about eight minutes before a team of doctors pronounced him dead.[21]

After the hanging, Sheriff Curtis thanked the crowd for being orderly and then ducked back inside the jail. McDaniel's body was cut down and placed in a hearse to be turned over to his family. He was buried on April 15 at Hazelwood Cemetery following a brief funeral service at his mother's home in the 900 block of South Main Street.[22]

Not only was McDaniel's execution just the second legal hanging in Greene County history, it also marked the last, because a state law was passed in 1937 moving all executions to the gas chamber at the state prison in Jefferson City.

20
Caught in a Police Trap
The Double Murder of Victor Spinetto
and Virgil Usrey

By mid-December, 1957, seventy-five-year-old Victor Spinetto had been in the grocery and produce business in Springfield for almost fifty years. An immigrant from Italy, he'd come to America in 1906 and, shortly afterward, he moved to Springfield and opened up his first business in the 500 block of Boonville Avenue. Later he moved his store to 425 Boonville. A lifelong bachelor, he lived nearby on Boonville, and he kept the store open seven days a week. In recent years, he'd stayed open from early morning until eight o'clock at night, but during earlier years he'd stayed open even later. His grocery store wasn't just his job; it was his whole life.[1]

Spinetto had been the victim of numerous petty crimes over the years and even a few serious ones. In 1944, he'd been slugged and robbed, and on November 21, 1957, he'd again been assaulted at his store, this time with a piece of metal pipe. Suffering from a fractured skull, he'd spent about two weeks in the hospital and was released around the sixth of December.

Maybe he should have retired. After all, he was an old man, but instead he went straight back to work.

And ten days later he was dead.[2]

About noon on Sunday, December 15, March Stokely and Everett Binegar, who'd been staying at Cavalry Mission in the 300 block of Boonville, walked down the hill to Spinetto's grocery to get something to eat. When Stokely opened the door, he was shocked to find Spinetto and another elderly man lying in the middle of the floor with blood all over the place. Both men had suffered numerous cuts and stab wounds. A basket of unshelled peanuts had been overturned and were scattered all around. Stokely and Binegar hurried back to the mission to report their gruesome discovery, and the manager called police.[3]

For the Sunday Dinner

SPECIALS

**Elberta
Peaches**

**10c, 15c, 20c
per basket**

California Pears.

Fresh Fruits of All
Kinds.

Victor Spinetto

527 Boonville St.

Victor Spinetto had been in business on Boonville Street for many years at the time he was killed in December 1957, as this advertisement from a July 1913 edition of the *Springfield Missouri Republican* illustrates.

When help arrived, the unknown man was already dead, having bled to death from a severed artery. He was later identified as sixty-seven-year-old Virgil Usrey, owner of the Brown Derby liquor store next door to the grocery. Spinetto was clinging to life, suffering from multiple wounds about his head and body. He was rushed to Burge Hospital, where he died fourteen hours later without regaining consciousness.[4]

Investigators learned from Usrey's wife that he'd left their home about eleven o'clock to get some cardboard boxes from his liquor store, which was not open on Sundays. He'd apparently stopped in to visit Spinetto when the attack happened. From the similarity of the wounds and other evidence, officers thought the bloody attack was the work of just one knife-wielding madman.[5]

Stokely and Binegar told investigators they'd seen no one suspicious during their walk to the store, and police questioning of several other people in the area turned up no suspects or leads. Officers concluded from the spilled peanuts and several overturned boxes that the two old men had put up a struggle against their assailant. Also found on the floor near the bodies was a broken metal object, later identified as part of a pellet gun. Police theorized that the gun might have been used as a weapon during the attack, since the victims had been bludgeoned with some blunt instrument as well as cut with a knife. The market's rear door was slightly ajar, leading officers to believe the assailant had left through that entrance. A pair of pants that appeared to be bloodstained were found stuffed in a basket in an alley at the rear of the store.[6]

Coroner Ralph Thieme examined Usrey and found twenty-one stab wounds on his body. The depth of the wounds indicated a knife with a blade about six and a half inches long, although some of the wounds were slicing cuts. The large number of wounds led police to theorize that the assailant was either viciously insane or very frightened. Officers did not know whether the motive for the crime was robbery, a personal grudge, or the bloodlust of a maniac, but they were inclined to rule out robbery. Little of value had apparently been taken from the store, but it was possible a would-be robber had fled after meeting more resistance than anticipated. There were some parallels between the current attack and the November 21st bludgeoning. Both had involved a silent weapon, and no money was taken in either case. However, there were not enough similarities to make a definite connection. The 1944 attack on Spinetto did involve robbery, but the perpetrator of that crime was nonetheless checked out. He had returned to Springfield after his parole from prison, but officers learned he had left the area several years ago.[7]

Officers questioned numerous witnesses and potential suspects throughout the remainder of December and into January 1958 without making much headway in solving the double murder of Spinetto and Usrey. Their first real lead came in early January when they discovered pellet gun parts on a flatbed railroad car that had been sitting idle on a side track near the Frisco depot about two blocks west of Spinetto's store since December 9. Tests conducted at the Missouri Highway Patrol lab determined that the newly discovered parts matched the part found earlier at Spinetto's store. Then on January 13, investigators found a butcher knife beneath an ice dock of the Springfield Ice and Refrigeration Company. The dock was about a block west of Spinetto's store between the store and the spur track where the pellet gun parts had been found. The knife was identified as having belonged to Spinetto, and it was believed to have been the primary murder weapon. Despite the promising lead, police were no closer to solving the crime unless they could identify who had disposed of the knife.[8]

They decided to lay a trap.

Authorities announced to the media on January 14 that the next day the police were going to conduct a thorough search for the murder weapon, combing the entire area between the store and the spur track where the pellet gun parts had been found. If lawmen found the knife used in the heinous crime, the announcement said, it likely would lead them to the killer. What the general public and the perpetrator of the crime did not know was that the knife had already been found. A similar but phony second knife had been planted in its place, and officers already had the area staked out when the announcement was made.[9]

Officers admitted the scheme sounded "fantastic and 'Dick Tracyish,'" but would it work? Would the killer take the bait and return to the scene under cover of darkness looking to retrieve the murder weapon before the concentrated police search scheduled for the next day?

It didn't take long to learn the answer. On the night of the 14th, five officers lay in wait, watching the area where the knife had been found. About 10:30 p.m., they spotted a man approaching through an alley. He paused and then suddenly ducked into a well house adjacent to and just west of the ice dock where the knife had been found. As the officers converged on the well house, the suspect emerged from the well house and offered no resistance as he was taken into custody.[10]

Two detectives, who were among the five officers, took charge of the suspect and began questioning him. Asked what he was doing in the area, he claimed he was there to "catch a train to St. Louis." When the detectives informed him that a person couldn't catch a train in this vicinity, he replied, "Well, if you want to know the truth, I'll tell you." He said he was there to retrieve the knife he'd used to kill "Vic Spinetto and that Usrey fellow." His conscience had been bothering him, and he might as well get it off his chest.[11]

Taken to the police station, the suspect was questioned by Springfield assistant police chief Sam Robards and Greene County sheriff Glenn Hendrix. The suspect identified himself as twenty-year-old Herman Joseph Flood, Jr. of Ash Grove. He said that, on that fateful Sunday in December, he was in Springfield to visit his grandmother. On his way to the train depot to return to Ash Grove, he stopped at Spinetto's store to get a cupcake and a bottle of pop, and he consumed them in the store. He claimed that he did not plan to rob the place when he entered, but after a customer departed, leaving Flood alone with Spinetto, he pulled out the pellet gun and pointed it at the storekeeper. Unfazed, Spinetto came toward him and started batting at the gun. Flood picked up the pop bottle that he'd just emptied and hit Spinetto with it. He said that he might have also hit Spinetto with the pellet gun and that it took at least two or three blows to knock the old man down. Spinetto was lying on the floor crying feebly when Usrey came to the door and started to enter. Flood told him Spinetto was closed up, but Usrey noticed his friend on the floor and snarled, "Yes, he looks like he's closed up." The liquor store owner made a move toward the assailant, and Flood struck him with the pop bottle and pellet gun the same way he'd hit Spinetto. Usrey begged him to quit hitting him, but Flood didn't stop until Usrey collapsed to the floor beside the groceryman. Flood then picked up a butcher knife belonging to Spinetto and stabbed both men repeatedly. After his bloody work, Flood washed his hands in a lavatory, grabbed a pair of pants hanging on the wall, and used them to wipe his hands. He exited through the back door and discarded the pants behind the store. He told his interrogators the exact route he'd taken from the store to the depot and the precise location where he'd gotten rid of the weapons and shattered the pop bottle.[12]

Herman Joseph Flood, Jr., pictured here shortly after his arrest for the double murder of Spinetto and Usrey. *Courtesy Rob Schroeder and the Springfield Police Museum.*

Investigators found a few inconsistencies in the young man's account, and the general story of the crime was well known to anyone who'd followed it in the media. Still, Flood knew enough details that had not been made public to convince lawmen that he was involved in the murders, although they thought it possible he might have had an accomplice.[13]

The young man told reporters his parents were separated and he was not living with either one of them. Instead, he worked as a farmhand near Ash Grove. Two years earlier, he'd spent ninety days in the US Army before receiving a medical discharge, but he did not specify the precise reason for the discharge. He said the three months he'd spent in the army were the best days of his life.[14]

Information gleaned within twenty-four hours after Flood's arrest showed that he had one previous arrest for theft, and he had been considered mentally disturbed for years. He had been questioned in the Spinetto-Usrey case right after the killings but was not considered a definite suspect at that time. He was now being investigated as a suspect in the November beating of Spinetto as well, but Flood said he'd never even seen Spinetto until the day he killed him. He'd been to the store once before, but that was when Spinetto was in the hospital after the November attack and someone else was minding the store. Contradicting his initial confession, Flood now admitted that he intended to rob the store when he entered it on December 15 and that he took twelve dollars from the cash register and got five dollars from Usrey's billfold.[15]

On January 16, the day after his arrest, Flood was arraigned on a first-degree murder charge in the death of Victor Spinetto. Later in the month, a coroner's inquest concluded that both Spinetto and Usrey had died "due to being beaten with a blunt instrument and by stabbing with a butcher's knife inflicted by the hands of one Herman Joseph Flood, Jr., in a holdup and robbery." Still later in January, a second charge of first-degree murder was filed against Flood in the death of Usrey. After a preliminary hearing in the Spinetto case on January 30, Flood was bound over to the circuit court for trial, and he then waived a hearing in the Usrey case.[16]

In mid-February 1958, Flood signed a written confession that agreed in almost every detail with the oral confession he had given earlier. Flood's trial for the double slaying came up in April, and he pleaded guilty to first-degree murder. During the sentencing phase of the trial, Flood's attorneys painted "a sordid picture of a child who was disfigured by malnutrition and disease, beaten 'from pillar to post,' and unwanted by any member of society." They recommended leniency, and even Sheriff Hendrix, Chief Robards, and prosecutor Lyndon Sturgis agreed that Flood's was a pitiful case deserving of special consideration. Therefore, Judge Warren L. White gave Flood two sentences of life imprisonment to run concurrently rather than imposing the death penalty.[17]

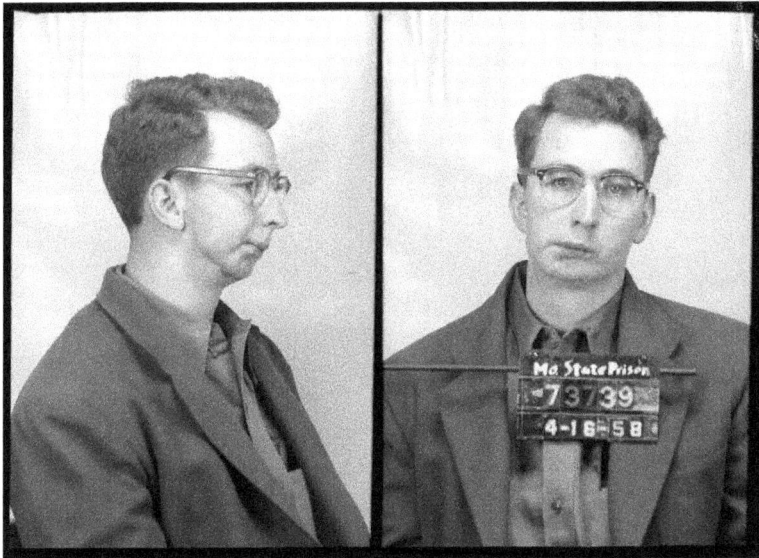

Mugshots of Flood at the time he was received at the Missouri State Prison.
Courtesy Missouri State Archives.

Flood was received at the state prison in Jefferson City on April 16, 1958. In January 1969, he was transferred to the Moberly Correctional Center, a medium to minimum security facility. The following year, Flood filed a motion to have his guilty plea vacated and to be granted a new trial. He claimed he "didn't know what was going on" when he pleaded guilty, but his motion was denied. Flood appealed to the Missouri Supreme

Court, but the high court upheld the convictions in January 1972.[18]

Flood was paroled on September 22, 1975, and discharged altogether on August 25, 1981. He died in Moberly on August 9, 2010, leaving a wife and two children.[19]

21

The Bizarre History of a Long-Unsolved Murder
Johnny Vaughn Killed at Water Valley Mill

About eight o'clock Sunday morning, August 2, 1964, the Greene County sheriff's office received a call from a fisherman who reported a bloodstained vehicle abandoned at the Water Valley Mill just northeast of Springfield. Hurrying to the scene, deputies found a bloody 1961 Ford with bullet holes in the windshield and the left front door. A short distance away, they found a man lying in a ditch near death. He was rushed to Burge Protestant Hospital in critical condition, suffering from five gunshot wounds. Identified as thirty-four-year-old John Franklin "Johnny" Vaughn, he had been shot at least three times in the head, once in the back, and once in the chest with a small-caliber weapon. He'd also apparently been beaten.[1]

The Ford, identified as belonging to Vaughn, had blood smears both inside and outside, and investigators could not say whether the victim had been shot inside or outside the vehicle. From the surroundings, it appeared that there had been a struggle and that Vaughn had stumbled and crawled a considerable distance after being shot. Lawmen theorized that robbery was not the motive for the crime, since Vaughn's billfold still contained seven or eight dollars. In addition about $300 in cash was found in the car's trunk. Although the trunk was locked, the key was found on a ring near a bloody spot on the ground about six feet from the driver's side door.[2]

Photo of Johnny Vaughn that appeared in the *Springfield Leader and Press* the day
after he died from gunshot wounds.

Exploring every avenue of investigation, officers interviewed several friends and acquaintances of Vaughn, who ran the V & E Grocery at 1551 Colgate in Springfield and had formerly taught school at Reeds Spring, Spokane, and other area towns. They located a man who had talked to Vaughn about 2:15 a.m. on Sunday morning; so they knew he'd been killed after that time. Other than turning up this tidbit, however, the investigation mostly hit dead ends.[3]

Vaughn died of his wounds early Monday morning, August 3. During an autopsy later that day, a pathologist removed four bullets or fragments from the victim's head and two from the body. A suspect in Vaughn's murder was questioned, but he was cleared by a lie detector test. Within a week after the crime, more than a hundred people had been interviewed in reference to the case, but to no avail. By the end of August, authorities were no closer to solving the murder than they had been right after it was first committed, and the case was already turning cold. In February 1965, a man named Crawford was arrested in Laclede County for the killing of a man who was shot five times and left in a ditch near Conway, and Greene County officials thought he could well be tied to the Vaughn case as well. Crawford denied involvement, and ballistic tests showed that neither gun he had in his possession at the time of his arrest was used in Vaughn's killing. About the first of August 1966, two years after Vaughn's murder, a Greene County deputy traveled to California to run down another lead in the case, but it, like all the others, proved fruitless.[4]

Nothing more was heard about the Johnny Vaughn murder case for over two years.

Then, on Sunday evening, December 8, 1968, a man registered at a motel in Corpus Christi, Texas, and shortly after checking in, went across the street to a Baptist church. He found the pastor, the Rev. Jack D. Walker, in the parsonage and said he had something he wanted to confess. He said his name was Donald D. Campbell of Central Point, Oregon, and that he'd killed a man in Springfield, Missouri, four years earlier.

Campbell said that, since he'd been saved, the crime had been weighing on him and that he needed to get it off his chest.[5]

Pastor Walker called a juvenile officer he knew who was a member of the Corpus Christi Police and made arrangements for authorities to come to the church to take Campbell into custody. Meanwhile, Campbell went with the preacher to the sanctuary for Sunday evening worship and sat through the service. When the invitation was given at the end, Campbell came forward, declared his Christian faith, and repeated to the entire congregation the confession he'd made to the pastor. After the meeting was dismissed, an old woman came up and gave Campbell a hug, and others in the congregation came forward to shake his hand. Two police officers then took custody of Campbell and escorted him to the police station.[6]

Campbell signed a written confession while still in Corpus Christi. Although Campbell's home was in Oregon, he was a drifter, and he'd been passing through Missouri the evening before the killing when he stopped and booked a hotel. A man named Johnny picked him up at either the Greyhound or Trailways bus station in downtown Springfield and drove him out into the country. They were outside the car when Johnny made homosexual advances toward Campbell, and the two men got into a heated argument. The suspect said he lost his temper, pulled out a .22 caliber pistol, and started firing. He shot Johnny in the back as the latter ran toward the car. Johnny made it into the car, but Campbell kept shooting him though the windshield. After the shooting, Campbell struck out on foot toward the highway and disposed of the weapon in a field.[7]

After the murder, Campbell went back to Oregon and became a Christian sometime after his return. Described as "clean-cut and well-dressed," he'd been doing volunteer work with the Central Point Police, but his conscience continued to bother him. He'd left Oregon in late November 1968, telling his mother that he'd done "a very bad thing" and was "going East to clear it up."[8]

Campbell said he'd come through Springfield on November 29 and tried to turn himself in for car theft but couldn't bring himself to mention the murder. A man who'd given Campbell a ride from the Kansas City area to Springfield confirmed his story. The man said Campbell confessed to an old murder during the drive to Springfield and that he'd taken Campbell to see his pastor. Campbell repeated his confession to the pastor, who called the Greene County sheriff's office and asked about unsolved murders and whether Donald D. Campbell was a suspect in any such case. Told "no," the pastor passed Campbell's story off as fantasy. The man who'd given Campbell a ride from Kansas City didn't believe him either, but, acting on Campbell's request, he took him to the courthouse building and dropped him off. Campbell said he was going to eat at Hamby's Restaurant and then go turn himself in. The man recalled later that Campbell was carrying only a suitcase and a Bible when he left him.[9]

Instead of going to the courthouse, Campbell went to the nearby post office and asked about turning himself in for a car theft. He was directed to the FBI, but FBI agent Jim Mitchell could find no record of the car theft described by Campbell and turned him loose. Leaving Springfield, the twenty-eight-year-old Campbell made his way to San Antonio, then caught a ride with a truck driver to Corpus Christi. He was on his way back to Oregon, but his conscience was still nagging him. He decided he couldn't go back without making a full confession. The day after his confession, Campbell said he wasn't really a bad person at the time he killed Vaughn, but he was only twenty-four and was "pretty wild as a kid." He said there had been a big change in him since he confessed and that, if he ever got out of prison, he'd like to become a minister or maybe an evangelist.[10]

Charged with first-degree murder, Campbell waived extradition, and two Greene County deputies drove to Texas to pick up the suspect. He was brought back to Springfield on December 13, lodged in the Greene County Jail, and arraigned in magistrate court three days later. Campbell was bound over to circuit court in late December. In early January 1969, circuit court judge Douglas Greene sustained a defense motion that Campbell undergo psychiatric evaluation prior to trial. In late March, he was found mentally capable of standing trial, but his court-appointed attorney, Ben Francka, said that his client would nevertheless plead not guilty by reason of mental disease or defect at his upcoming trial.[11]

The trial got underway in Greene County Circuit Court on May 19 with jury selection. In making its case, the prosecution relied heavily on the multiple confessions Campbell had given. When it came Francka's turn, he put his client on the stand to try to bolster the defense's insanity plea. Campbell told of a troubled childhood and youth. His mother had left his father when he was a young child. He stayed with his father at first but later went to live with his mother. Sometimes he didn't have enough to eat. He mentioned suffering a brain concussion in an automobile accident, and he said he once got so mad at his little sister that he almost choked her, even though he was very fond of her. During his young adulthood, he'd drifted from place to place and had never been able to hold a job for very long. He'd served briefly in the army but was discharged because of an incident in which he shot off a gun, wounding himself.[12]

On the evening of the murder, Campbell continued, Vaughn pulled up outside his hotel in downtown Springfield and offered to buy him a cup of coffee and show him around town. After Campbell got in the car, the subject of fishing came up, and Vaughn suggested they go to a lake outside town. When they got near the lake, Vaughn turned off onto a gravel road, stopped the car, and turned the lights off. Vaughn lay one hand on Campbell's neck and put the other one between his legs. Campbell hit the man with an elbow and got out of the car, but Vaughn followed and grabbed him by the shoulder. Campbell told Vaughn to leave him alone as he whipped out his .22 revolver. He pointed the gun at Vaughn's face and it went off, although Campbell claimed not to remember pulling the trigger. Vaughn got back into the car, and Campbell shot him again. When Vaughn tumbled out of the car, he shot him a couple of more times and then rolled him into a ditch. "I didn't want to kill a man," Campbell declared. "It didn't seem like me doing it; yet I know I did." He even remembered yelling, "No, no!" as he was shooting but couldn't seem to stop himself. "It seemed as if I was two people and watching myself do it."[13]

Campbell's attorney emphasized his client's sense of detachment, suggesting that it amounted to a split personality, but Prosecutor John Crow called expert witnesses who had examined Campbell to rebut the insanity plea. Crow argued that Campbell's murder of Vaughn was deliberate and premeditated because he shot the victim as he was retreating to his car and continued to shoot him after he'd fallen to the ground. Largely siding with the state, the jury came back on the night of May 21, after three hours of deliberation, with a guilty verdict. However, the conviction was for second-degree murder, not first-degree, and the jury assessed a punishment of twenty-five years in the state penitentiary.[14]

On June 6, Campbell waived his right to seek a new trial, and he was transported to the state penitentiary in Jefferson City three days later. After spending a little over two years at the big house, he changed his mind about wanting a new trial. In September 1971, he filed a motion to have his conviction set aside, claiming the mental evaluation he was given was incomplete and that he was under the influence of an hallucinatory drug at the time of his trial.[15]

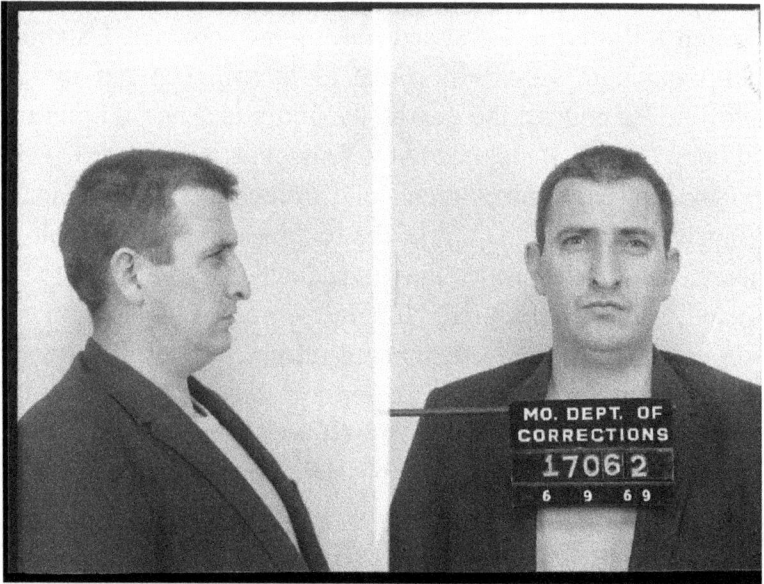

Mugshots of Donald D. Campbell. *Courtesy of Missouri State Archives.*

Granted a hearing on the motion in early November, Campbell was brought to Springfield to testify. He explained that he did not kill Johnny Vaughn but had only confessed so he could get help for his drug problem. He'd kept up the pretense because he enjoyed the attention and publicity he got. During his trial, he'd been high on mescaline, which he got from one of his jailers, and he'd been "drunk on dope" when he was in Springfield at the time of the killing. He said he'd first started lying about having killed Vaughn when he called his sister from Springfield a day or two after the murder and falsely confessed to her. He'd learned the details of the crime from newspapers and from hearing people talk about it. He said he told the lie for so long that he almost convinced himself he'd killed Vaughn, and he only came to his senses after he went to prison and got off drugs. Campbell offered to take a lie detector test. A Springfield newspaper reporter commented at the time that Campbell's latest claims "added another chapter" to the "bizarre history" of the Vaughn murder case.[16]

To refute Campbell's claims, the prosecution called a number of Greene County deputies and other law enforcement officials to testify that nothing in Campbell's behavior during the time he was incarcerated in the county jail led them to believe he was under the influence of drugs. While awaiting Judge James Keet's decision, Campbell cut his wrist in an apparent suicide attempt, although he was not seriously wounded. In mid-November, Keet denied Campbell's motion for a new trial and ordered him returned to the custody of state prison officials. Keet also denied Campbell's request to take a lie detector test, saying that such a test should have been requested and administered at the time of his trial.[17]

Campbell then appealed to the Missouri Supreme Court, but in November 1974 the justices upheld his conviction and Judge Keet's refusal to grant him a new trial. Their opinion pointed out that Campbell's claim that he had continued to lie about killing Vaughn because he delighted in the publicity he received did not mesh with his failure to seek a new trial in the immediate aftermath of his conviction. If he really enjoyed the publicity, why did he not prolong it by seeking a new trial when first convicted?[18]

On August 31, 1976, Campbell escaped from prison by walking away from a work farm near Jefferson City, but he was recaptured the next day. Charged in Cole County with prison escape, he was convicted and given a two-year sentence in addition to the twenty-five-year sentence he was already serving.[19]

Shortly afterward, on December 22, 1976, Campbell was transferred to the Kansas State Penitentiary. He was paroled on

January 16, 1978, but he was returned to the Missouri State Penitentiary on October 17, 1980, on a parole violation. He was paroled again on January 4, 1984, and he was discharged altogether on September 11, 1987. In 2011, a Donald Dee Campbell, the name Vaughn's killer usually went by, showed up on a sex registry in California. He was seventy-one years old, the age Vaughn's killer would have been. So, it's very likely, although not completely certain, that the two men were one and the same.[20]

Chapter 22
A Tangled Tale of Murder and Flight
Robert Fay Adams Slays His Wife

When twenty-one-year-old Adela Adams and her nineteen-year-old sister Donna left their Springfield home for school on the early morning of February 3, 1970, their father, Robert Fay Adams, was lying on the couch, and their mother, Willa Lee Adams, was getting ready for work. Just before the young women stepped out the door, Willa asked their advice on which dress she should wear. It was the last time the girls would see their mom alive.[1]

When Adela and Donna came home from school that afternoon, their father said Willa had left after he fell asleep on the couch, taking some clothes and other personal items with her, and he didn't know where she'd gone. The daughters knew their parents had been having marital problems. Their father had even left home and lived in an apartment for a while before recently coming back to help out with living expenses. Maybe their mother had decided it was her turn to leave. Although her car was still in the driveway, it was possible she'd left with someone else. But other suspicious circumstances nagged at the sisters and weren't so easy to rationalize. They learned from Ball

Supply Co, where Willa Lee had been employed for fourteen years, that she hadn't shown up for work and hadn't picked up her paycheck. That wasn't like their mother. Checking Willa's closet and bureau, they realized the number of missing clothes and personal items was too small to suggest an extended absence, and she'd taken no cosmetics at all. So, the longer their mother stayed gone, the more concerned the young women became.[2]

Photo of Willa Lee Adams from the *Springfield Leader and Press* shortly after her disappearance.

Later in February, the forty-one-year-old Adams made a trip to Florida, and when he came back, he told his daughters he'd found their mother there and had lunch with her. He told them Willa had promised to come back home by the first of March or thereabouts. On March 3rd, with the expected arrival date having come and gone, Adela and Donna confronted their father, demanding that, if he wasn't going to help them locate their mother, they'd find someone who would. He denied any knowledge of his wife's whereabouts beyond what he'd already told them, and thirty minutes later he left the house, saying he was going to Kansas City to visit his mother.[3]

A few days later, the young women, now suspecting foul play, went to the Springfield Police, who initiated an investigation. A check with Adams's mother in Kansas City revealed that he'd never arrived there. On March 12, the story of Willa's and Robert's separate disappearances, as the girls had related it to authorities, made front-page news in the *Springfield Leader and Press,* and police stepped up their efforts to find the missing couple. Two days later, Robert Fay Adams was located in a hospital in Pensacola, Florida. He'd been admitted the night before when a young woman named Shirley Grayson sought help for him after he took an overdose of medicine. Just twenty-two, Ms. Grayson and her two-year-old daughter had run away from Springfield with the older man about ten days earlier. After spending a few days in Jackson, Mississippi, the three had come to Pensacola and had been living in a local trailer park for the past week. Before Adams passed out on the evening he overdosed, he gave Ms. Grayson several thousand dollars in cash and a will leaving one-third of everything he owned to her and one-third each to his two daughters. Although he'd instructed Shirley to keep the money for herself and not tell anybody about it, she voluntarily turned it over to officers in Pensacola.[4]

Adams's stomach was pumped when he was admitted to the hospital, and he was expected to live. Police were eager to question him about the whereabouts of his missing wife, and when he regained consciousness on March 18, he admitted that he must have killed her but claimed not to remember how. All he remembered, he said, was seeing her lifeless, bloody body on the floor of their bedroom with a gun beside the body. He'd loaded his wife's body into a vehicle, cleaned up the mess in the house, and buried the body with a bulldozer at a gravel bar southeast of Forsyth in the Kissee Mills area a couple of days after the killing. He also disposed of the gun in the same general area.[5]

Bulldozer operator Elmer Claussen led investigators to the likely burial site, a Kissee Mills campground, after he identified a photo of Adams as a man who'd briefly used his bulldozer in early February. Claussen said the man told him he was on vacation, and he'd hung around Claussen's work site a couple of days. The man remarked, when Claussen let his ten-year-old granddaughter briefly run the machine, that he thought he could learn to do so, too. One day, Claussen recalled, he left the work site for a couple of hours, and when he returned, the bulldozer had been moved. Claussen remembered, also, that the man had been very careful about keeping his automobile locked at all times.[6]

A search in the area of the gravel bar was undertaken on the evening of March 18. Hampered by darkness and snow cover, the search was resumed the next morning, and the body of thirty-nine-year-old Willa Lee Adams, clad only in underclothes, was discovered about 8:30 a.m. buried in a ditch that ran beside the gravel bar along the banks of Beaver Creek.[7]

On the day Willa Lee's body was found, reporters interviewed some of her husband's former colleagues to try to get a sense of what kind of person would kill his own wife.

Adams, who previously worked at Hermann Lumber Company and a couple of other places before starting his own engineering firm, was described as "capable and friendly" but "distant." His mind wandered, and he was "distressed over something all the time."[8]

After Willa Lee Adams's body was retrieved from the muddy ditch on the 19th, it was taken back to Springfield, where a post mortem examination later that day concluded that Willa Lee had died from a gunshot wound to the head. On March 20, Greene County prosecutor John Crow filed a charge of first-degree murder against Robert Fay Adams, and a warrant for his arrest was wired to Pensacola police, who were temporarily holding Adams after his release from the hospital. Adams waived extradition, and he was turned over to Greene County deputies, who'd been previously dispatched to Pensacola. Driving through the night, they arrived back in Springfield on March 21 and lodged the prisoner in the Greene County Jail.[9]

During the trip back from Pensacola, Adams told the deputies escorting him that he'd thrown the murder weapon into Bull Shoals Lake at the Highway 86 overpass, and it was retrieved by divers near that location after a brief search on March 22. The pistol was identified by serial number as one Adams had purchased the previous September.[10]

At his arraignment in magistrate court on March 25, Adams was denied bail, and he was returned to jail to await a preliminary examination. At the preliminary hearing in mid-April, the state introduced, over a defense objection, the admission Adams had made that he didn't remember killing his wife but that he loaded her bloody, lifeless body into the trunk of his car and later buried it near Kissee Mills. Prosecutors also called a Springfield woman named Patricia Weidmann to the stand to establish motive. She testified that she had accompanied Adams in his automobile on the evening before his wife's death as he followed Willa when she left the Adams home in her own vehicle. They briefly lost track of Mrs. Adams but found her car parked at the Travelodge Motel on St. Louis Street. A man arrived shortly afterward and went to an upper level of the motel. Several hours later, the unidentified man and Mrs. Adams emerged from the same area of the motel and left in their separate cars. Near the conclusion of the hearing, a defense motion to reduce the charge to second-degree murder was overruled, and Adams was held without bond for trial in circuit court.[11]

Arraigned in the Greene County Circuit Court on May 1, Adams pleaded not guilty by reason of mental disease or defect. After a mental examination in early September determined he was competent to stand trial, the trial was set for November. However, it was continued until February 1971 because further psychiatric reports requested by the defense were not yet available.[12]

Jury selection for the Adams trial began on Monday, February 15. Testimony started late the next day and continued throughout the week. Two of the prosecution's important witnesses were the defendant's daughters. Both young women testified that they'd seen their father's revolver in his closet right before their mother disappeared but that it was gone after she disappeared. Both daughters also testified about their parents' marital problems. Adela said her mother and father slept in separate rooms and argued "all the time," and Donna said her mom had been "dating" other men for about five years. Adela added that her mother told her on the morning of her disappearance that the girls' father had followed her the night before and that her mother was irritated by his action.[13]

Another state witness, Mrs. Weidmann, may have hindered the prosecution about as much as she helped. Called primarily to tell the jury about accompanying Adams as he followed his wife the night before she was killed, Mrs. Weidmann testified to considerably more than that, and Prosecutor Dee Wampler ended up treating her as an adverse witness. Mrs. Weidmann said Adams told her his wife had been "motel hopping" for some time. Adams had shown the witness a number of love letters his wife had received from various men, sometimes accompanied by pictures of the men. One letter, in particular, was a point of contention, because it suggested that Donna, the youngest daughter, might not be Robert Fay Adams's biological child. Mrs. Weidmann also said another woman had told her that one of the daughters once caught her mother with a lover at the Adams home. Mrs. Weidmann, who was divorced, claimed she herself was not intimate with Adams and had never done more than share a couple of root beers with him.[14]

In his opening statement, defense attorney Jack Yocum claimed Adams killed his wife during a heated argument that ensued after she confronted him on the morning of February 3 about following her the night before. During the quarrel, Willa Lee threw up to the defendant the fact that he'd raised a child that wasn't even his, told him who Donna's real father was, and called Adams a "damn fool." Willa Lee went for her husband's pistol, but it fell to the floor and he picked it up. She then retrieved a knife and came at him with it. Robert tried to knock the knife away with the butt of the gun, but he got cut and shot his wife in a fit of anger. He couldn't remember actually pulling the trigger, though.[15]

The chief defense witness was the defendant himself. Asked directly by Yocum whether he'd killed his wife, Adams sobbed and answered "No," adding that he had never hurt his wife in his life.

The only other defense witnesses were a psychologist and a psychiatrist who testified that Adams had a hysterical personality that might lead to a mental breakdown when confronted with his wife's infidelities. Such a condition might very well cause him to suffer amnesia and, therefore, have no memory of killing his wife.[16]

During rebuttal, the prosecution, seeking to refute the idea that the murder was not premeditated, called a woman to the stand who said Adams had discussed with her in 1969 possible ways of killing his wife.[17]

The courtroom was packed during closing arguments late Saturday afternoon, February 20, as it had been for every session of the trial. Arguments wrapped up about 5:30 p.m., and the jury came back two and a half hours later with a verdict of second degree murder and a sentencing recommendation of forty years in the state prison.[18]

A Springfield newspaper reporter said at the time that the conviction "climaxed one of the most bizarre murder cases in Greene County history." But the bizarre elements of the case were not quite over.[19]

Adams's lawyers filed motions for a new trial, for a reduction in sentence, and for their client's release on bond. Judge James Keet overruled the first two motions, and the defense appealed to the Missouri Supreme Court. Keet approved the third motion, setting bond at $25,000, and Adams was released in early April pending the outcome of the appeal.[20]

Adams disappeared in the first half of 1973, while his appeal was still waiting to be heard in the supreme court. In early June, he was thought to be in Mexico. He was officially declared a fugitive after his appeal was turned down in mid-July and he could not be located.[21]

Adams was captured on November 9, 1973, at Chicago's O'Hare Airport as he returned from Germany, where he and his new wife, a young woman he'd met in Colorado, had been to visit her parents. FBI agents knew the fugitive was on the flight because the passport he'd used to board bore his real name. Adams waived extradition, and a few days later he was brought back to Missouri and taken directly to Jefferson City to begin serving his prison term.[22]

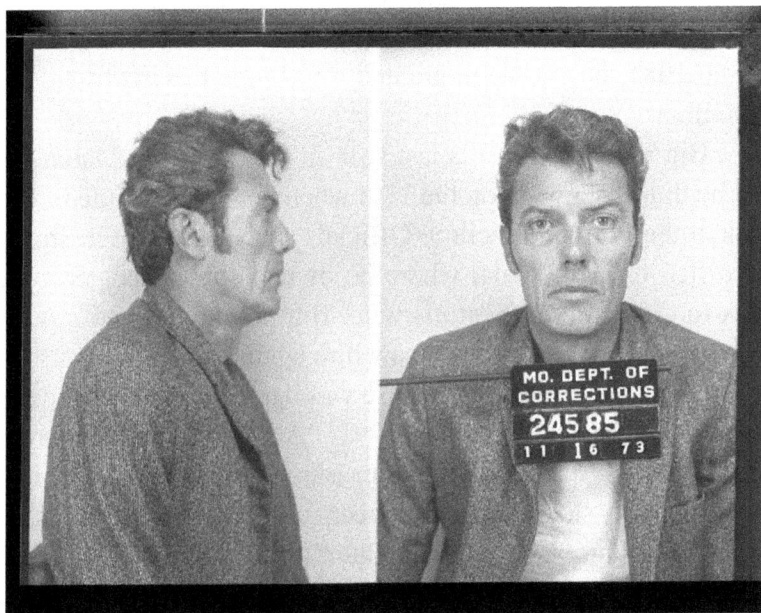

Mugshots of Robert Fay Adams when he was received at the Missouri State Penitentiary in November 1973. *Courtesy Missouri State Archives.*

He was brought back to Springfield in early December to face a new charge of bond-jumping. While still in Springfield, he took an overdose of pills and was rushed to Cox Medical Center in critical condition, but he soon recovered. Both Adams and his pretty, twenty-three-year-old wife, Friederike, testified for the defense at his trial on the bond-jumping charge in early March 1974, but he was convicted and given a five-year sentence, which was added to his previous forty-year-term. Adams was then returned to the state penitentiary.[23]

Some time prior to 1981, Adams was transferred from Jefferson City to the minimum-security Ozark Correctional Facility in Fordland because of his reported good behavior at the state prison. His behavior had been exemplary enough that it was thought he'd probably be released on parole in a few years, and he was being considered for a work-release program. In mid-March 1981, he was even granted a furlough to visit friends in Columbia.[24]

Big mistake! He was last seen in Columbia on March 14, and he didn't show up on the 17th when he was scheduled to be back at the Fordland facility. Officials speculated that he might have fled to Guatemala, where he owned some land, or gone back to Germany to meet his wife. But nobody knew for sure, and nobody in Missouri ever saw him again.[25]

The Robert Fay Adams case was depicted in an episode of "America's Most Wanted" in 1991. "A tangled tale of murder and flight," as Springfield reporter Barbara Clauser labeled it at the time, the story has since been called to mind by other Springfield journalists as well. But all to no avail. If Adams is still alive, he is a ninety-something-year-old fugitive who has escaped his just punishment in this world. More likely, he has passed over to the other side to face judgment in a court from which no one escapes.[26]

23
A Crime of the Greatest Magnitude
Bobby Lee Shuler and the I-44 Truck Explosion

About 1:10 a.m. on September 30, 1970, a tremendous explosion erupted on I-44 several miles west of Springfield near Route N. The blast thundered through the night, jolting people from their sleep for miles around and blowing out windows as far away as downtown Springfield.

Greene County deputy Ron Lindsey, patrolling near Route PP about five miles west of Route N, saw a "real bright flash" like a huge bolt of lightning and watched as it changed to a large orange ball. He hurried to the scene and was astonished by what he saw. The blast had blown a huge crater in the eastbound lane of the interstate, about thirty-five feet deep and forty feet wide. A nearby Stuckey's gift shop was virtually obliterated and two service stations also sustained heavy damage, as if from a violent tornado. Debris littered the eastbound and westbound lanes of the highway, blocking traffic in both directions.[1]

Other lawmen started arriving right after Sergeant Lindsey, and soon almost every available officer in the area had swarmed to the scene to set up blockades, control traffic, and begin an investigation. From witness accounts, the officers quickly learned that the source of the blast was a semi-trailer truck loaded with dynamite that had exploded when snipers fired into it. The driver, later identified as forty-eight-year-old John Galt, was killed instantly, as both he and his truck were blown to bits. Norman Hopkins, a twenty-two-year-old driver for Tri-State Trucking of Joplin, had been driving the lead truck in a two-truck convoy, and he witnessed the explosion in his rearview mirror. He turned around and came back, and he told officers the grille of his truck had also been fired into. However, he was driving a flatbed that wasn't carrying any explosives.[2]

The Teamsters union was on strike against Tri-State Trucking, and both Galt and Hopkins had recently been hired as replacements for striking drivers. Authorities had received reports during the previous week of rocks being thrown at Tri-State trucks, and they were aware that a company convoy was scheduled to come through Greene County on this night. This was why Lindsey was in the area, but the trucks had arrived sooner than expected.[3]

One witness told officers he was driving westbound on I-44 a half mile west of Route N when the explosion occurred. He stopped and soon a car in a battered condition passed him. His suspicion aroused, he followed the car and took down its license plate number, which he gave to officers, along with a description of the auto. Another witness said that, just before the explosion, he saw a car parked on the I-44 westbound entry ramp at Route N, and his description of the vehicle matched that of the first witness. Checking the designated ramp, officers found a blood-spattered 30-30 rifle believed to be involved in the shooting and a shattered windshield believed to be from the shooter's car lying a few feet north of the pavement. A spent cartridge was also found nearby.[4]

The explosion had flattened a tire on the suspect vehicle, and the tire came completely off shortly after the shooter or shooters drove the car away. The vehicle was thus riding on the rim, leaving a trail that was easy to follow. Officers trailed the damaged automobile to a farm on Route F about three miles north of Highway 266. The car had turned into a driveway, and officers found it abandoned behind a well house. A 1966 white-over-red Dodge, the car was missing its windshield, and there were bloodstains inside the vehicle. Officers fanned out looking for the car's occupants, but, as dawn approached, they had still found no sign of them.[5]

However, after three or four hours of skulking through the woods and fields to avoid the dragnet, one of the fugitives was ready to give herself up. Mrs. Lenora Kimmell went to the Trogdon farm two or three miles north of where she and her partners had abandoned the Dodge and asked to make a telephone call. The family let her in, and she called her husband, Earnest, at their Carl Junction home and told him she was in trouble. Meanwhile, using the license plate number provided by one of the witnesses, the highway patrol had already identified Kimmell as the owner of the Dodge. A patrolman was dispatched to the Kimmell home to see what he could learn, and he found Earnest Kimmell talking to his wife on the phone when he arrived.[6]

When Earnest told Lenora an officer was at their house, the thirty-one-year-old Mrs. Kimmell said she might as well talk to him now as later. Earnest put the patrolman on the phone, and Lenora told him where she was. The message was relayed to the search party, and lawmen quickly descended on the Trogdon home. They found Mrs. Kimmell at the house drinking a cup of coffee the family had prepared, and the officers took her into custody about 7:15 a.m. on the morning of the 30th. About fifteen minutes later, three other suspects; twenty-nine-year-old Bobby Lee Shuler, twenty-seven-year-old Gerald Bowden, and twenty-seven-year-old Sharron Lynn Bowden; all of Joplin, were spotted and arrested as they emerged from a clump of trees near the Trogdon home. Two other Joplin men, who had been trailing the Tri-State truck when it exploded, were arrested on suspicion at the scene of the blast but later released without charges.[7]

Shuler and the Bowdens were charged with second-degree murder and held in lieu of $100,000 bond. Lenora Kimmell was held as a material witness, and her bond was set at $50,000. Shuler and Bowden were identified as Teamsters drivers on strike against Tri-State Trucking. Based on Mrs. Kimmell's statement, Shuler was tentatively identified as the person who'd fired the shots into Galt's truck.[8]

Bobby Shuler, left, and Gerald Bowden after their arrest. *The Springfield Leader and Press*

A few days after the arrests, it was learned that Gerald Bowden was not legally married to Sharron Lynn Bowden, whom he had identified as his new bride. Bowden was the object of a divorce suit in McDonald County but was still legally married to his first wife.[9]

The three defendants' preliminary examination was held in magistrate court in Springfield in mid-December. Mrs. Kimmell testified that she got a telephone call on the evening of September 29 from Sharron Lynn "Kim" Bowden asking whether she wanted to go "partying" with Mrs. Bowden, Gerald Bowden, and Bobby Lee Shuler. Despite being married, Lenora had previously gone on several "dates" with Shuler, and she agreed to Sharron's suggestion. The four met at the Teamsters' union hall in Duenweg, where Shuler retrieved a rifle from his car and put it in Lenora's vehicle. The four then started for Springfield in Lenora's car with Shuler driving. Along the way, Shuler stopped for beer and let her take over driving. In Springfield, they stopped again to buy more beer and then headed south on Highway 65. When they met a Tri-State truck, Shuler told Lenora to turn around and catch up with it. She did, and as she passed the truck, Shuler stuck the barrel of his rifle out the passenger window and fired two shots. The foursome then headed back toward Joplin, and when they met the Tri-State trucks a few miles west of Springfield, Shuler again instructed Lenora to turn around and overtake them. Mrs. Kimmell passed the trucks, and Shuler ordered her to hurry ahead and cross over to the other side of the highway. She parked on the westbound access ramp at Route N, because Shuler said he had to "relieve himself." He stepped outside the car with his rifle. Lenora heard two shots and then saw and heard a terrific explosion. She was cut by flying glass fragments, but she helped Shuler push the shattered windshield to the side of the road. Then Shuler took the wheel, drove west on I-44, turned at the next exit (Route PP), and went northwest until he turned into the driveway and ditched the car. The four occupants got out and started running. After crossing fields and climbing several fences, Lenora decided to call her husband. She said that Mr. and Mrs. Bowden had sat in the back seat during the entire misadventure, and at no point during her testimony did she indicate that either had handled the gun.[10]

Testifying in her own defense, Sharron Lynn admitted that her legal name was Moritz and that she'd only started calling herself Mrs. Bowden after she moved into Bowden's trailer southwest of Joplin. She said that she'd been taking nerve pills and Darvon on the night of the explosion and that she was awakened from sleep by the blast. Despite her testimony, she was bound over for trial in Greene County Circuit Court at the end of the hearing, as were Shuler and Bowden, who'd declined to testify.[11]

The three defendants were granted separate trials, and Shuler's trial began first, in early May 1971. Prosecutor Dee Wampler summarized the facts of the case in his opening statement, and, Henry Sheldon, one of Shuler's attorneys, stipulated to almost every detail that Wampler had outlined. However, the two sides differed markedly in their interpretation of the incident. Wampler painted Shuler's firing into a truck loaded with dynamite as a heinous, premeditated act deserving of a second-degree murder conviction and the maximum sentence, while the defense claimed it was a reckless, thoughtless act that warranted no more than a manslaughter conviction.[12]

Near the end of the trial, Shuler took the stand in his own defense. He said that he didn't know Galt's truck was carrying dynamite and that he was aiming at the grille in any case, trying only to disable the truck. He said the thought never occurred to him that he might kill or seriously injure anyone. He added that, when the explosion occurred, he was knocked down and the rifle blown out of his hands.[13]

Throughout the trial, prosecutors pored over law books studying legal precedent in manslaughter cases. In closing arguments, they urged upon Judge Jack Powell their conclusion that a verdict of manslaughter was not appropriate for cases in which a person's death occurred as a result of an act that, even without the death, would be considered felonious. Powell agreed, and he instructed the jury to decide only between a guilty verdict and a not guilty verdict on the second-degree murder charge. After deliberating an hour and a half, the jury came back at midday on May 7 with a verdict of guilty and a sentencing recommendation of ninety-nine years in prison.[14]

On May 21, Bowden pleaded guilty to second-degree murder in an agreement with the prosecution, and he received a sentence of ten years imprisonment. Bowden's lawyer said that, even though his client and Shuler were originally in cahoots in menacing Tri-State trucks, Bowden had tried to break the conspiracy by urging Shuler to "forget it" and go on back to Joplin. At the same time, though, the attorney realized that the offense Bowden was being charged with was "the crime of the greatest magnitude ever committed in Greene County," and his client was willing to serve a reasonable amount of time.[15]

Bowden's common-law wife, Sharron Lynn Moritz, was released on $5,000 bond on June 10, 1971, but a month later she was back in jail, returned by her bondsman. In mid-November she was convicted of being an accessory after the fact to Galt's murder and was given a three-year prison term by Judge Powell, with credit for time served. The rest of her sentence was suspended, and she was released on probation. Powell commented at the time that, of all those involved in the case, Moritz had "the least to do with it."[16]

Sharon Moritz (aka Bowden) got off with a light sentence. *Springfield Leader and Press.*

A few weeks after Shuler's trial concluded, Judge Powell denied a defense motion for a new trial and pronounced the ninety-nine-year sentence recommended by the jury. Shuler was then transported to the state prison. His lawyers filed an appeal with the Missouri Supreme Court, but it was denied in late 1972. Not long after his arrival in Jefferson City, Shuler was placed in minimum security because of his exemplary behavior.[17]

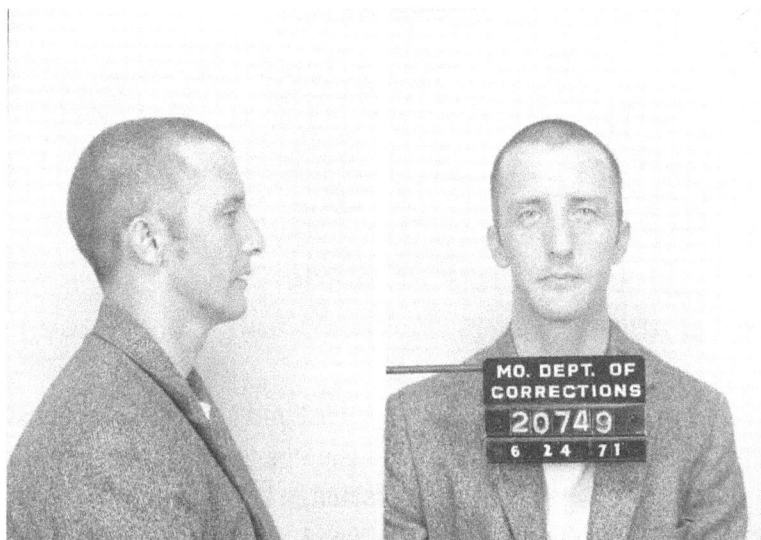

Mugshots of Bobby Lee Shuler. *Courtesy of the Missouri State Archives.*

Bowden was paroled in 1977 after serving a little over half of his ten-year term. Over protests from Greene County officials, Shuler was also paroled in 1979 after serving about eight and a half years of his ninety-nine-year term. He was released from parole in 1986. A retired truck driver named Bobby Lee Shuler, presumably the same Bobby Lee Shuler, died in Tennessee in 2010.[18]

Because she gave herself up, almost immediately agreed to turn state's evidence, and played a minor role in the crime, Lenora Kimmell was never charged in the case.

24
Double Murder or Murder-Suicide?
The Burning Deaths of Willard and Viola Blades

The seven-acre lot where Willard and Viola Blades lived at the corner of Grant Avenue and Catalpa Street in Springfield was so ringed with trees and shrubs that, when their home caught fire late Saturday night, June 16, 1984, no one discovered the blaze until it was raging out of control. A passing motorist finally noticed the fire about 11:45 p.m. and called it in, but the house was already consumed in flames. After the fire was extinguished, investigators found the charred remains of the couple in the rubble, but the bodies were so badly burned that investigators said they might never know the exact cause of their deaths. Fire and police detectives did not suspect foul play, and an initial examination of the bodies yielded no clues, leaving authorities to speculate that the couple must have died of smoke inhalation.[1]

But some things just didn't seem quite right from the very beginning. The sixty-four-year-old Blades and his sixty-three-year-old wife were both known as "sticklers for fire safety" and had several smoke detectors in their home. Mrs. Blades's body was found in an upstairs room stretched out in the middle of a bed "kind of in a strange and unusual position," while her husband's body was found on its back nearby in the bedroom floor. Victims of fire were more often found in a curled up position.[2]

Suspicions were further aroused on Monday, June 18, when forensics tests on Viola Blades revealed that she had two head injuries. She also had a piece of rope tied around one wrist and what appeared to be a piece of cloth tied around her neck, suggesting that she might have been assaulted and tied up prior to her death. Upon close examination of the burned-out house, investigators discovered that the bed mattress where Viola was found was soaked with a considerable amount of blood, a finding that was consistent with her head injuries, and they also concluded from the burn pattern beneath the bed that the fire had probably started there. Unlike his wife's body, Willard Blades's body had no signs of injury, and investigators tentatively concluded that he had, in fact, died of smoke inhalation. Although officials were reluctant to declare publicly that foul play was involved, they strongly suspected that they were looking at either a homicide-suicide or a double homicide.[3]

But which one? There were no signs of forced entry and no signs that anything of substantial value had been taken from the house. Several thousand dollars in currency and old coins were found undisturbed in a hiding place in the basement of the home. Had Blades assaulted his wife and then burned her and himself up in the fire, or was the arson an attempt to cover up a heinous double murder? Although investigators couldn't say for sure on Wednesday, four days after the fire, they were leaning toward the theory that Blades and his wife had been victims of a double-homicide. Since the previous day, forensics experts had determined that Mrs. Blades died before she was consumed by fire but that her head injuries were insufficient to have caused death. Investigators also concluded that her husband had definitely died of smoke inhalation and that his body showed no signs of external injury and or restraint that would have prevented him from escaping from the fire. In addition, three or four other spots, besides the spot under the bed, had been found where an accelerant had been used to start the fire.[4]

The police now knew for sure that, one way or the other, they were dealing with an arson, and a $5,000 reward was offered for any significant information about the case.[5]

On June 21, Springfield detectives traveled to Oklahoma to talk to friends and relatives of the Bladeses, and based on those interviews, they identified an acquaintance of the couple as a person of interest in the case. The man, whose name was not revealed at first, was known to have been in Springfield on the Saturday that the Blades house burned down. The detectives then traveled to Mount Vernon, Illinois, where the man was thought to be living, and they learned he was wanted there for jumping bond after an arrest for felony stealing. Two women told the detectives they had traveled through Missouri with the man in mid-June and had stayed in a Springfield motel on June 15, the night before the arson.[6]

The "acquaintance" of the couple turned out to be Willard Blades's thirty-eight-year-old nephew, Ronald Conn. By July 24, Springfield officers had accumulated enough evidence to charge him and two accomplices with two counts each of capital murder in the deaths of Mr. and Mrs. Blades. The accomplices were twenty-four-year-old Ann Marie Dulany of Wayne City, Illinois, and forty-five-year-old Paul Richard Schmitt of Mount Vernon, Illinois. Conn and Ms. Dulany, who'd been living together, were already in custody in Illinois when the charges were filed, and Schmitt was arrested later that day. The suspects were brought back to Springfield on July 26. Conn and Schmitt were arraigned in circuit court on Friday the 27th and Ms. Dulany the following Monday. The three were held in the Greene County Jail without bond to await their preliminary hearing. Frustrated by two continuances, authorities referred the case to a grand jury in hopes that doing so might expedite proceedings against the three defendants, and the jury indicted them for capital murder in mid-September 1984.[7]

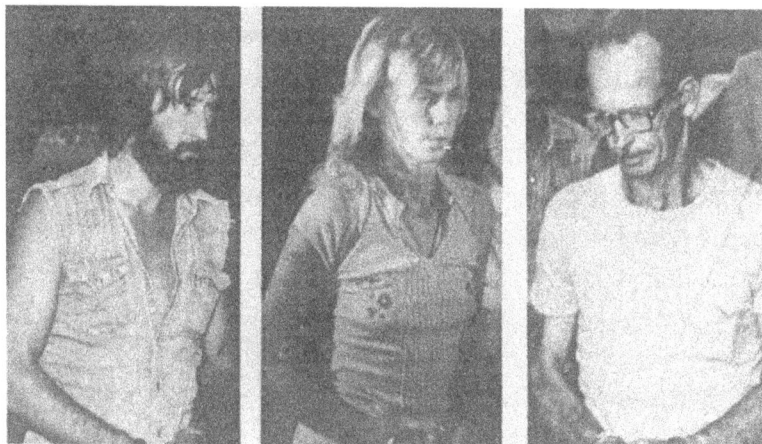

Left to right, Ronald Conn, Ann Marie Dulany, and Paul Richard Schmitt shortly after they were arrested for the double murder of Willard and Viola Blades. *From the Springfield Leader and Press.*

The action of the grand jury, however, scarcely sped up the legal proceedings in the case. The three defendants had their cases separated, and Conn, whose case came up first, finally went on trial on capital murder charges in early June 1986. As the trial opened, Greene County prosecutor Tom Mountjoy announced that he planned to seek the death penalty.[8]

On June 5, after a jury had already been selected, Conn pleaded guilty to first-degree murder in a deal with the state that allowed him to escape the death penalty. Prosecutor Mountjoy said he had consulted with relatives of the Bladeses before agreeing to the plea bargain. Conn, who had grown up in the Republic area, was sentenced to two concurrent life terms.[9]

Schmitt had previously reached a deal of his own that called for him to plead guilty to second-degree murder and receive a twenty-year sentence in exchange for his testimony against Conn, but now Conn had turned the tables, laying primary blame for the crime on Schmitt. In a statement he gave at the time of his plea-bargain agreement, Conn admitted to stealing power tools, firearms, and cameras from his uncle and aunt, but he claimed he and Ms. Dulany were already outside the house at the time Schmitt set the fire. He and Dulany, Conn said, had left while the couple was tied up on the bed after Schmitt told Conn, if he didn't like it, to "get the hell out."[10]

Ann Marie Dulany's trial on charges of capital murder got underway in December 1986. Prosecutor Mountjoy waived the death penalty, which meant that, under the law then in effect, Dulany, if convicted, would be sentenced to life imprisonment with no possibility of parole for at least fifty years.[11]

After the prosecution presented its case, the defendant took the stand in her own defense. She admitted being present at the fire. She, Conn, and Schmitt had driven from Illinois on their way to Oklahoma and stopped in Springfield on June 15. They drove by the Bladeses' house that evening, and on the way there Conn announced he meant to kill his uncle for not lending him bail money earlier that year. However, the three did not stop because they thought no one was home. The next day Dulany and Conn drove by the house again and saw Blades mowing his lawn, but they again did not stop.[12]

When the three returned to the house on the night of the 16th, Conn brought along two cans of flammable roofing cement. The three were admitted into the Bladeses' home, but Conn and Willard Blades quickly started arguing over some property that Conn's mother, who was Willard's sister, had left when she died. Conn struck Blades in the head knocking him down. Conn then tied Mr. Blades's hands behind his back with rope that Dulany fetched from Conn's truck. After the three intruders made a fruitless search of the house, Conn told Blades that he knew there was a collection of guns and a large cache of money hidden in the house and that, if Blades didn't say where they were, Conn would kill him. Blades revealed the whereabouts of a couple of guns but wouldn't tell where anything else was. Mrs. Blades was seated on the couch beside her husband, and Dulany held a gun on them while Conn and Schmitt continued searching the house. Unable to find the gun collection or any money, Conn went to the truck and brought back the two cans of roofing cement.[13]

Dulany helped Conn herd his uncle and aunt into a bedroom, while Schmitt went outside and did not come back into the house. Willard and Viola were made to lie on the bed, their hands and feet were bound, and they were tied to each other. Mr. and Mrs. Blades begged and prayed that their nephew would not kill them as they were being bound. At Conn's instruction, Dulany searched for something to gag Mrs. Blades, but she stopped when Conn decided a gag wasn't needed. Dulany then took two sacks of items scavenged from the house to the truck, and when she returned, Conn was throwing the roofing cement on Mr. and Mrs. Blades and on the bed. Viola was lying still on the bed with blood around her head, and her husband was also on the bed but was moving. The sight made Dulany sick, she said, and as soon as Conn had finished spreading the cement, she carried the empty cans back to the truck and did not return.[14]

It didn't help Dulany's cause, however, that she had given conflicting statements. Her trial testimony essentially agreed with a statement she'd given to police prior to the trial, but it conflicted with a still-earlier statement she'd given shortly after her arrest in which she laid most of the blame for the murders on Schmitt.[15]

Throughout the proceedings and during closing arguments, defense attorney Ray Gordon tried to portray Dulany as a victim of Conn's domineering control over her. Dulany was a prostitute, and Conn was her pimp, Gordon told the jurors. She had been forced into prostitution after running away from her foster home when she was just eleven years old, and she'd been abused ever since. It was not illogical to think that she would do whatever Conn told her to do.[16]

Prosecutor Mountjoy countered with just the facts in the case. He said the evidence showed that Dulany went to a car outside the Bladeses' home and brought back the rope with which the victims were bound, that she held a gun on them at one point, that she helped search the house for money and valuables, and that she carried some of the stolen items from the house. Mountjoy asked that jurors judge the case strictly on these circumstances and not let their emotions sway them. If they thought Dulany was an active and willing participant in the crime, even if she did not actually set the fire, she was guilty of capital murder.[17]

After deliberating about two hours, the jury came back on the afternoon of December 13 with a guilty verdict. On January 30, 1987, Judge David Anderson denied a defense motion for a new trial. Dulany, now twenty-six, was sentenced to life in prison with no possibility of parole until she was seventy-four years old.[18]

On February 7, the plea-bargain agreement with Paul Richard Schmitt, the third defendant, was consummated. In exchange for his guilty plea to second-degree murder, he received two concurrent twenty-year prison terms without the possibility for parole.[19]

Dulany's verdict was appealed to the Missouri Court of Appeals, Southern District, which ruled in late July 1988 that she must be given a new trial because of an error in the instructions to the jury. In lieu of immediately holding a new trial, the prosecution asked that the Missouri Supreme Court review the case first.[20]

At the same time the appellate court ruling in Dulany's case was announced, it was also reported that Conn was trying to get his guilty pleas set aside. He claimed now that he did not kill his uncle and aunt and did not even see them when they were tied up. He said the only items he took from the Blades residence were things that belonged to him or had been given to him. The only reason he'd confessed otherwise, he explained, was so that prosecutors would accept his guilty pleas. He claimed he'd been coerced into pleading guilty by Mountjoy and his assistants in the prosecutor's office.[21]

In mid-September, the Missouri Supreme Court agreed to review the appellate court's decision in the Dulany case, and in a separate appeal process, Dulany filed a motion to have her convictions set aside. In mid-October, Greene County judge Don Bonacker ruled that Conn's guilty pleas should stand.[22]

Later in October, Judge Bonacker also conducted the hearing on Dulany's motion to have her convictions overturned. In her testimony Dulany said her previous attorneys did not adequately portray the extent to which she was under the control of Ronnie Conn nor the extent of her prior abuse by men. She had been abused and battered for years and was under the complete domination of Conn. Dulany said her testimony at her original trial was true as far as it went but that her attorneys failed to ask her about Conn holding a gun on her. In late December, Judge Bonacker ruled against Dulany, but her motion was forwarded to the supreme court to hear at the same time it reviewed the appellate court's decision granting her a new trial.[23]

Conn asked the Missouri Court of Appeals-Southern District to review Judge Bonacker's decision to deny his motion to have his guilty pleas set aside, but on May 2, 1989, the appeals court agreed with Bonacker and refused to set aside the pleas.[24]

In mid-November 1989, the Missouri Supreme Court upheld Dulany's convictions. In May 1990, Paul Richard Schmitt's petition for early release from his twenty-year sentence was denied.[25]

So, even though the evidence suggested that Conn was the one who actually started the fire that burned up his uncle and aunt and destroyed their house, Ann Marie Dulany ended up getting a tougher sentence than her male sidekick, in that he was eligible for parole sooner. One might say that's the risk she ran by refusing to cop a plea. However, Mother Nature stepped in to rectify the seeming inequity. Conn died of natural causes at the age of sixty-eight in 2014 while still serving time at the Farmington Correctional Center.[26]

25
Unlike Anything Ever in Greene County
The Murder of Wilma Plaster

After the dismembered body of a woman was found Friday afternoon, October 6, 1989, north of Willard at the side of Farm Road 105, authorities said "the crime was unlike anything ever discovered in Greene County." The woman's legs and pelvic area were stacked on top of her torso with her feet pointing skyward. Nearby were several white plastic trash bags, one of them containing the woman's head. A knife, a pair of garden shears, and a brown toilet seat cover made of rug-like material were found in another bag. The woman's arms had been severed from her body, but they were nowhere to be seen. The dismembered body was nude except for a pair of gray stockings encasing the woman's legs. The missing arms and a lack of blood at the scene caused investigators to conclude that the woman had been murdered elsewhere and brought to where the body parts were found. Because of the way the body parts were arranged, investigators further concluded that the parts had not been tossed from a moving vehicle, but rather the culprit had stopped at the side of the road and positioned them.[1]

A passing motorist had discovered the dismembered body about 4:00 p.m., and other motorists soon came forward to swear

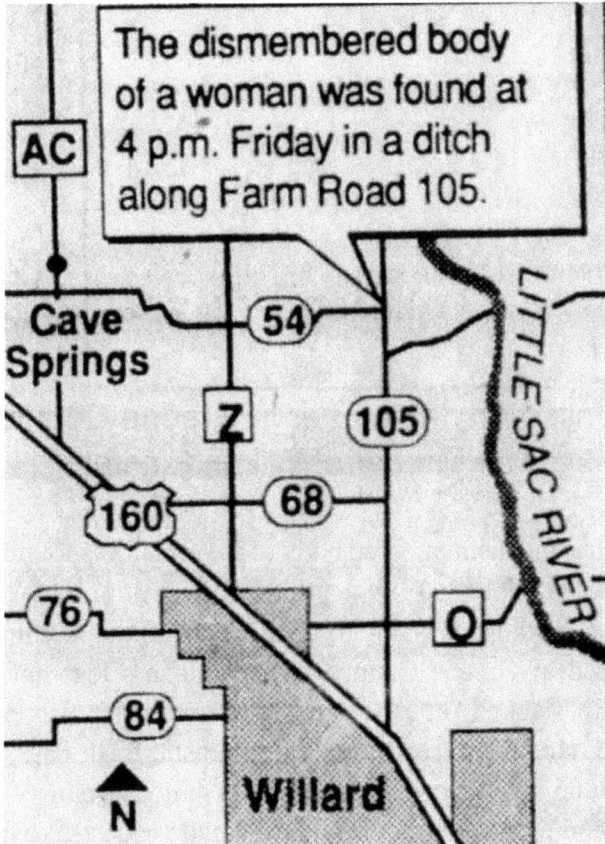

Map showing where a woman's dismembered body was found on October 6, 1989, published in the *Springfield News-Leader* the day after the gruesome discovery.

that the body was not there when they passed about 3:45 p.m. Thus, the time at which the body was placed at the side of the road was narrowed to that fifteen-minute window, but the time of death was uncertain. No clues to the woman's identity were found at the scene. Her body was taken at first to Cox Medical Center South in Springfield but was sent to St. Louis the next day for an autopsy, which, investigators hoped, would determine a cause of death.[2]

On October 8, two days after the body was found, the victim was tentatively identified as sixty-six-year-old Wilma Plaster of Hollister, Missouri, whose daughter had reported her missing the day before. The widow of a Church of Christ minister, Wilma was described by people who had known her as a friendly person and a regular churchgoer. Meanwhile, police were trying to locate the victim's red 1969 Chevy Beretta, in which she'd left her Hollister home for Springfield on October 3. Witnesses had reported seeing a car matching the Beretta's description in the Springfield-Willard area on October 6 before the body was found.[3]

On October 9, Wilma's automobile was found in the parking lot of the Ramada Inn on North Glenstone in Springfield, and investigators began combing it for clues. Although not yet complete, the autopsy determined on the same day that the victim had been killed by a gunshot to the back of the head fired by a small caliber weapon. On October 10, investigators learned that someone had forged a check for over $4,000 on Wilma's bank account about two weeks before her death. Officers theorized that the forgery was probably connected to her death and that she had been acquainted with her murderer.[4]

Later the same day, Tuesday the 10th, a woman from Olvey, Arkansas, contacted authorities after she discovered a number of suspicious items on her property that had apparently been left there by fifty-three-year-old Shirley Jo Phillips, a friend of hers from Springfield who'd visited her on Monday and left early Tuesday. The woman said that Phillips appeared very nervous during her stay and that she had insisted on washing her car. Investigators went to Olvey, and the woman pointed them to two plastic bags and a paper sack stashed beneath a wooden porch adjoining her mobile home. They contained pieces of evidence that seemed to link Phillips to the forgery as well as the

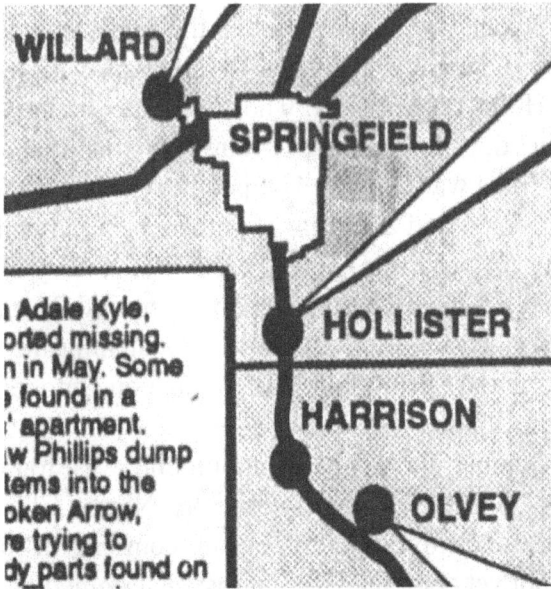

Map from the *Springfield News-Leader* showing Wilma Plaster's hometown of
Hollister, where her dismembered body was found near Willard, and where evidence
in the murder was found at Olvey, Arkansas.

murder, including bloody floor mats, a bloody trunk liner, a car
jack with blood spattered on it, several canceled checks on
Wilma Plaster's account, a blank book of checks on the same
account, and a .38 caliber revolver with a box of cartridges.
Further investigation revealed that Phillips and Plaster had met
each other in Hollister about September 20 and that the forged
check had been written just a day or two later.[5]

Phillips was arrested Tuesday night in Springfield on
suspicion of forgery and held on $150,000 bond. Missouri law
dictated that she could only be held twenty hours without being
charged, but she was re-arrested the next day on probable cause
of first-degree murder. On Thursday morning, October 12,
Phillips was formally charged with Wilma's murder, and her
identity was made public for the first time. She was charged in
Greene County because it was thought Wilma was killed there,

although the site of the murder had not been definitely determined. Just hours after Phillips was charged, a judge ordered her bank account frozen to prohibit her from using funds for her criminal defense that were thought to have been stolen from her victim. The suspect, also known as Jo Ann Phillips, lived on west College Street in Springfield and had recently worked as a secretary through a temporary employment agency. She also served as vice-president of the fan club for Branson entertainers John and Paul Cody, and it was apparently through her connection to Branson that she had met Wilma Plaster.[6]

About a week after Phillips's arraignment on the murder charge, her mother, seventy-six-year-old Lela Kyle, was reported missing. Kyle had moved out of her Branson home in May, and neighbors thought she planned to get an apartment in Springfield. Later they heard she'd gone to Oklahoma to stay with an ailing brother, but now, five months later, she couldn't be located. On October 18, a daughter from Texas (Shirley Jo's sister) flew into Springfield and filed a missing person's report with the Springfield Police Department. The report said Shirley Jo was known to have been in her mother's company after the older woman left Branson, but police would not say whether Phillips was a suspect in Kyle's disappearance.[7]

After learning of the Plaster murder and the disappearance of Lela Kyle, Oklahoma authorities contacted Springfield Police to report that an elderly woman's dismembered and mutilated body had been discovered in the north part of Broken Arrow on May 12. This was near the same time that Kyle was last seen, and the general description of the dismembered body seemed to match the Kyle woman. Scars on the dead woman's nose also suggested a match, but evidence to establish the identity of the deceased with certainty was inconclusive. A month later, in November 1989, authorities tentatively concluded that the dismembered body in Oklahoma was indeed Lela Kyle, based on matching fingerprints taken from the body and from a mixing bowl that Kyle had owned. Shirley Jo Phillips was considered a prime suspect in her mother's murder, but she was not charged in the crime.[8]

After a couple of continuances, Phillips's preliminary hearing was held in Springfield on March 19, 1990. The items found at the Arkansas mobile home and blood found in the defendant's 1976 Cadillac were among the key pieces of evidence presented by the prosecution. Nora Martin, the Arkansas woman that Phillips visited a couple of days after Plaster's body was found, testified that the defendant seemed very upset during her visit, especially when the subject of Plaster's murder came up. Phillips's public defender argued that all the evidence was circumstantial, but the defendant was bound over without bond for trial in the Greene County Circuit Court on a first-degree murder charge. At her initial appearance in the circuit court in late March, her lawyer entered a not guilty plea.[9]

In July 1990, Lela Kyle's Texas daughter, Wanda Moorer, filed suit against her mother's Springfield bank in an effort to recoup almost $38,000 allegedly paid out for checks forged on Kyle's account as far back as February 1987. Moorer's name was also on the account.[10]

In October 1990, Phillips entered a second plea of not guilty by reason of mental illness, and a psychiatric examination to determine her sanity was ordered. At the same time, her trial, which had previously been set for November, was continued until June 1991.[11]

Later the trial was delayed at least twice more, and it was finally scheduled for late January 1992. A defense motion for a change of venue was overruled, but the judge said a jury could be brought to Greene County from another county. Jasper County was selected as the jurisdiction from which the panel of jurors would be imported.[12]

Phillips's trial began on January 27 with jury selection in Joplin. The jury was brought to Springfield the next day, and the testimony phase of the trial began on January 29. Much of the prosecution testimony centered around Phillips's visit to Nora Martin, her Arkansas friend, and the items found under the mobile home porch. Martin testified that Phillips cut a seatbelt out of the front passenger seat of her car during her stay in Arkansas and that she thoroughly washed and vacuumed the vehicle even though it already appeared clean. Phillips seemed very nervous when a newscast about Wilma Plaster's murder came on TV, and she admitted that police probably wanted to question her about Wilma's death. Forensics experts linked the incriminating items found under the porch to the defendant and the victim. They testified that the .38 caliber weapon found among the items was the gun that killed Mrs. Plaster.[13]

Another expert witness for the state testified that traces of blood were found in Phillips's automobile and in Plaster's Hollister home. However, the blood had been contaminated by detergents to the point that it could not be matched to Plaster. A handwriting expert testified that the $4,000-plus check written on Plaster's bank account was endorsed by Phillips and deposited into her account. He couldn't say for sure whether Plaster's forged signature had been written by Phillips, however, because whoever wrote it had disguised it to try to make it look like Plaster's signature.[14]

Phillips's public defender called her thirty-two-year-old son, Glen "Buddy" Minster, to the stand and tried to shift the blame for Plaster's murder to him. Minster, who was currently serving a prison term unrelated to the Plaster case, said he didn't remember what he did or where he was at any given time during the fall of 1989 because he was drinking heavily at the time. The defense also called witnesses from the Branson area who had been with Phillips near the time Plaster was presumably killed and near the time her body was dumped to try to establish an alibi.[15]

After deliberating about three hours on the morning of February 4, 1992, the jury announced that they had reached a verdict finding Phillips guilty of first-degree murder. The defendant showed no emotion, but, as she was escorted from the courtroom, she told reporters, "I didn't do it."[16]

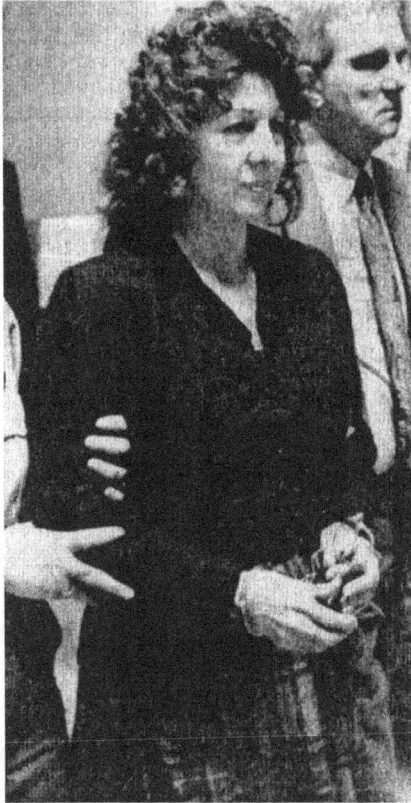

Shirley Joe Phillips is led back to jail after her 1992 murder conviction. *From the Springfield News-Leader.*

The penalty phase of the trial was held the next day, and the jury came back after deliberations with a recommendation of death. In early April, Greene County circuit judge Don Bonacker denied a defense motion for a new trial and officially sentenced Phillips to die.[17]

In 1994, Phillips filed an appeal, claiming that the evidence in her case was botched, that her lawyers did not adequately represent her, that her son was the one who actually committed the murder, and that, if she did have anything to do with it, her mental illness influenced her actions. After a post-conviction relief hearing held during late 1994 and early 1995, her request for a new trial was denied. However, the Missouri Supreme Court threw out her death penalty in February 1997 and ordered a new sentencing hearing because a statement Phillips's son, Buddy Minster, had allegedly made claiming he had dismembered Plaster's body was not allowed into evidence.[18]

In March 1998, Minster refused to give a deposition for his mother's new hearing, and he was sentenced to a year in jail for contempt of court. In October of the same year, Greene County prosecutor Ron Carrier decided not to pursue another death penalty, because he felt that circumstances, such as Minster's refusal to cooperate and the fact that at least two witnesses were now dead, would make obtaining another death sentence very difficult. Phillips was then resentenced to life imprisonment. Confined at the Chillicothe Correctional Center, Phillips could not be reached for comment after the decision sparing her life.[19]

The Only Good Witness Is a Dead Witness
Career Criminal Donald Joe Hall and the Murder of William Roscoe White

In 1994, Donald Joe Hall had a criminal history stretching back twenty-nine years to 1965 when, as a seventeen-year-old kid, he broke into a Thrifty Mart on North Grant in Springfield and later pleaded guilty to burglary. Graduating to the big time in 1970, he was charged with the murder of a fifty-year-old woman during the robbery of another convenience store on North Glenstone, but he managed to beat the rap. The close call didn't stop him from resuming his criminal ways, and he spent the next twenty-plus years in and out of prison on charges ranging from burglary to assault. Then in December 1992, someone walked into a College Street jewelry store and shot the owner in the head during a jewelry heist, and Donald Joe Hall, just paroled from prison seven months earlier, was arrested for the crime. Would the forty-six-year-old Hall beat another murder rap when he went on trial in 1994, or would be finally have to pay the full penalty of the law?[1]

The Thrifty Mart burglary only scratched the surface of Hall's teenage misadventures, because he was actually implicated in a whole string of burglaries. The first couple of times he got caught he was given suspended sentences and placed on probation. In June of 1966, he was finally sentenced to three years in prison, but he was released on parole in time to become involved in a burglary ring with several other Springfield youths the following year.[2]

In March of 1969, Hall paid a $17 fine for reckless driving. Then, two months later officers were called to the West Norton neighborhood where Hall lived in response to a report of someone driving carelessly in the area. A policeman arriving on the scene after 9:00 p.m. spotted a blue sports car driving down the street with no lights on. The driver proved to the Donnie Hall, and the cop followed him as he pulled into his family's driveway. The twenty-one-year-old Hall jumped from his vehicle and ran into the house. The policeman got out of his car and was walking toward the house when Hall pointed a rifle at him and yelled, "I'll shoot that SOB cop." Hall's mother-in-law and another person in the house helped subdue the young man, however, and he was taken into custody. Hall pleaded guilty to displaying a deadly weapon in a threatening manner and was placed on probation in October 1969.[3]

Hall couldn't stay out of trouble for long, though. In early December of the same year, he was charged with trespassing and car tampering after a security guard interrupted him in the act of removing tires and wheels from some vehicles on a Reliable Chevrolet used car lot on East St. Louis. He pleaded not guilty and was released on bond to await trial.[4]

Apparently tired of his shenanigans, Donald's first wife divorced him in January 1970, but the dissolution of his marriage did little to deter further misdeeds on his part. In early March, while still awaiting action on the Reliable Chevrolet case, Hall was arrested, along with several other men, as part of a burglary ring allegedly responsible for a number of break-ins and thefts in the Springfield area dating back to the previous fall.

Charges were filed against Hall but later dropped pending further investigation. In mid-May, he was found guilty of the trespassing and car tampering charges. He was fined $25 and sentenced to thirty days in jail, but he appealed the verdict.[5]

On the morning of August 27, 1970, fifty-year-old Violet Brewer, clerk at a Quick Shop at 3328 N. Glenstone, was shot to death during a holdup as she was opening the store for business

Donald Joe Hall was charged with killing Violet Brewer in 1970. This picture of her appeared in the *Springfield Leader and Press* the day after her murder.

about 7:00 a.m. Hall was arrested as a suspect in the case in mid-September on a tip from Warren Martin, who told police that Hall had given him a .32 caliber pistol to dispose of shortly after the Brewer murder. Martin, who was under arrest on suspicion of armed robbery, said he'd thrown the weapon into Lake

Springfield, and it was recovered a few days later. Hall was charged with first-degree murder, and, at the same time, he had his probation revoked on the charge of displaying a deadly weapon and was sentenced to five years in prison. At Hall's trial, Martin, a former cellmate of Hall's at the state prison, testified that Hall told him, after he gave him the pistol to get rid of, that he'd "had to shoot a gal" with it during a holdup when the woman reached for a phone to call police, and Hall admitted it was the murder and holdup that had been in the news so much lately. Forensic experts linked the weapon taken from Lake Springfield to the bullet removed from Mrs. Brewer's head. However, Hall took the stand in his own defense to deny killing Brewer. He admitted giving the pistol to Martin but said he'd done so before the murder. Although one is left to wonder why Martin would point police toward a murder weapon if he'd committed the murder himself, Hall planted enough doubt in the minds of jurors to win an acquittal. He still faced five years in the penitentiary on the charge of displaying a deadly weapon.[6]

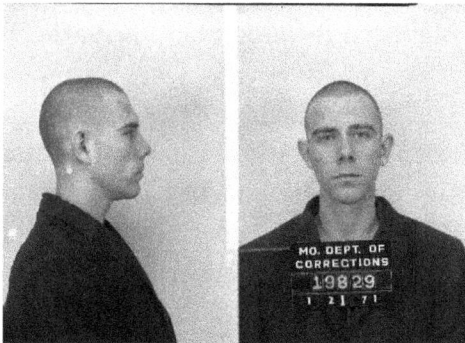

1971 mugshots of Donald Joe Hall. *Courtesy Missouri State Archives.*

After Hall was released from prison on August 20, 1973, it took him less than three weeks to get in trouble again when he was arrested September 7 in Springfield on a public drunkenness charge. Released on bond, Hall teamed up with another ex-con to assault a Wright County couple two nights later, and five nights after that, on September 14, he pulled off a drugstore holdup in Springfield. Pursued by the highway patrol when he was spotted shortly after the holdup driving a vehicle that matched the description of the robber's vehicle, Hall rammed another automobile broadside and was arrested. He was charged with first-degree robbery in the Springfield case and with felonious assault with intent to kill in the Wright County case, Hall was also suspected in a string of other store robberies that had occurred in Springfield since his release.[7]

In April 1974, while still being held in the Greene County Jail, Hall was charged with assault for striking two deputies with a club made from a broom handle. In late May, he pleaded guilty to the robbery charge and was sentenced to ten years in prison. In October, he received a twelve-year sentence in the Wright County case on a reduced charge of accessory to assault. The charges against him for allegedly clubbing the deputies were dropped. Hall applied for but was refused admittance to a drug program which would have suspended the prison sentences if he successfully completed the program. When officers prepared to take Hall to Jefferson City in early December, he refused to go quietly and had to be subdued.[8]

Hall returned to Springfield after he was released from the penitentiary in September 1980. In the wee hours of April 5, 1981, Hall and another man were interrupted by a homeowner during a burglary on South Estate Avenue in Springfield. The pair fled, and Hall fired shots at the homeowner as he gave chase. A policeman responded to the homeowner's emergency call and spotted the getaway car going in the opposite direction as he was approaching the scene. After a short chase, the officer apprehended Hall and his sidekick without further incident. The two were charged with burglary and assault but released on $50,000 bond.[9]

Less than three weeks later, Hall pulled a gun on Brenda Wells in the garage of her home on East Cherokee, where items were still on display from a sale she'd had the day before, but he fled when Wells resisted. He was taken into custody at his bail bondsman's office later that day on a charge of displaying a deadly weapon in a threatening manner. This time bail was set at a quarter of a million dollars, and Hall was held in lieu of bond.[10]

In a plea bargain agreement, Hall pleaded guilty in late July 1981 to burglary and displaying a dangerous weapon in the Estate Avenue incident while charges against him in the Brenda Wells case were dropped. Hall was assessed a fifteen-year prison sentence.[11]

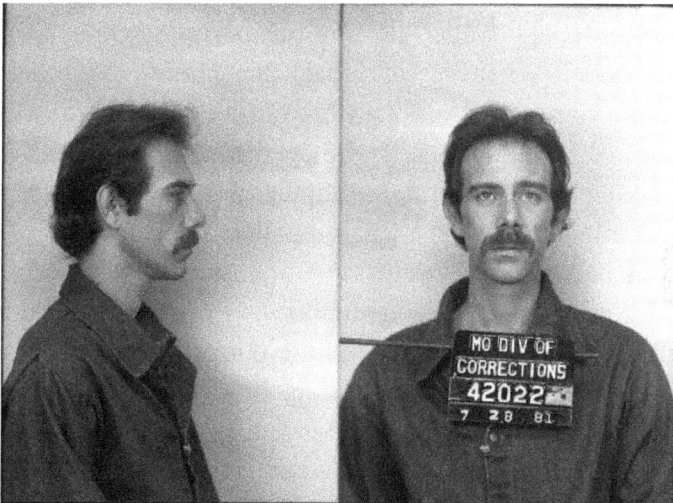

1981 mugshots of Donald Joe Hall. *Courtesy Missouri State Archives.*

Paroled in early May 1992, Hall once again returned home to Springfield. On December 15, William Roscoe White, owner of Custom Made Jewelry and Repair at the corner of Broadway and College in Springfield, was found dead in his shop, shot once in the back of the head. There were no suspects in the immediate aftermath of the crime.[12]

But that would soon change.

On January 8, 1993, Donald Hall was arrested on a charge of possession of marijuana with intent to distribute. The next day, his ex-wife, Donna Hicks, with whom he'd been living, contacted Springfield police to implicate Hall in the murder of William White. Another witness, Kimball Morton, an ex-cellmate of Hall's, came forward about the same time to give a statement that also incriminated Hall in the murder.[13]

Hall was indicted for first-degree murder, and at his trial in Greene County Circuit Court in September 1994, Hicks was the star witness for the prosecution, which was seeking the death penalty. Hicks said she drove Hall to the jewelry shop on the day of the murder and waited for him nearby in the car as he went into the shop. When he came back ten minutes later, he was carrying a paper sack and had blood on his hands. She asked what he'd done, and he said he "blew the man's brains out." The sack contained the murder weapon, a box of jewelry, and White's bloody wallet. Explaining the blood, Hall said that someone had approached the store after he shot White and that he'd locked the door, grabbed White by the head, and pushed him down so he couldn't be seen. He'd then retrieved the wallet from White's pocket and grabbed the box of jewelry. Hicks said she drove Hall to Lake Springfield at his instruction, and he threw the murder weapon into the water. Whenever Hicks questioned Hall about killing White, he kept repeating, "The only good witness is a dead witness." Hicks said she and Hall pawned the jewelry in Springfield and Kansas City during the weeks following the murder. Much of Hicks's testimony was corroborated by physical evidence in the case. For instance, the murder weapon was found in Lake Springfield as she said, and it was matched to the bullet that killed White. Several items taken from the jewelry shop were found in Hall's possession, and several receipts for items he had pawned matched items taken from the shop. In addition, a photo was found showing Hall wearing a pinky ring that had belonged to White.[14]

The defense attacked Hicks as an untrustworthy witness because of her habitual use of illegal drugs and her severe depression. Hicks admitted she'd been hospitalized twice for depression and had undergone shock treatments. Defense lawyers also attacked Hicks's motive, suggesting that she was only testifying against Hall out of jealousy.[15]

The trial took a surprise turn when Hall announced halfway through the proceeding that he had, in fact, shot White but that he'd done so in self-defense. He said that he went to White's shop on the fateful day to collect a debt White owed him, that White became angry and pulled a gun on him, and that he shot the man in self-defense during a struggle over the weapon. Hall said he'd known White, who had killed a lawman in southeast Missouri, when they were in prison together during the early 1970s and that White was known as a violent man. He said that he panicked and hurried out of the store immediately after the shooting and that it was his ex-wife, Donna, who went back into the store and took the jewelry and wallet. He said Donna's attempt to lay the blame on him for the murder and robbery of White was just her attempt to get back at him for an affair he'd had with her son's fiancée.[16]

Prosecutor Darrell Moore subjected Hall to a grueling cross-examination, suggesting he'd just made his story up on the spur of the moment after listening to the state's evidence against him. Moore then called Kimball Morton to the stand to refute Hall's testimony. Morton had been unwilling to testify against Hall when the state was presenting its case unless he was offered an immediate parole on two separate crimes he'd committed, but he'd changed his mind, he said, because he "couldn't sleep" with himself. Morton contradicted Hall's claim that White was a violent person, and he said that Hall had asked him to help rob White's store. Morton said Hall told him such a crime would be easy—that all they'd have to do was walk in and shoot White in the head—but Morton told Hall he "wasn't up to it."[17]

On September 13, 1994, the jury found Hall guilty of first-degree murder after deliberating only an hour and forty-three minutes. During the penalty phase of the trial, which took place the next day, the prosecution called three victims of prior crimes Hall had committed to testify to his violent nature and criminal proclivity. The three witnesses were Harvey Rector, the police officer who'd answered the disturbance call in 1969 and been met by Hall pointing a gun at him and threatening to shoot that "SOB cop;" James Williams, whom Hall had fired shots at after burglarizing his home on South Estate Avenue in 1981; and Brenda Craig (formerly Brenda Wells), whom Hall had threatened with a gun at her home on Cherokee Street later in 1981. After deliberating for slightly less time than it took to find Hall guilty of murder, the jury came back with a recommendation of death. Following the jury's suggestion, Judge David Anderson sentenced Hall to die by lethal injection.[18]

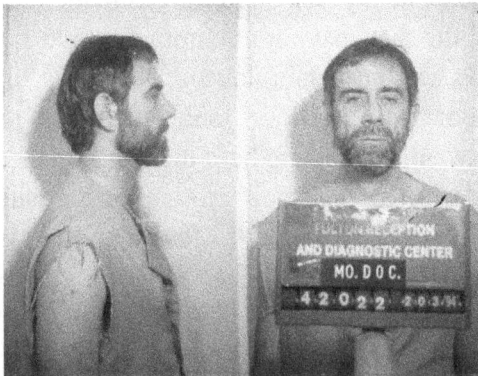

1994 mugshots of Donald Joe Hall. *Courtesy Missouri State Archives.*

After a defense motion for a new trial was denied, Hall's lawyers appealed the verdict to the Missouri Supreme Court. In early December 1998, the justices unanimously upheld the verdict of the lower court. Hall then filed a motion for a writ of habeas corpus with the US District Court. The motion was denied, and the US Court of Appeals for the Eight Circuit upheld the district court's ruling in September 2002. However, in August 2005, the Missouri Supreme Court reversed itself and ordered that a new penalty phase in Hall's trial be held because he had been shackled during the original penalty phase. In light of a recent ruling by the US Supreme Court in a similar case, the justices said the shackles likely prejudiced the jury. In May of 2007, Hall was resentenced to life imprisonment without parole.[19]

End Notes

Short forms of bibliographic sources, such as the author's last name only, are used in the endnotes. Sources cited only once or twice may be fully identified in the endnotes and omitted from the bibliography. Following is a list of frequently used abbreviations.

KCS	*Kansas City Star*
MSPD	Missouri State Penitentiary Database
SDN	*Springfield Daily News*
SDR	*Springfield Daily Republican*
SL	*Springfield Leader*
SLP	*Springfield Leader and Press*
SLPD	*St. Louis Post-Dispatch*
SNL	*Springfield News-Leader*
SMR	*Springfield Missouri Republican*
SMWP	*Springfield Missouri Weekly Patriot*
SP	*Springfield Press*
SR	*Springfield Republican*

1
Two Pre-Civil War Murders

[1] Holcombe, 177-178. Campbell's home was often used as a courthouse in Springfield's early days, which might account for his presence at this 1836 legal proceeding. It is interesting to note that, although Campbell was the founder of Springfield and was widely respected among its early white citizens, his reputation is not without stain. Earlier in 1836, he was among a mob who beat a recently-freed black woman in Springfield.

Yancey was also implicated in the incident for his failure to disperse the mob. (See *SNL*, Mar. 21, 2018.)

[2] *SMWP*, Feb. 7, 1867; Abstracts of Greene County Circuit Court Records; *SL*, Sep. 7, 1899.

[3] Holcombe, 177-178; Abstracts of Circuit Court Records.

[4] Abstracts of Circuit Court Records; Holcombe, 178.

[5] *SMWP*, Feb. 7, 1867; Holcombe, 178.

[6] Holcombe, 178-179; Abstracts of Circuit Court Records.

[7] Holcombe, 228-230.

[8] Holcombe, 228-229; *SL*, Apr 28, 1886; *Kansas City Daily Times*, Apr. 24, 1882.

[9] Holcombe, 228.

[10] *Kansas City Daily Times*, Apr., 24, 1882; Holcombe, 228; *SL*, Sep. 7, 1899.

[11] Holcombe, 228-229.

[12] Holcombe, 229.

[13] *Ibid*.

[14] Holcombe, 229-230.

[15] Holcombe, 231; *SL*, Apr. 28, 1886, Sep. 7, 1899, Jan. 23, 1923.

[16] Holcombe, 231.

2
The Lynching of Mart Danforth

[1] *Huntsville (MO) Randolph Citizen*, Sep. 2, 1859, quoting the *Boonville Observer*; *Nashville (TN) Republican Banner*, Sep. 1, 1859, quoting the *Springfield Mirror*, Aug. 20, 1859; Holcombe, 265. The identity of John Morrow, whose wife Danforth allegedly raped, is unclear. The only married man named Morrow who lived south of Springfield in Greene County during the appropriate time frame and had a relatively young wife was L. J. Morrow. His wife, Harriet, was about twenty-eight at the time of the Morrow woman's rape, but she

had three or four children, not one or two as Holcombe said. This Morrow family moved to California about the time of the rape. Perhaps immediately afterward?

[2] *Nashville Republican Banner*, Sep 1, 1859, quoting the *Springfield Mirror*.

[3] Holcombe, 265; *Nashville Republican Banner*, Sep. 1, 1859, quoting the *Springfield Mirror*.

[4] *Nashville Republican Banner*, Sep. 1, 1859, quoting the *Springfield Mirror*.

[5] *Nashville Republican Banner*, Sep. 1, 1859, quoting the *Springfield Mirror*; Holcombe, 266.

[6] *Huntsville Randolph Citizen*, Sep. 2, 1859, quoting the *Boonville Observer*.

[7] Holcombe, 266.

[8] Fairbanks and Tuck, 222.

3
The Murder of Miss Mary Willis

[1] *Columbia (MO) Statesman*, Jun. 13, 1862, quoting the *Springfield Missourian;* US Census 1840, 1850, 1860.

[2] Tennessee Marriage records; US Census, 1840, 1850, 1860, familysearch.org; Wayne Glenn, Facebook post, https://www. facebook.com/148151331884826/posts/my-glenn-ancestors-immediate-neighbors-in-christian-county-in-1860this-is-not-an/2082876988412241/.

[3] Soldiers Records; Glenn, Facebook post; *New York Times*, Jul. 28, 1862.

[4] Soldiers Records; *Columbia Missouri Statesmen*, Jun. 18, 1862, quoting *Springfield Missourian*.

[5] *Columbia Missouri Statesman*, Jun. 18, 1862, quoting the *Springfield Missourian*; Trego.

[6] *Columbia Missouri Statesman*, Jun. 18, quoting the *Springfield Missourian*; Trego; *New York Times*, Mar. 10, 1863.

[7] *Columbia Missouri Statesman*, Jun. 18, quoting the *Springfield Missourian*; *New York Times*, Mar. 10, 1863.

[8] *New York Times*, Mar. 10, 1863.

[9] Abstracts of Greene County Circuit Court Records; Phelps County Circuit Court Records; Holcombe, 418.

[10] Soldiers Records; US Census 1870; *New York Times*, Jul. 28, 1862.

4
Hickok and Tutt Shoot It Out

[1] Greene County Coroners Reports, Davis K. Tutt, Greene County Archives and Records Center; *SL*, Aug. 8, 1867; conversation with Robert Neumann, former director of Greene County Archives, fall 2011.

[2] "'Wild Bill' Hickok in Nebraska," *History Nebraska* blog, https://history.nebraska.gov/blog/ wild-bill-hickock-nebraska; "James 'Wild Bill' Hickok," *Community and Conflict: The Impact of the Civil War in the Ozarks*, http://ozarkscivilwar. org/archives/585.

[3] Abstracts of Greene County Circuit Court Records; Holcombe, 763.

[4] J. W. Orr testimony, Tutt coroner's report.

[5] Rosa, "What Really Happened...," 7; US Census, 1860.

[6] Orr testimony; Rosa, "What Really Happened...," 7; Holcombe, 764-765.

[7] Oliver Scott testimony, Tutt coroner's report.

[8] A. T. Budlong testimony, Tutt coroner's report.

[9] Rosa, "What Really Happened...," 4, 6.

[10] Orr testimony; F. W. Scholten testimony, Tutt coroner's report.

[11] Scholten testimony.

[12] Testimony of A. T. Budlong, Scholten, and Dr. Edwin Ebert, Tutt coroner's report; Rosa, "What Really Happened...," 6-7.

[13] Scholten testimony.

[14] Tutt coroner's report; "Maple Park Cemetery Part of Springfield History," *SNL*, Mar. 21, 2014.

[15] Rosa, "What Really Happened...," 10; Greene County Circuit Court Records; Holcombe, 766; Brunitz diary.

[16] *SMWP*, Jul. 27, 1865.

[17] Abstracts of Circuit Court Records; *SMWP*, Aug. 10, 1865.

[18] "150 YEARS AGO: Radical 'Drake Constitution' approved by narrow margin in state vote," *Columbia Tribune*, Jun. 6, 2015; *SMWP*, Aug. 10, 1865.

[19] Rosa, "What Really Happened...," 13-14.

[20] *SMWP*, Aug. 10, 1865; Holcombe, 766.

[21] *SMWP*, Aug 10, 1865.

[22] *SMWP*, Aug 10, 1865; Rosa, 13.

[23] Holcombe, 762.

[24] Rosa, "George Ward Nichols...," 144-150; Abstracts of Greene County Circuit Court Records.

[25] Holcombe, 765-766. Whether James Orr, who played cards with Hickok and Tutt, and John Orr were related is unclear.

[26] "James 'Wild Bill' Hickok," *Community and Conflict;* *SMWP*, Aug. 24, 1876.

[27] "James 'Wild Bill' Hickok," *Community and Conflict;* Rosa, What Really Happened, 15.

[28] Wood, *Wicked Springfield*, 40; conversation with Robert Neumann, fall 2011. The fact that Hickok stood well west of where the marker is can be deduced from a careful study of the Tutt coroner's report, early day maps, newspapers, etc.

5
The Reign of the Regulators

[1] Holcombe, 498-499; US Census, 1860.

[2] Holcombe, 499.

[3] *SMWP*, Apr. 12, 1866.

[4] Holcombe, 498; *SMWP*, May 31, Aug. 9, 23, 1866.

[5] Holcombe, 499; Order Book, Enrolled Missouri Militia, 4th Military District, pp. 24-26, Missouri Digital Heritage, http://mdh.deepwebaccess.com/mdh/desktop/en/results.html; Yen, "Horse-Stealing and Man-Hanging; Abstracts of Greene County Circuit Court Records.

[6] Holcombe, 499; *SMWP*, May 31, 1866; Soldiers' Records; US Census, 1860.

[7] *SMWP*, May 31, 1866; Holcombe, 500.

[8] *SMWP*, May 31, 1866; Yen, 60-61.

[9] *SMWP*, May 31, 1866; Holcombe, 500; Stringfield, 122.

[10] *SMWP*, May 31, 1866.

[11] *Ibid.*

[12] *Ibid.*

[13] *SMWP*, May 31, *Springfield Southwest Union Press*, Jun. 9, 1866.

[14] *SMWP*, Jun. 7, 1866; Soldiers' Records; Missouri Marriages; US Census, 1850.

[15] *Howard County Advertiser*, Jun. 28, 1866, quoting the *Springfield Press*; Fairbanks and Tuck, 226.

[16] *Howard County Advertiser*, Jun. 28, 1866, quoting the *Springfield Press*.

[17] *SMWP*, Jun. 21, 1866.

[18] *SMWP*, Aug. 9, 1866.

[19] Yen, 57, 66-68, 78.

[20] *SMWP*, Aug. 23, 1866.

[21] *SMWP*, Oct. 4, 1866.

[22] *SMWP*, Apr. 18, 1867; Yen, 76-77, 79.

[23] Yen, 79; Missouri Judicial Records, Mary Rush, Plaintiff.

6
The Lynching of Bud Isbel

[1] *SL*, Jun 22, 1871; US Census, 1860, 1870; Wood, *Civil War*

Springfield, 91.

[2] *SL*, Jun. 22, 1871; *SMWP*, Jun. 22, 1871.

[3] *SL*, Jun. 22, 1871; *SMWP,* Jun. 22, 1871.

[4] *SL*, Jun. 29, 1871, *SMWP*, Jun. 29, 1871.

[5] *SL*, Jun. 29, *SMWP*, Jun. 29, 1871.

[6] *SMWP*, Jun. 29, 1871.

[7] *SL*, Jun. 29, 1871.

[8] *Ibid.*

[9] *Ibid.*

[10] *Ibid.*

[11] *SL*, Jun. 29, 1871; Fairbanks and Tuck, 223; Holcombe, 266. Whether Isbel was lynched on the south side or north side of Jordan Creek is not altogether clear. The *Leader* said the south side a few days after the incident. However, the reporter's own description of the route the mob took seems to suggest the north side, and later evidence supports the idea of the north side. Holcombe's 1883 *History of Greene County* recalled that Isbel was taken "across 'Jordan'" and lynched very near the spot where Mart Danforth was lynched in 1859, which the history had previously identified as being on the north side. An 1886 reminiscent account in a Springfield newspaper agreed that Danforth was taken to "the north side of Jordan" and that Isbel was hanged near the same spot. Neither the *Leader*'s contemporaneous report that the spot was about equidistant between the two black churches nor the recollection in Holcombe's history that it was "just west of the cotton factory" (located on the north side of Mill Street) does much to clear up the incongruence.

[12] *SL*, Jun. 29, 1871.

[13] *SMWP*, Jun. 29, 1871.

[14] *SL* Jun. 29, 1871; Folder 24, Greene County Coroner's Records.

[15] *SL*, Jun. 29, 1871; Folder 24, Coroner's Records.

[16] *SL*, Jun. 29, 1871.

[17] *SL*, Jun. 29, 1871; US Census, 1870.
[18] *SMWP*, Jun. 29, 1871.
[19] *SMWP*, Jun. 29, 1871.

7
The Lynching of Greenberry Buis

[1] *SMWP*, Jul 10, 1873; US Census, 1870.
[2] MSPD; *SMWP*, Jul 10, 1873.
[3] MSPD; *SMWP*, Jul 10, 1873.
[4] *SMWP*, Jul. 10, 1873.
[5] *SMWP*, Jul. 10, 1873; Folder 32, Greene County Coroner's Records.
[6] Folder 32, Coroner's Records.
[7] *Ibid.*
[8] *Ibid.*
[9] *SMWP*, Jul. 10, 1873.
[10] *SMWP*, Jul, 10, 1873; Folder 32, Coroner's Records.
[11] *SMWP*, Jul. 10, 1873.

8
The Murder of Sarah Graham

[1] The information for this chapter is drawn almost entirely from my book on the same subject, *Bigamy and Bloodshed: The Scandal of Emma Molloy and the Murder of Sarah Graham.*
[2] Some of Emma Molloy's harshest critics suggested that the lynching of George Graham was instigated and orchestrated by her powerful Springfield friends, particularly Judge Baker, to keep Graham from revealing more incriminating details about Mrs. Molloy. In arguing against this notion, I asserted in *Bigamy and Bloodshed* that the Colonel Baker who largely excused the actions of the Regulators in 1866 and Judge Baker,

Mrs. Molloy's confidant, were not the same person. This was an error. I knew there were two different James Bakers who lived in post-Civil War Springfield, and I knew Judge Baker had never served as a full colonel in the Union Army (although he was a lieutenant colonel). In addition, a number of sources mistakenly identify the James Baker who spoke to the Regulators as Colonel James H. Baker, who was, in fact, a full colonel in the Union Army in Missouri during the Civil War. Also, the 1893 *Pictorial and Genealogical Record of Greene County* says that Judge James Baker strongly opposed the Regulators. However, additional research has convinced me that the James Baker who spoke to the Regulators and Judge James Baker who befriended Emma Molloy twenty years later were the same person. The truth is that, while Baker may not have openly condoned the actions of the Regulators, neither did he speak out strongly against the group, as the *Pictorial and Genealogical Record* claims. Still, I am no less convinced than when I wrote *Bigamy and Bloodshed* that the vigilantes who lynched George Graham were not organized or directed by Judge James Baker and his prominent Springfield friends. The mob came from and returned to Brookline.

9
The Murder of Frank Keller

[1] *SDR*, Sep. 29, 1895.

[2] *Ibid.*

[3] *SL*, Jul 12, 1887, Apr. 12, 1888; *SDR*, Apr. 20, 1888.

[4] *Springfield Democrat*, Jun. 23, 1895; *SDR* Sep. 29, 1895; MSPD.

[5] *MVLC*, Jan. 7, 1892; *MVLC*, Jan. 21, 1892, quoting the *Pierce City Empire*.

[6] *Springfield Democrat,* Jan. 24, 1892.

[7] *MVLC*, Jan. 28, 1892.

[8] *MVLC*, April 21, 1892, quoting the *Peirce City Democrat;* *MVLC*, Jun. 26, 1892, quoting the *Carterville Republican.*

[9] *MVLC*, Sep. 15, Oct. 13, 1892.

[10] *MVLC*, Feb. 16, Mar. 9, 1893.

[11] *MVLC*, Mar. 30 1893, quoting the *Aurora Advertiser.*

[12] *Joplin Weekly Herald*, Jun. 26, 1893; MSPD.

[13] *MVLC*, Apr. 11, 1895, quoting the *Joplin News.*

[14] *Springfield Democrat*, Jun. 23, 1895.

[15] *Ibid.*

[16] *SL*, Jul. 10, 1895.

[17] *Ibid.*

[18] *Ibid.*

[19] *Springfield Leader-Democrat*, Aug. 13, 1895.

[20] *Springfield Leader-Democrat*, Sep. 27, 1895; *SDR*, Sep. 28, 1895.

[21] *SDR*, Sep. 28,1895.

[22] *SDR*, Sep. 29, 1895.

[23] *SDR*, Oct. 1-2, 1895; *Springfield Leader-Democrat*, Oct. 2, 1895.

[24] MSPD; *Springfield Leader-Democrat*, Oct. 3, 1895; *SDR*, Jun. 3, 1904; *SMR*, Sep. 19, 1915; *SL*, Jun. 15, 1929.

10
Anna McMahan and the Prettiest Boy

[1] *SR*, Dec. 9, 1902.

[2] *Ibid.*

[3] *Ibid.*

[4] *SR*, Dec. 9, 1902; Folder 170, Coroner's Records.

[5] *SR*, Dec. 9, 1902, Apr. 11, 1903.

[6] *SR*, Dec. 9, 1902.

[7] *Ibid.*

[8] *SR,* Feb. 28, Apr. 10, 1903.

[9] *SR*, Apr. 10, 1903.

[10] *Ibid.*

[11] *SR*, Apr. 11, 1903.

[12] *Ibid.*

[13] *Ibid.*

[14] *Ibid.*

[15] *Ibid.*

[16] *Ibid.*

[17] *SR,* Apr. 11, 1903; *Springfield Leader and Democrat*, Dec. 8, 1902.

[18] *SR*, Apr. 14, 1903

[19] *SR*, Apr. 18 1903.

[20] MSPD.

11
The 1906 Easter Weekend Lynchings

[1] *SDR*, Apr. 14, 1906.

[2] US Census, 1900, 1910; *St. Louis Globe-Democrat*, Apr. 16, 1906; *KCS*, Apr. 18, 1906; *SL*, Apr. 16, 1906; Charles Cooper testimony, Grand Jury Report, March term, 1906, Greene County Records and Archives.

[3] *SDR*, Apr. 14, 1906.

[4] *Ibid.*

[5] Katherine Lederer, "And They Sang a Sabbath Song," *Springfield! Magazine*, Part 1, (Apr. 1981), 26; *KCS*, Apr. 15, 1906; *SLPD*, Apr. 15, 16, 1906.

[6] *SDR*, Apr. 15, 1906.

[7] *Ibid.*

[8] *Ibid.*

[9] *SDR*, Apr. 15, 1906; *SLPD*, Apr. 16, 1906.

[10] *SDR*, Apr. 15, 1906.

[11] *SDR*, Apr. 15, 1906; *KCS*, Apr. 15, 1906.

[12] *SDR*, Apr. 15, 1906.

[13] *Ibid.*

[14] *Ibid.*

[15] *SDR*, Apr. 15, 1906; "Historic Postcards."

[16] *SDR*, Apr, 15, 1906.

[17] *Ibid.*

[18] *KCS*, Apr. 15, 1906; *SDR*, Apr. 15, 1906; *SLPD*, Apr. 16, 1906.

[19] *KCS*, Apr. 15, 1906; *SDR*, Apr. 15, 1906; *St. Louis Globe-Democrat*, Apr. 16, 1906; *SLPD* Apr. 16, 1906.

[20] *SDR*, Apr. 15, 1906; *St. Louis Globe-Democrat,* Apr. 16, 1906.

[21] *SDR*, Apr. 15, 1906.

[22] *Ibid.*

[23] *Ibid.*

[24] *Kansas City Star & Times*, Apr. 16, 1906.

[25] *Kansas City Star & Times*, Apr. 16, 1906; *SDR*, Apr. 16, 1906.

[26] *SL*, Apr. 16, 1906; *SLPD* Apr. 16, 1906.

[27] *KCS*, Apr 18, 1906; *SDR*, Apr. 17, 1906; *SLPD*, Apr. 18, 1906.

[28] *SDR*, May 24, 1906.

[29] *SL*, May 24, 31, 1906; Record of Special Grand Jury, April 25-May 23, 1906, Greene County Archives and Records Center; Larry Wood, "Martha Misner and the Plain View Hotel," *Missouri and Ozarks History*, http://ozarks-history.blogspot.com/2016/08/martha-misner-and-plain-view-hotel.html.

[30] *SL*, Jun. 6, 7, Aug. 8, 17, 19, 1906.

[31] *SL*, Aug. 20, 22, 24, 25, 27, 1906.

[32] *SL*, Oct 7, 1906; *KCS*, Aug. 25, 1907.

12
The Murder of Joshua and Elizabeth Ellis

[1] "State v. Tucker," 1-22; *SMR*, Feb. 23, 1909.

[2] MSPD; "State v. Tucker," 1-22.

[3] "State v. Tucker," 1-22; *SMR*, Feb. 23, 1909.

[4] *SMR*, Feb. 23, 1909; "State v. Tucker," 1-22.

[5] "State v. Tucker," 1-22.

[6] "State v. Tucker," 1-22; US Census, 1900, 1910; *SMR*, Feb. 23, 1909.

[7] "State v. Tucker," 1-22; *SMR,* Feb. 23, 1909.

[8] "State v. Tucker," 1-22; *SMR* Feb. 23, 1909.

[9] "State v. Tucker," 1-22; *SMR* Feb. 23, 1909.

[10] "State v. Tucker," 1-22; *SMR* Feb. 23, 1909.

[11] *SMR* Feb. 25, 1909; "State v. Tucker," 1-22.

[12] *SMR*, Feb. 28, 1909.

[13] *SMR*, May 4, 1909.

[14] *SMR*, May 5, 1909.

[15] *SMR*, May 6, 1909.

[16] *SMR*, May 6, 29, 1909.

[17] State v. Tucker," 1-22; *SMR* Dec. 14, 18, 1910.

[18] *SMR*, Dec. 18, 20, 1910.

[19] *SMR*, Dec 29, 1910, Jan, 13, Mar. 7, 1911.

[20] *SMR*, Mar. 10, 12, 1911.

[21] *SMR*, Mar. 15, 1911.

[22] *SMR*, Mar. 15, Jul. 1, Jul. 4, 1911; US Census, 1900.

[23] MSPD; US Census, 1920; California Marriages, familysearch.org; *SLPD*, Mar. 14, 1918; *St. Louis Globe-Democrat*, Mar. 14, 1918.

13
The Death of Mollie Bass

[1] "State v. Bass," 107-134; *SMR*, Jan. 25, 1911.

[2] "State v. Bass."

[3] "State v. Bass"; *SMR*, Apr. 27 1911; US Census, 1910.

[4] *SMR*, Jan. 25, 26, 1911.

[5] *SMR*, Jan. 27, Feb. 7, 1911.

[6] *SMR*, Feb. 7. 1911.

[7] *SMR*, Feb. 7, 1911.

[8] *SMR*, Feb. 14, 16, 25, 1911.

[9] *SMR,* Apr. 27, 1911.

[10] *SMR*, Feb. 25, Apr. 27, 1911.

[11] *SMR*, Apr. 28, 1911.

[12] *SMR*, Apr. 29, 1911.

[13] *SMR*, Apr. 30, 1911.

[14] *Ibid.*

[15] *SMR*, May 2, 1911.

[16] *Ibid.*

[17] *SMR*, May 2, 3, 1911.

[18] *SMR*, May 3, 5, 1911, Nov. 22, 1912, Dec. 11, 1912.

[19] *SMR*, Jun. 3, 1913; MSPD; "State v. Bass."

[20] Colorado Statewide Marriage Index, 1853-2006, family search.org; US Census, 1920; Find A Grave, www.finda grave.com, Andrew Jackson Bass, Memorial #50778913.

14
The Kidnapping and Murder of Baby Keet

[1] *KCS*, May 31, 1917; *SMR*, Jun. 1, 1917; Steve Pokin, "Pokin' Around," *SNL*, Oct. 15, 2019.

[2] Pokin, *SNL*, Oct. 15, 2019; *SMR*, Jun. 1-3, 1917.

[3] *SMR*, Jun. 2, 5, 1917.

[4] *SLPD*, Jun. 4, 1917; *St. Louis Globe-Democrat*, Jun 4, 1917.

[5] *SMR*, Jun. 5, 1917.

[6] *SMR*, Jun. 6-7, 19017; *SLPD*, Jun. 6, 1917.

[7] *SLPD* Jun. 6-7, 1917.

[8] *SMR*, Jun. 7, 1917.

[9] *SMR*, Jun. 8-9, 1917.

[10] *SMR*, Jun. 9, 1917.

[11] *SLPD*, Jun. 9, 1917; *SMR*, Jun. 10, 1917; Pokin, *SNL*, Oct. 15, 2019.

[12] *SMR*, Jun. 10, 1917.

[13] SLPD, Jun. 11, 1917; *SMR*, Jun. 12, 1917.

[14] *SMR*, Jun. 10, 1917.

[15] *SMR*, Jun. 10, 1917.

[16] *SMR*, Jun. 12, 1917.

[17] *SMR*, Jun. 12, 1917; *SLPD* Jun. 12, 1917.

[18] *SLPD*, Jun. 18, 1917; *SMR*, Jun. 19-22, 1917.

[19] *SLPD*, Jun. 22, 1917; *SMR*, Jun. 23, 28, 1917.

[20] *SLPD*, Jun. 23-24, 1917; *SMR*, Jun. 27-28, 1917; *St. Louis Globe-Democrat*, Jun. 30, 1917.

[21] *SMR*, Jul. 1, 1917.

[22] *SMR*, Jul. 17, 1917; KCS, Jul. 16, 22, 30, 1917.

[23] *SMR*, Oct. 12, 14, 16, Dec. 23, 1917; MSPD.

[24] Larry Wood, *Missouri and Ozarks History*, "Kidnapping and Murder of Baby Keet," http://ozarks-history.blogspot.com/2018/07/kidnapping-and-murder-of-baby-keet.html; MSPD.

15
A Murder at Percy's Cave

[1] *SL*, Aug. 15, Sep. 6, 1922.

[2] *SL*, Sep. 5, 6, Dec. 3, 1922; US Census, 1920; Soldiers Database; "State vs. Aurentz," *Court Listener*.

[3] *SL*, Dec. 4, 1922.

[4] *SL*, Dec. 2, 1922.

[5] "State v. Aurentz," *Court Listener*; *SL*, Dec. 2-6, 1922.

[6] "State v. Aurentz," *Southwestern Reporter* 263:179-180; *SL*, Sep. 5, Dec. 2-6, 1922.

[7] *SL*, Aug. 15, 1922.

[8] *SL*, Aug. 16, 1922.

[9] *Ibid.*

[10] *SL*, Sep. 5, 6, 1922.

[11] *SL*, Dec. 2, 1922.

[12] *SL*, Dec. 2, 3, 1922.

[13] *SL*, Dec. 2-5, 1922; *SMR*, Dec. 5, 1922.

[14] *SL*, Dec. 6, 1922.

[15] *SL*, Dec, 8, 1922.

[16] *SMR*, Dec. 17, 1922, Jun. 6, 1924; *SL*, Dec. 28, 29, 1922.

[17] "State v. Aurentz," *Southwestern Reporter*, 263:178.

[18] *SL*, Jan. 7-8, 10, 1925.

[19] "State v. Aurentz," *Court Listener*; *SL*, May 27, Jun. 3, 8, 1926; MSPD.

[20] *SL*, Oct. 31, 1930; MSPD; *Find A Grave*, Memorial #19739229; *Jefferson City Post-Tribune*, Oct. 31, 1930.

16
Dobb Adams Goes on a Rampage

[1] *SL*, Jun. 19, 1928.

[2] *Ibid.*

[3] *SL*, Jun. 19, Jul. 17, 1928. Zella's name was usually spelled St. Clair in newspapers, but her tombstone says Sinclair.

[4] *SL*, Jun. 19, 1928; "State v. Dobbs."

[5] *SL*, Jun. 19, Jul. 17, 1928

[6] *SL*, Jun. 19, Jul. 17, 1928.

[7] *SL*, Jun. 19, 20, 1928·

[9] *Ibid.*

[10] *Ibid.*

[11] *Ibid.*

[12] *SL*, Jun. 19, 20, 1928.

[13] *SL*, Jun. 19, 1928.

[14] *SL*, Jun., 20, 1928

[15] *SL*, Jun. 19, 20, 1928.

[16] *SL*, Jul. 17, 18, 1928

[17] *SL*, Jul. 18, 19, 1928.

[18] *SL*, Jul. 20, 1928.

[19] *SL*, Aug. 15, 1928.

[20] *SL*, May 25, 27, 1929.

[21] *SL*, Jun. 6, Sep. 10, 1929; "State v. Dobbs"; *St,. Louis Star and Times*, Aug. 14, 1929.

[22] *SL*, Oct. 22, 1929.

[23] *SL*, Jan. 6, 7, 1930.

[24] *SL*, Feb.12, 1930; MSPD.

17
Young Brothers Massacre

[1] *SLPD*, Jan. 3, 4, 1932.

[2] SL, Jan. 8, 1924, Jul 23, 1928; *SMR*, May 16, Dec. 16, 1924; MSPD; Paul W. Barrett and Mary H. Barrett, 19-20, 27-29.

[3] *Fort Worth Star-Telegram*, Mar. 31, 1930; Barrett and Barrett, 24-25, 37-38

[4] *SLPD*, Jan. 3, 4, 1932; *SL*, Jun. 3, 1929; MSPD; Davis, 25-26.

[5] *SLPD*, Jan. 4, 1932.

[6] *SLPD*, Jan. 4, 1932; Barrett and Barrett, 67.

[7] *SLPD*, Jan. 4, 1932; Barrett and Barrett, 69.

[8] *SLPD*, Jan. 4, 1932; Barrett and Barrett, 69.

[9] *SLPD*, Jan. 4, 1932; Barrett and Barrett, 70.

[10] Barrett and Barrett, 69; *SLPD*, Jan. 4, 1932.

[11] *SLPD*, Jan. 4, 1932.

[12] *Ibid.*

[13] *Ibid.*

[14] *Ibid.*

[15] *SLPD*, Jan. 4, 1932; Barrett & Barrett, 71-81.

[16] Barrett and Barrett, 91; *St. Louis Star and Times*, Jan. 4, 1932.

[17] Barrett and Barrett, 91-96, 99; *Corsicana (TX) Daily Sun*, Jan. 5, 1932.

[18] Barrett and Barrett, 119, 129-130; *St. Louis Star and Times*, Jan. 13, 1932; *Sedalia Democrat*, Jan. 13, 1932.

18
Bonnie and Clyde Kidnap Tom Persell

[1] *SP*, Jan. 27, 1933; *SL*, Jan. 27, 1933.

[2] *SP*, Jan. 27, 1933; *SL*, Jan. 27, 1933.

[3] *SP*, Jan. 27, 1933; *SL*, Jan. 27, 1933.

[4] *SP*, Jan. 27, 1933; *SL*, Jan. 27, 1933; *SDN*, Jan. 28, 1933.

[5] *SP*, Jan. 27, 1933; *SDN*, Jan. 28, 1933.

[6] *SL*, Jan. 27, 1933; *SP*, Jan. 27, 1933; *SDN*, Jan. 28, 1933.

[7] *SP*, Jan. 27, 1933; *SL*, Jan. 27, 1933.

[8] *SP*, Jan. 27, 1933; *SL*, Jan. 27, 1933.

[9] *SP*, Jan. 27, 1933.

[10] *Ibid.*

[11] *Ibid.*

[12] *SP*, Jan. 27, 1933; *Joplin Globe*, Dec. 1, 1932.

[13] *SP*, Jan. 27, 1933.

[14] *SP*, Jan. 27, 1933; US Census, 1930.

[15] *SP*, Jan. 27, 1933; *SL*, Jan. 27, 1933; *SDN*, Jan. 27, 1933.

[16] *SP*, Jan. 27, 29, 30, 1933; *SL*, Jan 30, 1933.

[17] *SP*, Apr. 16, 1933; *SNL*, Apr. 16, 1933.

[18] *SLP*, Feb. 13, 1934; *SDN*, Feb. 13, 1933.

[19] *SDN*, May 24, 1934; Jan. 22, 1956; *SLP*, Sep. 13, 1959, Apr. 23, 26, 1968; *SNL*, Jul. 25, 1989, Oct. 10, 1999, Jul. 24, 2020.

19
Last Legal Hanging in Greene County

[1] *SL*, Mar. 29, 1933; *SDN*, Apr. 5, 1933; "State vs. McDaniel," *Case Text*, https://casetext.com/case/state-v-mcdaniel-110; Folder 1170, Greene County Coroner's Records.

[2] *SL*, Mar. 29, 1933, Mar. 31, 1935; *SP*, Mar. 31, 1933; Folder 1170, Coroner's Records.

[3] *SL*, Mar. 29, 1933.

[4] *SL*, Mar. 30-31, 1933; *SP*, Mar. 31, 1933; Folder 1170.

[5] *SDN*, Mar. 31, 1933, Apr. 12, 1935; *SMR*, Apr. 19, 1924; *SP*, Aug. 13, 30, 1929, Oct 8, 1930; *SL*, Mar. 31, 1935; MSPD

[6] *SDN*, Apr. 5, 1933.

[7] *SDN*, Apr. 5, 1933; State v. McDaniel.

[8] *SDN*, Apr. 5, 1933.

[9] *SDN*, Apr. 5, 1933

[10] *SL*, Apr. 4, 14, 1933; *SDN*, Apr. 5, 1933; *SP*, Apr. 5, 1933.

[11] *SL*, Jun. 19, 1933;

[12] *SL*, Jun. 20, 1933; *SDN*, Jun. 20, 1933; State v. McDaniel.

[13] *SL*, Jun. 20-21, 1933; *SDN*, Jun. 27, 1933.

[14] *SDN*, Jun. 21, 1933.

[15] *SL*, Jun. 26, 1933; *SDN*, Jun. 29, 1933.

[16] State v. McDaniel; *SL*, Mar. 5, 1935.

[17] *SDN*, Mar. 9, 17, 28, 1935.

[18] *SDN*, Apr. 3, 11, 1935.

[19] *SDN*, Apr. 12, 1935.

[20] *SDN* , Apr. 12, 1935; *SL*, Apr. 12, 1935.

[21] *SL*, Apr. 12, 1935.

[22] *SDN*, Apr. 13, 16, 1935.

20
Double Murder of Spinetto and Usrey

[1] US Census, 1920; *SDN*, Dec, 16, 1957; *SLP*, Dec. 16, 1957.

[2] *SDN*, Dec. 16, 1957.

[3] *Ibid.*

[4] *SDN*, Dec. 16, 1957; SLP, Dec. 16, 1957.

[5] *SDN*, Dec. 16, 1957; SLP, Dec. 16, 1957.

[6] *SDN,* Dec. 16, 1957; SLP, Dec. 16, 1957.

[7] *SDN*, Dec. 16, 1957; SLP, Dec. 16, 1957.

[8] SLP, Jan. 8, 14, 15, 1958.

[9] SLP, Jan. 14, 15, 1958.

[10] SLP, Jan. 15, 1958.

[11] *Ibid.*

[12] *SLP*, Jan. 15, 1958; *SDN*, Jan. 16, 1958.

[13] *SLP*, Jan. 15, 1958; *SDN*, Jan. 16, 1958.

[14] *SLP*, Jan. 15, 1958; *SDN*, Jan. 16, 1958.

[15] *SLP*, Jan. 15-17, 1958; *SDN*, Jan. 16, 1958.

[16] *SLP*, Jan. 16, 21, 23, 30, 1958.

[17] *SLP*, Feb. 14, Apr. 11, 1958.

[18] *SLP*, Sep. 23, Oct. 8, 1970, Jan. 10, 1972; *SDN*, Oct. 30, 1970;
Register of Inmates.

[19] Register of Inmates; *Columbia Daily Tribune*, Aug. 10, 2010.

21
The Long-Unsolved Murder of Johnny Vaughn

[1] *SLP*, Aug. 3, 4, 1964.
[2] *SDN*, Aug. 3, 1964; *SLP*, Aug. 3, 1964.
[3] *SLP*, Aug. 3, 1964.
[4] *SLP*, Aug. 3, 5, 8, 11, 1964, Feb. 5, Mar. 3, 1965, Aug. 3, 1966.
[5] *SLP*, Dec. 10 1968.
[6] *Ibid.*
[7] *SLP*, Dec. 9, 10, 1968.
[8] *SLP*, Dec. 10, 1968.
[9] *SLP*, Dec. 10, 11, 1968.
[10] *Ibid.*
[11] *SDN*, Dec. 11, 17, 1968; *SLP*, Dec. 14, 27, 1968, Jan. 4, Mar. 28, 1969.
[12] *SLP*, May 19, 21, 1969.
[13] *SLP*, May 21, 1969.
[14] *SLP*, May 21, 22, 1969.
[15] *SLP*, Jun. 6, 1969, Sep. 16, 1971; *SDN*, Jun. 10, 1969.
[16] *SLP*, Nov. 3, 1971.
[17] *SLP*, Nov. 4, 1971; *SDN*, Nov. 17, 1971.
[18] *SDN*, Nov. 13, 1974; *SLP*, Nov. 14, 1974.
[19] Register of Inmates; *SLP*, Aug. 31, 1976; *Jefferson City Daily Capital News*, Nov. 27, Dec. 9, 1976.
[20] Register of Inmates; *Mugshots.com*—News, US States— California, https://mugshots.com/search.html?q=Donald% 20Redding&c=119043.

22
Robert Fay Adams Slays His Wife

[1] *SLP*, Mar. 12, 1970.
[2] *Ibid.*

[3] *SLP*, Mar. 12, Apr. 16, 1970.

[4] *SLP*, Mar. 12, 14, Apr. 16, 1970.

[5] *SDN*, Mar. 19, 1970; *SLP*, Mar. 14, 19, 1970.

[6] *SDN*, Mar. 19, 1970; *SLP*, Mar. 19, 1970.

[7] *SLP*, Mar, 19, 1970.

[8] *Ibid.*

[9] *SLP*, Mar. 20, 21, 1970.

[10] *SLP*, Mar. 23, 1970.

[11] *SLP*, Mar. 25, Apr. 16, 17, 18, 1970.

[12] *SLP*, Sep. 4, Nov. 24, 1970.

[13] *SLP*, Feb. 15, 16, 17, 1971.

[14] *SLP*, Feb. 17, 1971.

[15] *SLP*, Feb. 20, 1971.

[16] *Ibid.*

[17] *Springfield Sunday News and Leader*, Feb. 21, 1971.

[18] *Ibid.*

[19] *Ibid.*

[20] *SLP*, Mar. 24, Apr. 8, 1971.

[21] *SDN*, Jul. 11, 1973; *SLP*, Jul. 16, 19, 1973, Mar. 6, 1974; State v. Adams.

[22] *SLP*, Nov. 10, 16, 1973.

[23] *SLP*, Dec. 6, 23, 1973, Mar. 6, Apr. 5, 17, 1974.

[24] *SLP*, Feb. 27, Mar. 22, 1981.

[25] *SLP*, Mar. 22, 1981.

[26] *SLP*, Feb. 27, 1981; Feb. 12, 1991, Feb. 10, 2002, May 14, 2017, SNL.

23
The I-44 Truck Explosion

[1] *SLP*, Sep. 30, 1970.

[2] *SLP*, Sep. 30, Oct. 5, 1970.

[3] *SLP*, Sep. 30, 1970.

[4] *SLP*, Sep. 30, 1970, May 5, 1971.

[5] *SLP*, Sep. 30, Oct. 1, 1970.

[6] *SLP*, Sep. 30-Oct. 2, Dec. 10, 1970.

[7] *SDN*, Oct. 1, 2, 1970; *SLP*, Dec. 10, 1970, May 4, 1971.

[8] *SLP*, Oct. 2, 5, 1970.

[9] *SLP*, Oct. 5, 1970.

[10] *SLP*, Dec. 10, 1970.

[11] *Ibid.*

[12] *SDN*, Apr. 30, 1971; *SLP*, May 4, 1971.

[13] *SLP*, May 7, 1971.

[14] *Ibid.*

[15] *SLP*, May 21, 1971.

[16] *SLP*, Jun. 11, Jul. 14, Nov. 18, 1971.

[17] *SLP*, Jun. 23, Nov. 15, 1971, Nov. 14, 1972, Jul. 26, 1979.

[18] SNL, Jan. 6, 1980, Feb. 24, 2017; *SLP*, Oct. 11, 1979; Register of Inmates.

24
The Burning Deaths of Willard and Viola Blades

[1] *SLP*, Jun. 18, 1984.

[2] *Ibid.*

[3] *SLP*, Jun. 19, 1984.

[4] *SLP*, Jun. 20, 1984.

[5] *Ibid.*

[6] *SLP*, Jul. 3, 1984.

[7] *SLP*, Jul. 24, 27, Aug. 10, 30, Sep. 14, 1984.

[8] *SLP*, Jun. 2, 3, 1986.

[9] *SLP*, Jun. 5, 1986.

[10] *SLP*, Jun. 5, 6, 1986.

[11] *SLP*, Dec. 10, 11, 1986.

[12] "State v. Dulany."

[13] *Ibid.*

[14] "State v. Dulany"; *SNL*, Dec. 10, 11, 1986.

[15] "State v. Dulany."
[16] *SNL*, Dec. 14, 1986.
[17] *SNL*, Dec. 14, 1986; "State v. Dulany."
[18] *SNL*, Dec. 14, 1986, Jan. 31, Feb. 7, 1987.
[19] *SNL*, Feb. 7, 1987.
[20] *SNL*, Jul. 30, 1988.
[21] *SNL*, Jul. 30, Aug. 30, 1988.
[22] *SNL*, Sep. 15, Oct. 14, 22, 1988.
[23] *SNL*, Oct. 29, Dec. 29, 1988.
[24] *SNL*, May 3, 1989.
[25] *SNL*, Nov. 15, 1989, May 8, 1990.
[26] *Flat River (MO) Daily Journal*, Apr. 4, 2014.

25
The Murder of Wilma Plaster

[1] *SNL*, Oct. 7, 10, 1989.
[2] *SNL*, Oct. 7, 8, 1989.
[3] *SNL*, Oct. 9, 11, 13, 1989.
[4] *SNL*, Oct. 10, 1989.
[5] *SNL*, Oct. 12, 1989.
[6] *SNL*, Oct. 12, 13, 1989.
[7] *SNL*, Oct. 20, 1989.
[8] *SNL*, Oct. 26, 27, Nov. 22, 1989.
[9] *SNL*, Mar. 20, 31, 1990.
[10] *SNL*, Jul. 27, 1990.
[11] *SNL*, Oct. 24, 1990.
[12] *SNL*, May 1, Aug. 24, 1991, Jan. 7, 15, 1992.
[13] *SNL*, Jan. 27, 28, 30, 31, 1992.
[14] *SNL*, Feb. 1, 2, 4, 1992.
[15] *SNL*, Feb. 4, 1992.
[16] *SNL*, Feb. 5, 1992.
[17] *SNL*, Feb. 6, Apr. 7, 1992,

[18] *SNL*, Jul. 17, 26, Aug. 4, 1994, May 25, 1995, Feb. 26, 1997, Apr. 26, 1998.

[19] *SNL*, Mar. 29, Oct. 9, 16, 1998.

26
Donald Joe Hall and the Murder of William White

[1] *SLP*, Oct. 1 1967; *SNL,* Dec. 16, 1992, Sep. 9, 1994.

[2] *SLP*, May 2, 1967.

[3] *SLP*, Mar. 5, May 7, Sep. 5, Oct. 3, 1969.

[4] *SDN*, Dec. 2, 1969.

[5] *SLP*, Jan. 17, Mar. 5, May 19, 1970.

[6] *SLP*, Aug. 27, Sep. 12, Sep. 25, 1970, Jan. 12, 14, 15, 1971.

[7] *SLP*, Sep. 8, 11, 15, 1973.

[8] *SLP*, Apr. 19, Jun. 1, Oct. 21, Nov. 19, 1974; *SDN*, Nov. 22, Dec. 5, 1974.

[9] *SLP*, Apr. 6, 1981; *SNL* Sep. 9, 1994.

[10] *SLP*, Apr. 25, May 5, 1981.

[11] *SLP*, Jul 27, 1981.

[12] *SNL,* Dec. 16, 1992, Sep. 9, 1994.

[13] "State v. Hall,"; *SNL*, Apr. 6, 1993.

[14] *SNL,* Sep. 10, 1994.

[15] *SNL*, Sep. 11, 1994.

[16] *SNL*, Sep. 11, 13, 1994.

[17] *SNL*, Sep. 13, 1994.

[18] *SNL*, Sep. 14, 15, 1994, Dec. 2, 1998.

[19] "State v. Hall"; *SNL*, Dec. 2, 1998, Aug. 31, 2005; "Hall v. Luebbers"; "Donald J. Hall," *Murderpedia*, https:// murderpedia.org/male.H/h/hall-donald.htm.

Bibliography

Abstracts of Greene County Circuit Court Records. Springfield-Greene County Library. https://thelibrary.org/lochist/records/.

Barnitz, Albert. Papers (WA MSS S-1294), Folders 81-82. Beinecke Rare Books and Manuscripts Library. Yale University.

Barrett, Paul W. and Mary Barrett. *Young Brothers Massacre.* Columbia: University of Missouri Press, 1988.

Davis, Bruce. *We're Dead, Come On In.* Gretna, LA: Pelican Publishing, 2005.

"Donald Joe Hall, Petitioner/appellant, v. Allen Luebbers, Superintendent of Potosi Correctional Center, Respondent/appellee, 296 F.3d 685 (8th Cir. 2002)." *Justia Law.* https://law. justia.com/cases/federal/appellate-courts/F3/296/685/559803/.

Fairbanks, Jonathan, and Clyde Edwin Tuck. *Past and Present of Greene County, Missouri.* Indianapolis: A. W. Bowen and Company, 1915.

Find A Grave. https://www.findagrave.com/.

Glenn, Wayne. Facebook Post. https://www. facebook. com/148151331884826/posts/my-glenn-ancestors-immediate-neighbors-in-christian-county-in-1860this-is-not-an/2082876988412241/.

Greene County Coroner's Records. Greene County Archives and Records Center. Springfield, Missouri.

"Historic Postcards of Springfield, Missouri, Public Square." The Springfield-Greene County Library District. https://thelibrary.org/lochist/postcards/publicsquare.cfm.

Holcombe, R. I., ed. *History of Greene County, Missouri.* St. Louis: Western Historical Company, 1883.

Missouri Marriages. FamilySearch.org. https://www.family search.org/search/collection/1680838.

Missouri Judicial Records Historical Database. Missouri State Archives. Jefferson City. https://s1.sos.mo.gov/Records/Archives/ArchivesDb/JudicialRecords/.

Missouri State Penitentiary Database. Missouri State Archives. Jefferson City. https://s1.sos.mo.gov/records/archives/archivesdb/msp/.

Register of Inmates of the Missouri State Penitentiary. Missouri State Archives. Jefferson City.

Rosa, Joseph G. "George Ward Nichols and the Legend of Wild Bill Hickok." *Arizona and the West: A Quarterly Journal of History* 19. No. 2, Summer 1977.

———. "'Little Dave's' Last Fight: What Really Happened When Wild Bill Hickok and Davis K. Tutt Shot It Out at Springfield, Missouri." *Quarterly of the National Association of Outlaw and Lawman History*, 20. No. 4, Oct-Dec 1996.

Soldiers' Records, War of 1812 - World War I. Missouri State Archives. Jefferson City. https://s1.sos.mo.gov/records/archives/archivesdb/soldiers/#soldierSearch.

"State v. Adams, 497 S.W.2d 147 (1973)." *Justia US Law*. Supreme Court of Missouri. https://law.justia.com/cases/missouri/supreme-court/1973/56772-0.html.

"State v. Aurentz, 286 S.W. 69 (Mo. 1926)." *Court Listener*. https://www.courtlistener.com/opinion/3553489/state-v-aurentz/.

"State v. Aurentz." *Southwestern Reporter* 263. St. Paul: West Publishing Co., 1924.

"State v. A. J. Bass." *Reports of Cases Determined by the Supreme Court of the State of Missouri*, 251. Perry S. Rader, Reporter. Columbia, MO: E. W. Stephens, 1913.

"State v. Dobbs, 323, Mo. 729, Mo. Supreme Court (1929)." *Ravel*.https://www.ravellaw.com/opinions/d07aa8ded926b3830b33e44f0c75e50c.

"State v. Dulany, 781 S.W.2d 52 (1989)." *Justia US Law*.

https://law.justia.com/cases/missouri/supreme-court/
1989/70914-0.html.

"State v. Eugene Tucker, Appellant." *Cases Determined in the
Supreme Court of the State of Missouri Between Decem-
ber 27, 1910, and February 28, 1911.* Vol. 232. Perry S.
Rader, Reporter. Columbia, MO: E. W. Stephens, 1911.

"State v. Hall, Supreme Court of Missouri, En Banc. State of
Missouri, Respondent, v. Donald J. Hall, Appellant, No.
77481." *FindLaw.* https://caselaw.findlaw.com/mo-
supreme-court/1129892.html.

"State v. McDaniel." *Case Text.* https://casetext.com/case/state-
v-mcdaniel-110.

Stringfield, E. E. *Presbyterianism in the Ozarks.* Springfield,
MO: Presbytery of Ozark, U.S.A., 1909.

Tennessee Marriage Records. Familysearch.org.

Trego, Joseph. "Letters of Joseph H. Trego." Ed. by Edgar
Langsdorf. *Kansas Historical Quarterly* 19, no. 3 (August
1951).

Wood, Larry. *Civil War Springfield.* Charleston, SC: The
History Press, 2011.

———. *Wicked Springfield.* Charleston, SC: The History
Press, 2012.

Wood, Larry E. *Bigamy and Bloodshed: The Scandal of Emma
Molloy and the Murder of Sarah Graham.* Kent, OH: The
Kent State University Press, 2019.

Yen, Connie. "Horse-Stealing and Man-Hanging: An
Examination of Vigilantism in the Ozarks." Master's
Thesis, Missouri State University, Summer 2015.
https://bearworks.missouri_state.edu/cgi/view.content.
cgi?article=2175&context=theses.

Index

www.ingramcontent.com/pod-product-compliance
Lightning Source LLC
Chambersburg PA
CBHW051942090426
42741CB00008B/1236